The Causes of the Corruption of the Traditional Text of the Holy Gospels

The Corrupted Lore of Christian Scripture – The Accidental and Intentional Reasons

By John William Burgon

Edited by Edward Miller

PANTIANOS
CLASSICS

Published by Pantianos Classics

ISBN-13: 978-1-78987-194-4

First published in 1896

Contents

'Tenet ecclesia nostra, tenuitque semper firmam illam et immotam Tertulliani regulam "Id verius quod prius, id prius quod ab initio." Quo propius ad veritatis fontem accedimus, eo purior decurrit Catholicae doctrinae rivus.'

— Cave's *Prolog.* p. xliv.

'Interrogate de semitis antiquis quae sit via bona, et ambulate in ea.'

— Jerem. vi. 16.

'In summa, si constat id verius quod prius, id prius quod ab initio, id ab initio quod ab Apostolis; pariter utique constabit, id esse ab Apostolis traditum, quod apud Ecclesias Apostolorum fuerit sacrosanctum.'

— Tertull. *adv. Marc.* 1. iv. c. 5.

Preface

THE reception given by the learned world to the First Volume of this work, as expressed hitherto in smaller reviews and notices, has on the whole been decidedly far from discouraging. All have had some word of encomium on our efforts. Many have accorded praise and signified their agreement, sometimes with unquestionable ability. Some have pronounced adverse opinions with considerable candour and courtesy. Others in opposing have employed arguments so weak and even irrelevant to the real question at issue, as to suggest that there is not after all so much as I anticipated to advance against our case. Longer examinations of this important matter are doubtless impending, with all the interest attaching to them and the judgements involved: but I beg now to offer my acknowledgements for all the words of encouragement that have been uttered.

Something however must be said in reply to an attack made in the *Guardian* newspaper on May 20, because it represents in the main the position occupied by some members of an existing School. I do not linger over an offhand stricture upon my 'adhesion to the extravagant claim of a second-century origin for the Peshitto, because I am content with the companionship of some of the very first Syriac scholars, and with the teaching given in an unanswered article in the *Church Quarterly Review* for April, 1895. Nor except in passing do I remark upon a fanciful censure of my account of the use of papyrus in MSS. before the tenth century—as to which the reviewer is evidently not versed in information recently collected, and described for example in Sir E. Maunde Thompson's Greek and Latin Palaeography, or in Mr. F. G. Kenyon's Our Bible and the Ancient Manuscripts, and in an article in the just mentioned Review which appeared in October, 1894. These observations and a large number of inaccuracies shew that he was at the least not posted up to date. But what will be thought, when attention is drawn to the fact that in a question whether a singular set of quotations from the early Fathers refer to a passage in St. Matthew or the parallel one in St. Luke, the peculiar characteristic of St. Matthew—'them that persecute you'—is put out of sight, and both passages (taking the lengthened reading of St. Matthew) are represented as having equally only four clauses? And again, when quotations going on to the succeeding verse in St. Matthew (v. 45) are stated dogmatically to have been wrongly referred by me to that Evangelist? But as to the details of this point in dispute, I beg to refer our readers to the present volume. The reviewer appears also to be entirely unacquainted with

the history of the phrase μονογενὴς Θεός. in St. John i. 18, which was introduced by heretics and harmonized with Arian tenets, and was rejected
on the other side. That some orthodox churchmen fell into the trap, and
like those who in these days are not aware of the pedigree and use of the
phrase, employed it even for good purposes, is only an instance of a
strange phenomenon. We must not be led only by first impressions as to
what is to be taken for the genuine words of the Gospels. Even if phrases
or passages make for orthodoxy, to accept them if condemned by evidence and history is to alight upon the quicksands of conjecture.

A curious instance of a fate like this has been supplied by a critic in the
Athenaeum, who, when contrasting Dean Burgon's style of writing with
mine to my discredit, quotes a passage of some length as the Dean's
which was really written by me. Surely the principle upheld by our opponents, that much more importance than we allow should be attributed to
the 'Internal evidence of Readings and Documents,' might have saved him
from error upon a piece of composition which characteristically proclaimed its own origin. At all events, after this undesigned support, I am
the less inclined to retire from our vantage ground.

But it is gratifying on all accounts to say now, that such interpolations
as in the companion volume I was obliged frequently to supply in order
to fill up gaps in the several MSS. and in integral portions of the treatise,
which through their very frequency would have there made square
brackets unpleasant to our readers, are not required so often in this part
of the work. Accordingly, except in instances of pure editing or in simple
bringing up to date, my own additions or insertions have been so marked
off. It will doubtless afford great satisfaction to others as well as the admirers of the Dean to know what was really his own writing: and though
some of the MSS., especially towards the end of the volume, were not left
as he would have prepared them for the press if his life had been pro-
longed, yet much of the book will afford, on what he regarded as the chief
study of his life, excellent examples of his style, so vigorously fresh and so
happy in idiomatic and lucid expression.

But the Introduction, and Appendix II on 'Conflation' and the 'Neutral
Text,' have been necessarily contributed by me. I am anxious to invite attention particularly to the latter essay, because it has been composed upon request, and also because—unless it contains some extraordinary mistake—it exhibits to a degree which has amazed me the baselessness of
Dr. Hort's theory.

The manner in which the Dean prepared piecemeal for his book, and
the large number of fragments in which he left his materials, as has been
detailed in the Preface to the former volume, have necessarily produced
an amount of repetition which I deplore. To have avoided it entirely,
some of the MSS. must have been rewritten. But in one instance I discov-

ered when it was too late that after searching for, and finding with difficulty and treating, an example which had not been supplied, I had forestalled a subsequent examination of the same passage from his abler hand. However I hope that in nearly all, if not all cases, each treatment involves some new contribution to the question discussed; and that our readers will kindly make allowance for the perplexity which such an assemblage of separate papers could not but entail.

My thanks are again due to the Rev. G. H. Gwilliam, B.D., Fellow of Hertford College, for much advice and suggestion, which he is so capable of giving, and for his valuable care in looking through all the first proofs of this volume; to 'M. W.,' Dean Burgon's indefatigable secretary, who in a pure labour of love copied out the text of the MSS. before and after his death; also to the zealous printers at the Clarendon Press, for help in unravelling intricacies still remaining in them.

This treatise is now commended to the fair and candid consideration of readers and reviewers. The latter body of men should remember that there was perhaps never a time when reviewers were themselves reviewed by many intelligent readers more than they are at present. I cannot hope that all that we have advanced will be finally adopted, though my opinion is unfaltering as resting in my belief upon the Rock; still less do I imagine that errors may not be discovered in our work. But I trust that under Divine Blessing some not unimportant contribution has been made towards the establishment upon sound principles of the reverent criticism of the Text of the New Testament. And I am sure that, as to the Dean's part in it, this trust will be ultimately justified.

EDWARD MILLER.
9 BRADMORE ROAD, OXFORD:
Sept. 2, 1896.

Introduction

In the companion volume to this, the Traditional Text, that is, the Text of the Gospels which is the resultant of all the evidence faithfully and exhaustively presented and estimated according to the best procedure of the courts of law, has been traced back to the earliest ages in the existence of those sacred writings. We have shewn, that on the one hand, amidst the unprecedented advantages afforded by modern conditions of life for collecting all the evidence bearing upon the subject, the Traditional Text must be found, not in a mere transcript, but in a laborious revision of the Received Text; and that on the other hand it must, as far as we can judge, differ but slightly from the Text now generally in vogue, which has been generally received during the last two and a half centuries.

The strength of the position of the Traditional Text lies in its being logically deducible and to be deduced from all the varied evidence which the case supplies, when it has been sifted, proved, passed, weighed, compared, compounded, and contrasted with dissentient testimony. The contrast is indeed great in almost all instances upon which controversy has gathered. On one side the vast mass of authorities is assembled: on the other stands a small group. Not inconsiderable is the advantage possessed by that group, as regards numerous students who do not look beneath the surface, in the general witness in their favour borne by the two oldest MSS. of the Gospels in existence. That advantage however shrinks into nothing under the light of rigid examination. The claim for the Text in them made at the Semiarian period was rejected when Semiarianism in all its phases fell into permanent disfavour. And the argument advanced by Dr. Hort that the Traditional Text was a new Text formed by successive recensions has been refuted upon examination of the verdict of the Fathers in the first four centuries, and of the early Syriac and Latin Versions. Besides all this, those two manuscripts have been traced to a local source in the library of Caesarea. And on the other hand a Catholic origin of the Traditional Text found on later vellum manuscripts has been discovered in the manuscripts of papyrus which existed all over the Roman Empire, unless it was in Asia, and were to some degree in use even as late as the ninth century before and during the employment of vellum in the Caesarean school, and in localities where it was used in imitation of the mode of writing books which was brought well-nigh to perfection in that city.

It is evident that the turning-point of the controversy between ourselves and the Neologian school must lie in the centuries before St.

Chrysostom. If, as Dr. Hort maintains, the Traditional Text not only gained supremacy at that era but did not exist in the early ages, then our contention is vain. That Text can be Traditional only if it goes back without break or intermission to the original autographs, because if through break or intermission it ceased or failed to exist, it loses the essential feature of genuine tradition. On the other hand, if it is proved to reach back in unbroken line to the time of the Evangelists, or to a period as near to them as surviving testimony can prove, then Dr. Hort's theory of a 'Syrian' text formed by recension or otherwise just as evidently falls to the ground. Following mainly upon the lines drawn by Dean Burgon, though in a divergence of my own devising, I claim to have proved Dr. Hort to have been conspicuously wrong, and our maintenance of the Traditional Text in unbroken succession to be eminently right. The school opposed to us must disprove our arguments, not by discrediting the testimony of the Fathers to whom all Textual Critics have appealed including Dr. Hort, but by demonstrating if they can that the Traditional Text is not recognized by them, or they must yield eventually to us[1].

In this volume, the other half of the subject will be discussed. Instead of exploring the genuine Text, we shall treat of the corruptions of it, and shall track error in its ten thousand forms to a few sources or heads. The origination of the pure Text in the inspired writings of the Evangelists will thus be vindicated anew by the evident paternity of deflections from it discoverable in the natural defects or iniquities of men. Corruption will the more slim itself in true colours:—

Quinquaginta atris immanis hiatibus hydra[2]:

and it will not so readily be mistaken for genuineness, when the real history is unfolded, and the mistakes are accounted for. It seems clear that corruption arose in the very earliest age. As soon as the Gospel was preached, the incapacity of human nature for preserving accuracy until long years of intimate acquaintance have bred familiarity must have asserted itself in constant distortion more or less of the sacred stories, as they were told and retold amongst Christians one to another whether in writing or in oral transmission. Mistakes would inevitably arise from the universal tendency to mix error with truth which Virgil has so powerfully depicted in his description of 'Fame':—

Tam ficti pravique tenax, quam nuntia veri[3].

And as soon as inaccuracy had done its baleful work, a spirit of infidelity and of hostility either to the essentials or the details of the new religion must have impelled such as were either imperfect Christians, or no Christians at all, to corrupt the sacred stories.

Thus it appears that errors crept in at the very first commencement of the life of the Church. This is a matter so interesting and so important in the history of corruption, that I must venture to place it again before our readers.

Why was Galilee chosen before Judea and Jerusalem as the chief scene of our Lord's Life and Ministry, at least as regards the time spent there? Partly, no doubt, because the Galileans were more likely than the other inhabitants of Palestine to receive Him. But there was as I venture to think also another very special reason.

'Galilee of the nations' or 'the Gentiles,' not only had a mixed population[4] and a provincial dialect[5], but lay contiguous to the rest of Palestine on the one side, and on others to two districts in which Greek was largely spoken, namely, Decapolis and the parts of Tyre and Sidon, and also to the large country of Syria. Our Lord laid foundations for a natural growth in these parts of the Christian religion after His death almost independent as it seems of the centre of the Church at Jerusalem. Hence His crossings of the lake, His miracles on the other side, His retirement in that little understood episode in His life when He shrank from persecution[6], and remained secretly in the parts of Tyre and Sidon, about the coasts of Decapolis, on the shores of the lake, and in the towns of Caesarea Philippi, where the traces of His footsteps are even now indicated by tradition.[7] His success amongst these outlying populations is proved by the unique assemblage of the crowds of 5000 and 4000 men besides women and children. What wonder then if the Church sprang up at Damascus, and suddenly as if without notice displayed such strength as to draw persecution upon it! In the same way the Words of life appear to have passed throughout Syria over congenial soil, and Antioch became the haven whence the first great missionaries went out for the conversion of the world. Such were not only St. Paul, St. Peter, and St. Barnabas, but also as is not unreasonable to infer many of that assemblage of Christians at Rome whom St. Paul enumerates to our surprise in the last chapter of his Epistle to the Romans. Many no doubt were friends whom the Apostle of the Gentiles had met in Greece and elsewhere: but there are reasons to shew that some at least of them, such as Andronicus and Junias or Junia[8] and Herodion, may probably have passed along the stream of commerce that flowed between Antioch and Rome, and that this interconnexion between the queen city of the empire and the emporium of the East may in great measure account for the number of names well known to the apostle, and for the then flourishing condition of the Church which they adorned.

It has been shewn in our first volume that, as is well known to all students of Textual Criticism, the chief amount of corruption is to be found in what is termed the Western Text; and that the corruption of the West is so closely akin to the corruption which is found in Syriac remains, that practically they are included under one head of classification. What is the reason of this phenomenon? It is evidently derived from the close commercial alliance which subsisted between Syria and Italy. That is to say, the corruption produced in Syria made its way over into Italy, and there in many instances gathered fresh contributions. For there is reason to suppose, that it first arose in Syria.

We have seen how the Church grew of itself there without regular teaching from Jerusalem in the first beginnings, or any regular supervision exercised by the Apostles. In fact, as far as the Syrian believers in Christ at first consisted of Gentiles, they must perforce have been regarded as being outside of the covenant of promise. Yet there must have been many who revered the stories told about our Lord, and felt extreme interest and delight in them. The story of King Abgar illustrates the history: but amongst those who actually heard our Lord preach there must have been very many, probably a majority, who were uneducated. They would easily learn from the Jews, because the Aramaic dialects spoken by Hebrews and Syrians did not greatly differ the one from the other. What difference there was, would not so much hinder the spread of the stories, as tend to introduce alien forms of speech and synonymous words, and so to hinder absolute accuracy from being maintained. Much time must necessarily have elapsed, before such familiarity with the genuine accounts of our Lord's sayings and doings grew up, as would prevent mistakes being made and disseminated in telling or in writing.

The Gospels were certainly not written till some thirty years after the Ascension. More careful examination seems to place them later rather than earlier. For myself, I should suggest that the three first were not published long before the year 70 A.D. at the earliest; and that St. Matthew's Gospel was written at Pella during the siege of Jerusalem amidst Greek surroundings, and in face of the necessity caused by new conditions of life that Greek should become the ecclesiastical language. The Gospels would thus be the authorized versions in their entirety of the stories constituting the Life of our Lord; and corruption must have come into existence, before the antidote was found in complete documents accepted and commissioned by the authorities in the Church.

I must again remark with much emphasis that the foregoing suggestions are offered to account for what may now be regarded as a fact, viz., the connexion between the Western Text, as it is called, and Syriac remains in regard to corruption in the text of the Gospels and of the Acts of the Apostles. If that corruption arose at the very first spread of Christianity, before the record of our Lord's Life had assumed permanent shape in the Four Gospels, all is easy. Such corruption, inasmuch as it beset the oral and written stories which were afterwards incorporated in the Gospels, would creep into the authorized narrations, and would vitiate them till it was ultimately cast out towards the end of the fourth and in the succeeding centuries. Starting from the very beginning, and gaining additions in the several ways described in this volume by Dean Burgon, it would possess such vigour as to impress itself on Low-Latin manuscripts and even on parts of the better Latin ones, perhaps on Tatian's Diatessaron, on the Curetonian and Lewis manuscripts of the fifth century, on the Codex Bezae of the sixth; also on the Vatican and the Sinaitic of the fourth, on the Dublin Palimpsest of St. Matthew of the sixth, on the Codex Regius or L of the eighth, on the St. Gall MS. of the ninth in St. Mark, on the Codex Zacynthius of the eighth in St. Luke, and a few others. We on our side admit that the corruption is old even though the manuscripts enshrining it do not date very far back, and cannot always prove their ancestry. And it is in this admission that I venture to think there is an opening for a meeting of opinions which have been hitherto opposed.

In the following treatise, the causes of corruption are divided into (I) such as proceeded from Accident, and (II) those which were Intentional. Under the former class we find (1) those which were involved in pure Accident, or (2) in what is termed Homoeoteleuton where lines or sentences ended with the same word or the same syllable, or (3) such as arose in writing from Uncial letters, or (4) in the confusion of vowels and diphthongs which is called Itacism, or (5) in Liturgical Influence. The remaining instances may be conveniently classed as Intentional, not because in all cases there was a settled determination to alter the text, for such if any was often of the faintest character, but because some sort of design was to a greater or less degree embedded in most of them. Such causes were (1) Harmonistic Influence, (2) Assimilation, (3) Attraction; such instances too in their main character were (4) Omissions, (5) Transpositions, (6) Substitutions, (7) Additions, (8) Glosses, (9) Corruption by Heretics, (10) Corruption by Orthodox.

This dissection of the mass of corruption, or as perhaps it may be better termed, this classification made by Dean Burgon of the numerous causes which are found to have been at work from time to time, appears to me to be most interesting to the inquirer into the hidden history of the Text of the Gospels, because by revealing the influences which have been at work it sheds light upon the entire controversy, and often enables the student to see clearly how and why certain passages around which dispute has gathered are really corrupt. Indeed, the vast and mysterious ogre called corruption assumes shape and form under the acute penetration and the deft handling of the Dean, whose great knowledge of the subject and orderly treatment of puzzling details is still more commended by his interesting style of writing. As far as has been possible, I have let him in the sequel, except for such clerical corrections as were required from time to time and have been much fewer than his facile pen would have made, speak entirely for himself.

1   It must be always borne in mind, that it is not enough for the purpose of the other side to shew that the Traditional Text was in a minority as regards attestation. They must prove that it was nowhere in the earliest ages, if they are to establish their position that it was made in the third and fourth centuries. Traditional Text of the Holy Gospels, p. 95.

2 'A hydra in her direful shape, With fifty darkling throats agape.'— Altered from Conington's version, Aen. vi. 576.

3 'How oft soe'er the truth she tell, What's false and wrong she loves too well.'— Altered from Conington, Aen. iv. 188.

4   Strabo, xvi, enumerates amongst its inhabitants Egyptians, Arabians, and Phoenicians.

5   Studia Biblica, i. 50-55. Dr. Neubauer, On the Dialects spoken in Palestine in the time of Christ.

6   Isaac Williams, On the Study of the Gospels, 341-352.

7   My devoted Syrian friend, Miss Helanie Baroody, told me during her stay in England that a village is pointed out as having been traversed by our Lord on Ills way from Caesarea Philippi to Mount Hermon.

8   It is hardly improbable that these two eminent Christians were some of those whom St. Paul found at Antioch when St. Barnabas brought him there, and thus came to know intimately as fellow-workers (ἐπίσημοι ἐν τοῖς ἀποστόλοις, οἳ καὶ πρὸ ἐμοῦ γεγόνασιν ἐν Χριστῷ). Most of the names in Rom. xvi are either Greek or Hebrew.

'Jam pridem Syrus in Tiberim defluxit Orontes
Et *linguam* et mores . . . vexit.'—Juv. Sat. iii. 62-3.

Chapter One - General Corruption

§ 1.

WE hear sometimes scholars complain, and with a certain show of reason, that it is discreditable to us as a Church not to have long since put forth by authority a revised Greek Text of the New Testament. The chief writers of antiquity, say they, have been of late years re-edited by the aid of the best Manuscripts. Why should not the Scriptures enjoy the same advantage? Men who so speak evidently misunderstand the question. They assume that the case of the Scriptures and that of other ancient writings are similar.

Such remonstrances are commonly followed up by statements like the following:—That the received Text is that of Erasmus:—that it was constructed in haste, and without skill:—that it is based on a very few, and those bad Manuscripts:—that it belongs to an age when scarcely any of our present critical helps were available, and when the Science of Textual Criticism was unknown. To listen to these advocates for Revision, you would almost suppose that it fared with the Gospel at this instant as it had fared with the original Copy of the Law for many years until the days of King Josiah[9].

Yielding to no one in my desire to see the Greek of the New Testament judiciously revised, I freely avow that recent events have convinced me, and I suppose they have convinced the public also, that we have not among us the men to conduct such an undertaking. Better a thousand times in my judgement to leave things as they are, than to risk having the stamp of authority set upon such an unfortunate production as that which appeared on the 17th May, 1881, and which claims at this instant to represent the combined learning of the Church, the chief Sects, and the Socinian[10] body.

Now if the meaning of those who desire to see the commonly received text of the New Testament made absolutely faultless, were something of this kind:—That they are impatient for the collation of the copies which have become known to us within the last two centuries, and which amount already in all to upwards of three thousand: that they are bent on procuring that the ancient Versions shall be re-edited;—and would hail with delight the announcement that a band of scholars had combined to index every place of Scripture quoted by any of the Fathers:—if this were meant, we should all be entirely at one; especially if we could further gather from the programme that a fixed intention was cherished of abiding by the result of such an appeal to ancient evidence. But unfortunately something entirely different is in contemplation.

Now I am bent on calling attention to certain features of the problem which have very generally escaped attention. It does not seem to be understood that the Scriptures of the New Testament stand on an entirely different footing from every other ancient writing which can be named. A few plain remarks ought to bring this fact, for a fact it is, home to every thoughtful person. And the result will be that men will approach the subject with more caution,—with doubts and misgivings,—with a fixed determination to be on their guard against any form of plausible influence. Their prejudices they will scatter to the winds. At every step they will insist on proof.

In the first place, then, let it be observed that the New Testament Scriptures are wholly without a parallel in respect of their having been so frequently multiplied from the very first. They are by consequence contained at this day in an extravagantly large number of copies [probably, if reckoned under the six classes of Gospels, Acts and Catholic Epistles, Pauline Epistles, Apocalypse, Evangelistaries, and Apostolos, exceeding the number of four thousand]. There is nothing like this, or at all approaching to it, in the case of any profane writing that can be named[11].

And the very necessity for multiplying copies,—a necessity which has made itself felt in every age and in every clime,—has perforce resulted in an immense number of variants. Words have been inevitably dropped,—vowels have been inadvertently confounded by copyists more or less competent:—and the meaning of Scripture in countless places has suffered to a surprising degree in consequence. This first.

But then further, the Scriptures for the very reason because they were known to be the Word of God became a mark for the shafts of Satan from the beginning. They were by consequence as eagerly solicited by heretical teachers on the one hand, as they were hotly defended by the orthodox on the other. Alike from friends and from foes therefore, they are known to have experienced injury, and that in the earliest age of all. Nothing of the kind can be predicated of any other ancient writings. This consideration alone should suggest a severe exercise of judicial impartiality, in the handling of ancient evidence of whatever sort.

For I request it may be observed that I have not said—and I certainly do not mean—that the Scriptures themselves have been permanently corrupted either by friend or foe. Error was fitful and uncertain, and was contradicted by other error: besides that it sank eventually before a manifold witness to the truth. Nevertheless, certain manuscripts belonging to a few small groups—particular copies of a Version—individual Fathers or Doctors of the Church,—these do, to the present hour, bear traces incontestably of ancient mischief.

But what goes before is not nearly all. The fourfold structure of the Gospel has lent itself to a certain kind of licentious handling—of which in other ancient writings we have no experience. One critical owner of a Codex considered himself at liberty to assimilate the narratives: another to correct them in order to bring them into (what seemed to himself) greater harmony. Brevity is found to have been a paramount object with some, and Transposition to have amounted to a passion with others. Conjectural Criticism was evidently practised largely: and almost with as little felicity as when Bentley held the pen. Lastly, there can be no question that there was a certain school of Critics

16

who considered themselves competent to improve the style of the Holy Ghost throughout. [And before the members of the Church had gained a familiar acquaintance with the words of the New Testament, blunders continually crept into the text of more or less heinous importance.] All this, which was chiefly done during the second and third centuries, introduces an element of difficulty in the handling of ancient evidence which can never be safely neglected: and will make a thoughtful man suspicious of every various reading which comes in his way, especially if it is attended with but slender attestation. [It has been already shewn in the companion volume] that the names of the Codexes chiefly vitiated in this sort prove to be BאCDL; of the Versions,—the two Coptic, the Curetonian, and certain specimens of the Old Latin; of the Fathers,—Origen, Clement of Alexandria, and to some extent Eusebius.

Add to all that goes before the peculiar subject-matter of the New Testament Scriptures, and it will become abundantly plain why they should have been liable to a series of assaults which make it reasonable that they should now at last be approached by ourselves as no other ancient writings are, or can be. The nature of God,—His Being and Attributes:—the history of Man's Redemption:—the soul's eternal destiny:—the mysteries of the unseen world:—concerning these and every other similar high doctrinal subject, the sacred writings alone speak with a voice of absolute authority. And surely by this time enough has been said to explain why these Scriptures should have been made a battle-field during some centuries, and especially in the fourth; and having thus been made the subject of strenuous contention, that copies of them should exhibit to this hour traces of those many adverse influences. I say it for the last time,—of all such causes of depravation the Greek Poets, Tragedians, Philosophers, Historians, neither knew nor could know anything. And it thus plainly appears that the Textual Criticism of the New Testament is to be handled by ourselves in an entirely different spirit from that of any other book.

§ 2.

I wish now to investigate the causes of the corruption of the Text of the New Testament. I do not entitle the present a discussion of 'Various Readings,' because I consider that expression to be incorrect and misleading[12]. Freely allowing that the term 'variae lectiones,' for lack of a better, may be allowed to stand on the Critic's page, I yet think it necessary even a second time to call attention to the impropriety which attends its use. Thus Codex B differs from the commonly received Text of Scripture in the Gospels alone in 7578 places; of which no less than 2877 are instances of omission. In fact omissions constitute by far the larger number of what are commonly called 'Various Readings.' How then can those be called 'various readings' which are really not readings at all? How, for example, can that be said to be a 'various reading' of St. Mark xvi. 9-20, which consists in the circumstance that the last 12 verses are left out by two MSS.? Again,—How can it be called a 'various reading' of St. John xxi. 25, to bring the Gospel abruptly to a close, as

17

Tischendorf does, at v. 24? These are really nothing else but indications either of a mutilated or else an interpolated text. And the question to be resolved is,—On which side does the corruption lie? and, How did it originate?

Waiving this however, the term is objectionable on other grounds. It is to beg the whole question to assume that every irregularity in the text of Scripture is a 'various reading.' The very expression carries with it an assertion of importance; at least it implies a claim to consideration. Even might it be thought that, because it is termed a 'various reading,' therefore a critic is entitled to call in question the commonly received text. Whereas, nine divergences out of ten are of no manner of significance and are entitled to no manner of consideration, as every one must see at a glance who will attend to the matter ever so little. 'Various readings' in fact is a term which belongs of right to the criticism of the text of profane authors: and, like many other notions which have been imported from the same region into this department of inquiry, it only tends to confuse and perplex the judgement.

No variety in the Text of Scripture can properly be called a 'various reading,' of which it may be safely declared that it never has been, and never will be, read. In the case of profane authors, where the MSS. are for the most part exceedingly few, almost every plausible substitution of one word for another, if really entitled to alteration, is looked upon as a various reading of the text. But in the Gospels, of which the copies are so numerous as has been said, the case is far otherwise. We are there able to convince ourselves in a moment that the supposed 'various reading' is nothing else but an instance of licentiousness or inattention on the part of a previous scribe or scribes, and we can afford to neglect it accordingly[13]. It follows therefore,—and this is the point to which I desire to bring the reader and to urge upon his consideration,—that the number of 'various readings' in the New Testament properly so called has been greatly exaggerated. They are, in reality, exceedingly few in number; and it is to be expected that, as sound (sacred) Criticism advances, and principles are established, and conclusions recognized, instead of becoming multiplied they will become fewer and fewer, and at last will entirely disappear. We cannot afford to go on disputing for ever; and what is declared by common consent to be untenable ought to be no longer reckoned. That only in short, as I venture to think, deserves the name of a Various Reading which comes to us so respectably recommended as to be entitled to our sincere consideration and respect; or, better still, which is of such a kind as to inspire some degree of reasonable suspicion that after all it may prove to be the true way of exhibiting the text.

The inquiry therefore on which we are about to engage, grows naturally out of the considerations which have been already offered. We propose to ascertain, as far as is practicable at the end of so many hundred years, in what way these many strange corruptions of the text have arisen. Very often we shall only have to inquire how it has come to pass that the text exhibits signs of perturbation at a certain place. Such disquisitions as those which follow, let it never be forgotten, have no place in reviewing any other text than that of the New Testament, because a few plain principles would suffice to solve every difficulty. The less usual word mistaken for the word of mare frequent occurrence;—clerical carelessness;—a gloss finding its way from the margin into the text;—such explanations as these would probably in other cases suffice to account for every ascertained corruption of the text. But it is far otherwise here, as I propose to make fully apparent by and by. Various disturbing influences have been at work for a great many years, of which secular productions know absolutely nothing, nor indeed can know.

The importance of such an inquiry will become apparent as we proceed; but it may be convenient that I should call attention to the matter briefly at the outset. It frequently happens that the one remaining plea of many critics for adopting readings of a certain kind, is the inexplicable nature of the phenomena which these readings exhibit. 'How will you possibly account for such a reading as the present,' (say they,) 'if it be not authentic?' Or they say nothing, but leave it to be inferred that the reading they adopt,—in spite of its intrinsic improbability, in spite also of the slender amount of evidence on which it rests,—must needs be accepted as true. They lose sight of the correlative difficulty:—How comes it to pass that the rest of the copies read the place otherwise? On all such occasions it is impossible to overestimate the importance of detecting the particular cause which has brought about, or which at least will fully account for, this depravation. When this has been done, it is hardly too much to say that a case presents itself like as when a pasteboard mask has been torn away, and the ghost is discovered with a broad grin on his face behind it.

The discussion on which I now enter is then on the Causes of the various Corruptions of the Text. [The reader shall be shewn with illustrations to what particular source they are to be severally ascribed. When representative passages have been thus labelled, and the causes are seen in operation, he will be able to pierce the mystery, and all the better to winnow the evil from among the good.]

§ 3.

When I take into my hands an ancient copy of the Gospels, I expect that it will exhibit sundry inaccuracies and imperfections: and I am never disappointed in my expectation. The discovery however creates no uneasiness, so long as the phenomena evolved are of a certain kind and range within easily definable limits. Thus:—

1. Whatever belongs to peculiarities of spelling or fashions of writing, I can afford to disregard. For example, it is clearly consistent with perfect good faith, that a scribe should spell κράβαττον[14] in several different ways: that he should write οὕτω for οὕτως, or the contrary: that he should add or omit what grammarians call the ν ἐφελκυστικόν. The questions really touched by irregularities such as these concern the date and country where the MS. was produced; not by any means the honesty or animus of the copyist. The man fell into the method which was natural to him, or which he found prevailing around him; and that was all. 'Itacisms' therefore, as they are called, of what-

ever kind,—by which is meant the interchange of such vowels and diphthongs as ι-ει, αι-ε, η-ι, η-οι-υ, ο-ω, η-ει,—need excite no uneasiness. It is true that these variations may occasionally result in very considerable inconvenience: for it will sometimes happen that a different reading is the consequence. But the copyist may have done his work in perfect good faith for all that. It is not he who is responsible for the perplexity he occasions me, but the language and the imperfect customs amidst which he wrote.

2. In like manner the reduplication of syllables, words, clauses, sentences, is consistent with entire sincerity of purpose on the part of the copyist. This inaccuracy is often to be deplored; inasmuch as a reduplicated syllable often really affects the sense. But for the most part nothing worse ensues than that the page is disfigured with errata.

3. So, on the other hand,—the occasional omission of words, whether few or many,—especially that passing from one line to the corresponding place in a subsequent line, which generally results from the proximity of a similar ending,—is a purely venial offence. It is an evidence of carelessness, but it proves nothing worse.

4. Then further,—slight inversions, especially of ordinary words; or the adoption of some more obvious and familiar collocation of particles in a sentence; or again, the occasional substitution of one common word for another, as εἶπε for ἔλεγε, φώνησαν for κράξαν, and the like;—need not provoke resentment. It is an indication, we are willing to hope, of nothing worse than slovenliness on the part of the writer or the group or succession of writers.

5. I will add that besides the substitution of one word for another, cases frequently occur, where even the introduction into the text of one or more words which cannot be thought to have stood in the original autograph of the Evangelist, need create no offence. It is often possible to account for their presence in a strictly legitimate way.

But it is high time to point out, that irregularities which fall under these last heads are only tolerable within narrow limits, and always require careful watching; for they may easily become excessive or even betray an animus; and in either case they pass at once into quite a different category. From cases of excusable oscitancy they degenerate, either into instances of inexcusable licentiousness, or else into cases of downright fraud.

6. Thus, if it be observed in the case of a Codex (*a*) that entire sentences or significant clauses are habitually omitted:—(*b*) that again and again in the course of the same page the phraseology of the Evangelist has upon clear evidence been seriously tampered with: and (*c*) that interpolations here and there occur which will not admit of loyal interpretation:—we cannot but learn to regard with habitual distrust the Codex in which all these notes are found combined. It is as when a witness, whom we suspected of nothing worse than a bad memory or a random tongue or a lively imagination, has been at last convicted of deliberate suppression of parts of his evidence, misrepresentation of facts,—in fact, deliberate falsehood.

7. But now suppose the case of a MS. in which words or clauses are clearly omitted with design; where expressions are withheld which are confessedly harsh or critically difficult,—whole sentences or parts of them which have a known controversial bearing;—Suppose further that the same MS. abounds in worthless paraphrase, and contains apocryphal additions throughout:— What are we to think of our guide then? There can be but one opinion on the subject. From habitually trusting, we shall entertain inveterate distrust. We have ascertained his character. We thought he was a faithful witness, but we now find from experience of his transgressions that we have fallen into bad company. His witness may be false no less than true: confidence is at an end.

§ 4.

It may be regarded as certain that most of the aberrations discoverable in Codexes of the Sacred Text have arisen in the first instance from the merest inadvertency of the scribes. That such was the case in a vast number of cases is in fact demonstrable. [Inaccuracy in the apprehension of the Divine Word, which in the earliest ages was imperfectly understood, and ignorance of Greek in primitive Latin translators, were prolific sources of error. The influence of Lectionaries, in which Holy Scripture was cut up into separate Lections either with or without an introduction, remained with habitual hearers, and led them off in copying to paths which had become familiar. Acquaintance with 'Harmonies' or Diatessarons caused copyists insensibly to assimilate one Gospel to another. And doctrinal predilections, as in the case of those who belonged to the Origenistic school, were the source of lapsing into expressions which were not the *verba ipsissima* of Holy Writ. In such cases, when the inadvertency was genuine and was unmingled with any overt design, it is much to be noted that the error seldom propagated itself extensively.]

But next, well-meant endeavours must have been made at a very early period to 'rectify' (διορθοῦν) the text thus unintentionally corrupted; and so, what began in inadvertence is sometimes found in the end to exhibit traces of design, and often becomes in a high degree perplexing. Thus, to cite a favourite example, it is clear to me that in the earliest age of all (A.D. 100?) some copyist of St. Luke ii. 14 (call him X) inadvertently omitted the second EN in the Angelic Hymn. Now if the persons (call them Y and Z) whose business it became in turn to reproduce the early copy thus inadvertently depraved, had but been content both of them to transcribe exactly what they saw before them, the error of their immediate predecessor (X) must infallibly have speedily been detected, remedied, and forgotten,—simply because, as every one must have seen as well as Y and Z, it was impossible to translate the sentence which results,—ἐπὶ γῆς εἰρήνη ἀνθρώποις εὐδοκία. Reference would have been made to any other copy of the third Gospel, and together with the omitted preposition (ἐν) sense would have been restored to the passage. But unhappily one of the two supposed Copyists being a learned grammarian who had no other copy at hand to refer to, undertook, good man that he was, *proprio Marte* to force a meaning into the manifestly corrupted text of the copy before him: and he did it by affixing to εὐδοκία the sign of the genitive case (ς). Unhappy effort of misplaced skill! That copy [or those copies] became the immediate progenitor [or progenitors] of a large family,—from which all the Latin copies are descended; whereby it comes to pass that Latin Christendom sings the Hymn 'Gloria in excelsis' incorrectly to the present hour, and may possibly sing it incorrectly to the end of time. The error committed by that same venerable Copyist survives in the four oldest copies of the passage extant, B* and א*, A and D,—though happily in no others,—in the Old Latin, Vulgate, and Gothic, alone of Versions; in Irenaeus and Origen (who contradict themselves), and in the Latin Fathers. All the Greek authorities, with the few exceptions just recorded, of which A and D are the only consistent witnesses, unite in condemning the evident blunder[15].

I once hoped that it might be possible to refer all the Corruptions of the Text of Scripture to ordinary causes: as, careless transcription,—divers accidents,—misplaced critical assiduity,—doctrinal animus,—small acts of unpardonable licence.

But increased attention and enlarged acquaintance with the subject, have convinced me that by far the larger number of the omissions of such. Codexes as אBLD must needs be due to quite a different cause. These MSS. omit so many words, phrases, sentences, verses of Scripture,—that it is altogether incredible that the proximity of like endings can have much to do with the matter. Inadvertency may be made to bear the blame of some omissions: it cannot bear the blame of shrewd and significant omissions of clauses, which invariably leave the sense complete. A systematic and perpetual mutilation of the inspired Text must needs be the result of design, not of accident[16].

[It will be seen therefore that the causes of the Corruptions of the Text class themselves under two main heads, viz. (I.) Those which arose from Inadvertency, and (II.) Those which took their origin in Design.]

[9] 2 Kings xxii. 8 = 2 Chron. xxxiv.15.
[10] [This name is used for want of a better. Churchmen are Unitarians as well as Trinitarians. The two names in combination express our Faith. We dare not alienate either of them.]
[11] See The Traditional Text of the Holy Gospels (Burgon & Miller), p.21, note 1.
[12] See Traditional Text, chapter ii, § 6, p. 32.
[13] [Perhaps this point may be cleared by dividing readings into two classes, viz. (1) such as really have strong evidence for their support, and require examination before we can be certain that they are corrupt; and (2) those which afford no doubt as to their being destitute of foundation, and are only interesting as specimens of the modes in which error was sometimes introduced. Evidently, the latter class are not 'various' at all.]
[14] [I.e. generally κράβαττον, or else κράβατον, or even κράβακτον; seldom found as κράββαττον, or spelt in the corrupt form κράββατον.]
[15] I am inclined to believe that in the age immediately succeeding that of the Apostles, some person or persons of great influence and authority executed a Revision of the N. T. and gave the world the result of such labours in a 'corrected

Text.' The guiding principle seems to have been to seek to *abridge* the Text, to lop off whatever seemed redundant, or which might in any way be spared, and to eliminate from one Gospel whatever expressions occurred elsewhere in another Gospel. Clauses which slightly obscured the speaker's meaning; or which seemed to hang loose at the end of a sentence; or which introduced a consideration of difficulty:—words which interfered with the easy flow of a sentence:—every thing of this kind such a personage seems to have held himself free to discard. But what is more serious, passages which occasioned some difficulty, as the *pericope de adultera*; physical perplexity, as the troubling of the water; spiritual revulsion, as the agony in the garden:—all these the reviser or revisers seem to have judged it safest simply to eliminate. It is difficult to understand how any persons in their senses could have so acted by the sacred deposit; but it does not seem improbable that at some very remote period there were found some who did act in some such way. Let it be observed, however, that unlike some critics I do not base my real argument upon what appears to me to be a not unlikely supposition.

[16] [Unless it be referred to the two converging streams of corruption, as described in The Traditional Text.]

Chapter Two - Accidental Causes of Corruption - I. Pure Accident

[IT often happens that more causes than one are combined in the origin of the corruption in any one passage. In the following history of a blunder and of the fatal consequences that ensued upon it, only the first step was accidental. But much instruction may be derived from the initial blunder, and though the later stages in the history come under another head, they nevertheless illustrate the effects of early accident, besides throwing light upon parts of the discussion which are yet to come.]

§ 1.

We are sometimes able to trace the origin and progress of accidental depravations of the text: and the study is as instructive as it is interesting. Let me invite attention to what is found in St. John x. 29; where,—instead of, 'My Father, who hath given them [viz. My sheep] to Me, is greater than all,'—Tischendorf, Tregelles, Alford, are for reading, 'That thing which My (*or* the) Father hath given to Me is greater (i.e. is a greater thing) than all.' A vastly different proposition, truly; and, whatever it may mean, wholly inadmissible here, as the context proves. It has been the result of sheer accident moreover,—as I proceed to explain.

St. John certainly wrote the familiar words,—ὁ πατήρ μου ὃς δέδωκέ μοι, μείζων ἐστί. But, with the licentiousness [or inaccuracy] which prevailed in the earliest age, some remote copyist is found to have substituted for ὃς δέδωκε, its grammatical equivalent ὃς δεδωκώς. And this proved fatal; for it was only necessary that another scribe should substitute μεῖζον for μείζων (after the example of such places as St. Matt. xii. 6, 41, 42, &c.), and thus the door had been opened to at least four distinct deflections from the evangelical verity, — which straightway found their way into manuscripts:—(1) ο δεδωκως . . . μειζων—of which reading at this day D is the sole representative: (2) ος δεδωκε . . . . μειζον—which survives only in AX: (3) ο δεδωκε . . . . μειζων—which is only found in אL: (4) ο δεδωκε . . . . μειζον—which is the peculiar property of B. The 1st and 2nd of these sufficiently represent the Evangelist's meaning, though neither of them is what he actually wrote; but the 3rd is untranslatable: while the 4th is nothing else but a desperate attempt to force a meaning into the 3rd, by writing μειζον for μειζων; treating ο not as the article but as the neuter of the relative ὅς.

This last exhibition of the text, which in fact scarcely yields an intelligible meaning and rests upon the minimum of manuscript evidence, would long since have been forgotten, but that, calamitously for the Western Church, its Version of the New Testament Scriptures was executed from MSS. of the same vicious type as Cod. B[17]. Accordingly, all the Latin copies, and therefore all the Latin Fathers[18], translate,—'Pater [meus] quod dedit mihi, majus omnibus est[19].' The Westerns resolutely extracted a meaning from whatever they presumed to be genuine Scripture: and one can but admire the piety which insists on finding sound Divinity in what proves after all to be nothing else but a sorry blunder. What, asks Augustine, 'was the thing, greater than all,' which the Father gave to the Son? To be the Word of the Father (he answers), His only-begotten Son and the brightness of His glory[20]. The Greeks knew better. Basil[21], Chrysostom[22], Cyril on nine occasions[23], Theodoret[24]— as many as quote the place—invariably exhibit the *textus receptus* ὅς . . . μείζων, which is obviously the true reading and may on no account suffer molestation.

'But,'—I shall perhaps be asked,—'although Patristic and manuscript evidence are wanting for the reading ὃ δεδωκέ μοι . . μείζων,—is it not a significant circumstance that three translations of such high antiquity as the Latin, the Bohairic, and the Gothic, should concur in supporting it? and does it not inspire extraordinary confidence in B to find that B alone of MSS. agrees with them?' To which I answer,—It makes me, on the contrary, more and more distrustful of the Latin, the Bohairic and the Gothic versions to find them exclusively siding with Cod. B on such an occasion as the present. It is obviously not more 'significant' that the Latin, the Bohairic, and the Gothic, should here conspire with—than that the Syriac, the Sahidic, and the Ethiopic, should here combine against B. On the other hand, how utterly insignificant is the testimony of B when opposed to all the uncials, all the cursives, and all the Greek fathers who quote the place. So far from inspiring me with confidence in B, the present indication of the fatal sympathy of that Codex with the corrupt copies from which confessedly many of the Old Latin were executed, confirms me in my habitual distrust of it. About the true reading of St. John x. 29, there really exists no manner of doubt. As for the old uncials' they

24

are (as usual) hopelessly at variance on the subject. In an easy sentence of only 9 words,—which however Tischendorf exhibits in conformity with no known Codex, while Tregelles and Alford blindly follow Cod. B,—they have contrived to invent five 'various readings,' as may be seen at foot[25]. Shall we wonder more at the badness of the Codexes to which we are just now invited to pin our faith; or at the infatuation of our guides?

§ 2.

I do not find that sufficient attention has been paid to grave disturbances of the Text which have resulted from a slight clerical error. While we are enumerating the various causes of Textual depravity, we may not fail to specify this. Once trace a serious Textual disturbance back to (what for convenience may be called) a 'clerical error,' and you are supplied with an effectual answer to a form of inquiry which else is sometimes very perplexing: viz. If the true meaning of this passage be what you suppose, for what conceivable reason should the scribe have misrepresented it in this strange way,—made nonsense, in short, of the place? . . . I will further remark, that it is always interesting, sometimes instructive, after detecting the remote origin of an ancient blunder, to note what has been its subsequent history and progress.

Some specimens of the thing referred to I have already given in another place. The reader is invited to acquaint himself with the strange process by which the 276 souls' who suffered shipwreck with St. Paul (Acts xxvii. 37), have since dwindled down to 'about 76[26].'—He is further requested to note how a 'certain man' who in the time of St. Paul bore the name of 'Justus' (Acts xviii. 7), has been since transformed into '*Titus*,' '*Titus Justus*,' and even "*Titius Justus*[27].'—But for a far sadder travestie of sacred words, the reader is referred to what has happened in St. Matt. xi. 23 and St. Luke x. 15,—where our Saviour is made to ask an unmeaning question—instead of being permitted to announce a solemn fact—concerning Capernaum[28].—The newly-discovered ancient name of the Island of Malta, *Melitene*[29], (for which geographers are indebted to the adventurous spirit of Westcott and Hort), may also be profitably considered in connexion with what is to be the subject of the present chapter. And now to break up fresh ground.

Attention is therefore invited to a case of attraction in Acts xx. 24. It is but the change of a single letter (λόγοΥ for λόγοN), yet has that minute deflection from the truth led to a complete mangling of the most affecting perhaps of St. Paul's utterances. I refer to the famous words ἀλλ' οὐδενὸς λόγον ποιοῦμαι, οὐδὲ ἔχω τὴν ψυχήν μου τιμίαν ἐμαυτῷ, ὡς τελειῶσαι τὸν δρόμον μου μετὰ χαρᾶς: excellently, because idiomatically, rendered by our Translators of 1611,—'But none of these things move me, neither count I my life dear unto myself, so that I might finish my course with joy.'

For οὐδενὸς λοΓON, (the accusative after ποιοῦμαι), some one having substituted οὐδενὸς λοΓOΥ,—a reading which survives to this hour in B and C[30],—it became necessary to find something else for the verb to govern. Τὴν ψυχήν was at hand, but οὐδὲ ἔχω stood in the way. Οὐδὲ ἔχω must therefore go[31]; and go it did,—as B, C, and ℵ remain to attest. Τιμίαν should have gone also, if the sentence was to be made translatable but τιμίαν was left behind[32]. The authors of ancient embroilments of the text were sad bunglers. In the meantime, Cod. ℵ inadvertently retained St. Luke's word, ΛΟΓΟΝ; and because ℵ here follows B in every other respect, it exhibits a text which is simply unintelligible[33].

Now the second clause of the sentence, viz. the words οὐδὲ ἔχω τὴν ψυχήν μου τιμίαν ἐμαυτῷ, may on no account be surrendered. It is indeed beyond the reach of suspicion, being found in Codd. A, D, E, H, L, 13, 31,—in fact in every known copy of the Acts, except the discordant ℵBC. The clause in question is further witnessed to by the Vulgate[34],—by the Harkleian[35],—by Basil[36],—by Chrysostom[37],—by Cyril[38],—by Euthalius[39],—and by the interpolator of Ignatius[40]. What are we to think of our guides (Tischendorf, Tregelles, Westcott and Hort, and the Revisers) who have nevertheless surrendered the Traditional Text and presented us instead with what Dr. Field,—who is indeed a Master in Israel,—describes as the impossible ἀλλ' οὐδενὸς λόγου ποιοῦμαι τὴν ψυχὴν τιμίαν ἐμαυτῷ[41]?

The words of the last-named eminent scholar on the reading just cited are so valuable in themselves, and are observed to be so often in point, that they shall find place here:—'Modern Critics,' he says, in deference to the authority of the older MSS., and to certain critical canons which prescribe that preference should be given to the shorter and more difficult reading over the longer and easier one, have decided that the T. R. in this passage is to be replaced by that which is contained in those older MSS.

'In regard to the difficulty of this reading, that term seems hardly applicable to the present case. A difficult reading is one which presents something apparently incongruous in the sense, or anomalous in the construction, which an ignorant or half-learned copyist would endeavour, by the use of such critical faculty as he possessed, to remove; but which a true critic is able, by probable explanation, and a comparison of similar cases, to defend against all such fancied improvements. In the reading before us, ἀλλ' οὐδενὸς λόγου ποιοῦμαι τὴν ψυχὴν τιμίαν ἐμαυτῷ, it is the construction, and not the sense, which is in question; and this is not simply difficult, but impossible. There is really no way of getting over it; it baffles novices and experts alike[42]: When will men believe that a reading vouched for by only BℵC is safe to be a fabrication[43]? But at least when Copies and Fathers combine, as here they do, against those three copies, what can justify critics in upholding a text which carries on its face its own condemnation?

§ 3.

We now come to the inattention of those long-since-forgotten Ist or IInd century scribes who, beguiled by the similarity of the letters EN and AN (in the expression EN AN-θρωποις ευδοκια, St. Luke ii. 14), left out the preposition. An unintelligible clause was the consequence, as has been explained above (p. 21): which some one next sought to remedy by adding to εὐδοκία the sign of the genitive (C). Thus the Old Latin translations were made.

26

That this is the true history of a blunder which the latest Editors of the New Testament have mistaken for genuine Gospel, is I submit certain[44]. Most Latin copies (except 14[45]) exhibit 'pax hominibus bonae voluntatis,' as well as many Latin Fathers[46]. On the other hand, the preposition EN is retained in every known Greek copy of St. Luke without exception, while the reading εὐδοκίας is absolutely limited to the four uncials ABℵD. The witness of antiquity on this head is thus overwhelming and decisive.

§ 4.

In other cases the source, the very progress of a blunder,—is discoverable. Thus whereas St. Mark (in xv. 6) certainly wrote ἕνα δέσμιον, ΟΝΠΕΡ ἠτοῦντο, the scribe of Δ who evidently derived his text from an earlier copy in uncial letters is found to have divided the Evangelist's syllables wrongly, and to exhibit in this place ΟΝ . ΠΕΡΗΤΟΥΝΤΟ. The consequence might have been predicted. ℵAB transform this into ΟΝ . ΠΑΡΗΤΟΥΝΤΟ: which accordingly is the reading adopted by Tischendorf and by Westcott and Hort.

Whenever in fact the final syllable of one word can possibly be mistaken for the first syllable of the next, or *vice versa*, it is safe sooner or later to have misled somebody. Thus, we are not at all surprised to find St. Mark's ἃ παρέλαβον (vii. 4) transformed into ἅπερ ἔλαβον, but only by B.

[Another startling instance of the same phenomenon is supplied by the substitution in St. Mark vi. 22 of τῆς θυγατρὸς αὐτοῦ Ἡρωδιάδος. for τῆς θυγατρὸς αὐτῆς τῆς Ἡρωδιάδος. Here a first copyist left out τῆς as being a repetition of the last syllable of αὐτῆς, and afterwards a second attempted to improve the Greek by putting the masculine pronoun for the feminine (ΑΥΤΟΥ for ΑΥΤΗΣ). The consequence was hardly to have been foreseen.]

Strange to say it results in the following monstrous figment:—that the fruit of Herod's incestuous connexion with Herodias had been a daughter, who was also named Herodias; and that she,—the King's own daughter,—was the immodest one[47] who came in and danced before him, 'his lords, high captains, and chief estates of Galilee,' as they sat at the birthday banquet. Probability, natural feeling, the obvious requirements of the narrative, History itself—, for Josephus expressly informs us that 'Salome,' not Herodias,' was the name of 'Herodias' daughter[48],—all reclaim loudly against such a perversion of the truth. But what ought to be in itself conclusive, what in fact settles the question, is the testimony of the MSS.,—of which only seven (ℵBDLΔ with two cursive copies) can be found to exhibit this strange mistake. Accordingly the reading ΑΥΤΟΥ is rejected by Griesbach, Lachmann, Tregelles, Tischendorf and Alford. It has nevertheless found favour with Dr. Hort; and it has even been thrust into the margin of the revised Text of our Authorized Version, as a reading having some probability.

This is indeed an instructive instance of the effect of accidental errors—another proof that ℵBDL cannot be trusted.

Sufficiently obvious are the steps whereby the present erroneous reading was brought to perfection. The immediate proximity in MSS. of the selfsame combination of letters is observed invariably to result in a various reading. AYTHCTHC was safe to part with its second THC on the first opportunity, and the definitive article (τῆς) once lost, the substitution of AYTOY for AYTHC is just such a mistake as a copyist with ill-directed intelligence would be sure to fall into if he were bestowing sufficient attention on the subject to be aware that the person spoken of in verses 20 and 21 is Herod the King.

[This recurrence of identical or similar syllables near together was a frequent source of error. Copying has always a tendency to become mechanical: and when the mind of the copyist sank to sleep in his monotonous toil, as well as if it became too active, the sacred Text suffered more or less, and so even a trifling mistake might be the seed of serious depravation.]

§ 5.

Another interesting and instructive instance of error originating in sheer accident, is supplied by the reading in certain MSS. of St. Mark viii. 1. That the Evangelist wrote παμπόλλου ὄχλου 'the multitude being very great,' is certain. This is the reading of all the uncials but eight, of all the cursives but fifteen. But instead of this, it has been proposed that we should read, 'when there was again a great multitude,' the plain fact being that some ancient scribe mistook, as he easily might, the less usual compound word for what was to himself a far more familiar expression: i.e. he mistook ΠΑΜΡΠΟΛΛΟΥ for ΠΑΛΙΝ ΠΟΛΛΟΥ.

This blunder must date from the second century, for 'iterum' is met with in the Old Latin as well as in the Vulgate, the Gothic, the Bohairic, and some other versions. On the other hand, it is against 'every true principle of Textual Criticism' (as Dr. Tregelles would say), that the more difficult expression should be abandoned for the easier, when forty-nine out of every fifty MSS. are observed to uphold it; when the oldest version of all, the Syriac, is on the same side; when the source of the mistake is patent; and when the rarer word is observed to be in St. Mark's peculiar manner. There could be in fact no hesitation on this subject, if the opposition had not been headed by those notorious false witnesses אBDL, which it is just now the fashion to uphold at all hazards. They happen to be supported on this occasion by GMNΔ and fifteen cursives: while two other cursives look both ways and exhibit πάλιν παμπόλλου.

In St. Mark vii. 14, πάλιν irciaLv was similarly misread by some copyists for πάντα, and has been preserved by אBDLΔ (ΠΑΛΙΝ for ΠΑΝΤΑ) against thirteen uncials, all the cursives, the Peshitto and Armenian.

So again in St. John xiii. 37. A reads δύνασαί σοι by an evident slip of the pen for δύναμαί σοι. And in xix. 31 μεγαλΗ Η Ημερα has become μεγάλη ἡμέρα in אΑΕΓ and some cursive copies.

---

[17] See the passages quoted in Scrivener's Introduction, II. 270-2, 4th ed.
[18] Tertull. (Prax. c. 22): Ambr. (ii. 576, 607, 689 bis): Hilary (930 bis, 1089): Jerome (v. 208): Augustin (iii². 615): Maximinus, an Arian bishop (ap. Aug. viii. 651).

[19] Pater (*or* Pater meus) quod dedit mihi (*or* mihi dedit), majus omnibus est (*or* majus est omnibus: *or* omnibus majus est).

[20] iii². 615. He begins, '*Quid dedit Filio Pater majus omnibus? Ut ipsi ille esset unigenitus Filius.*'

[21] i. 236.

[22] viii. 363 *bis*.

[23] i. 188: ii. 567: iii. 792: iv. 666 (ed. Pusey): v¹. 326, 577, 578: *ap.* Mai ii. 13: iii. 336.

[24] v. 1065 (= Dial ^Maced *ap.* Athanas. 555).

[25] Viz. + μου ABD: — μου ℵ | ος A: ο BℵD | δεδωκεν BℵA: δεδωκως | μειζων ℵD: μειζον AB | μειζ. παντων εστιν A: παντων μειζ. εστιν BℵD.

[26] The Revision Revised, p. 51-3.

[27] The Revision Revised, p. 53-4.

[28] Ibid. p. 51-6.

[29] Ibid. p. 177-8.

[30] Also in Ammonius the presbyter, A.D. 458—see Cramer's Cat. p. 334-5, *last line.* Λόγου is read besides in the cursives Act. 36, 96, 105.

[31] I look for an approving word from learned Dr. Field, who wrote in 1875— 'The real obstacle to our acquiescing in the reading of the T. R. is, that if the words οὐδὲ ἔχω had once formed apart of the original text, there is no possibility of accounting for the subsequent omission of them.' The same remark, but considerably toned down, is found in his delightful Otium Norvicense, P. iii, p. 84.

[32] B and C read—ἀλλ᾽ οὐδενὸς λόγον ποιοῦμαι τὴν ψυχὴν τιμίαν ἐμαυτῷ: which is exactly what Lucifer Calarit. represents,—'*sed pro nihilo aestimo animam meam carom esse mihi*' (Galland. vi. 241).

[33] ℵ reads—ἀλλ᾽ οὐδενὸς λόγον ποιοῦμαι τὴν ψυχὴν τιμίαν ἐμαυτῷ ὡς τελειῶσαι τὸν δρόμον μου.

[34] '*Sed nihil horum* [τούτων, is found in many Greek Codd.] *vereor, nec facio animam meam pretiosiorem quam me.*' So, the *Cod. Amiat.* It is evident then that when Ambrose (ii. 1040) writes '*nec facio animam meam cariorem mihi,*' he is quoting the latter of these two clauses. Augustine (iii¹. 516), when he cites the place thus, '*Non enim facio animam meam pretiosiorem quam me*'; and elsewhere (iv. 268) '*pretiosam mihi*'; also Origen (*interp.* iv. 628 c), '*sed ego non facio cariorem animam meam mihi*'; and even the Coptic, '*sed anima mea, dico, non est pretiosa mihi in aliquo verbo*':—these evidently summarize the place, by making a sentence out of what survives of the second clause. The Latin of D exhibits '*Sed nihil horum cura est mihi: neque habeo ipsam animam caram mihi.*'

[35] Dr. Field says that it may be thus Graecized—ἀλλ᾽ οὐδένα λόγον ποιοῦμαι, οὐδὲ λελόγισταί μοι ψυχή μού τι τίμιον.

[36] ii. 296 e,—exactly as the T. R.

[37] Exactly as the T. R., except that he writes τὴν ψυχήν, without μου (ix. 332). So again, further on (334 b), οὐκ ἔχω τιμίαν τὴν ἐμαυτοῦ ψυχήν. This latter place is quoted in Cramer's Cat. 334.

[38] *Ap.* Mai ii. 336 ἔδει καὶ τῆς ζωῆς καταφρονεῖν ὑπὲρ τοῦ τελειῶσαι τὸν δρόμον, οὐδὲ τὴν ψυχὴν ἔφη ποιεῖσθαι τιμίαν ἑαυτῷ.

[39] λόγον ἔχω, οὐδὲ ποιοῦμαι τὴν ψυχὴν τιμίαν ἐμαυτῷ, ὥστε κ.τ.λ. (*ap.* Galland. x. 222).

[40] ἀλλ᾽ οὐδενὸς λόγου ποιοῦμαι τῶν δεινῶν, οὐδὲ ἔχω τὴν ψυχὴν τιμίαν ἐμαυτῷ. Epist. ad Tars. c. 1 (Dressel, p. 255).

[41] The whole of Dr. Field's learned annotation deserves to be carefully read and pondered. I speak of it espe-

cially in the shape in which it originally appeared, viz. in 1875.

[42] Ibid. p. 2 and 3.

[43] Surprising it is how largely the text of this place has suffered at the hands of Copyists and Translators. In A and D, the words ποιοῦμαι and ἔχω have been made to change places. The latter Codex introduces μοι after ἔχω,—for ἐμαυτῷ, writes ἐμαυτοῦ,—and exhibits τοῦ τελειῶσαι without ὡς. C writes ὡς τὸ τελειῶσαι. אB *alone of Codexes* present us with τελειώσω for τελειῶσαι, and are followed by Westcott and Hort *alone of Editors*. The Peshitto (*'sed mihi nihili aestimatur anima mea'*), the Sahidic (*'sed non facio animam meam in ullâ re'*), and the Aethiopic (*'sed non reputo animam means nihil quidquam'*), get rid of τιμίαν as well as of οὐδὲ ἔχω. So much diversity of text, and in such primitive witnesses, while it points to a remote period as the date of the blunder to which attention is called in the text, testifies eloquently to the utter perplexity which that blunder occasioned from the first.

[44] Another example of the same phenomenon, (viz. the absorption of EN by the first syllable of ANθρωποις) is to be seen in Acts iv. 12,—where however the error has led to no mischievous results.

[45] For those which insert *in* (14), and those which reject it (25), see Wordsworth's edition of the Vulgate on this passage.

[46] Of Fathers:—Ambrose i. 1298— Hieronymus i. 448[2], 693, 876: ii. 213: iv. 34, 92: v. 147: vi. 638: vii. 241, 281, 283,—Augustine 34 times,—Optatus (Galland. v. 472, 487),—Gaudentius Brix. (*ap.* Sabat.),—Chromatius Ag. (Gall. viii. 337),—Orosius (*ib.* ix. 134), Marius M. (*ib.* viii. 672), Maximus Taus. (*ib.* ix. 355),—Sedulius (*ib.* 575),—Leo M. (*ap.* Sabat.),—Mamertus Claudianus (Gall. x. 430,—Vigilius Taps. (ap. Sabat.),—Zacchaeus (Gall. ix. 241,— Caesarius Arel. (ib. xi. 11),—ps.- Ambros. ii. 394, 396,—Hormisdas P. (Conc. iv. 1494, 1496),—52 Bps. at 8th Council of Toledo (Conc. 395), &c., &c.

[47] See Wetstein on this place.

[48] Antiqq. i. 99, xviii. 5. 4.

Chapter Three - Accidental Causes of Corruption - II. Homoeoteleuton

No one who finds the syllable OI recurring six times over in about as many words,—e. g. καὶ ἐγένετο, ὡς ἀπῆλθον . . . OI ἄγγελOI, καὶ OI ἄνθρωπOI OI πOIμένες εἶπον,—is surprised to learn that MSS. of a certain type exhibit serious perturbation in that place. Accordingly, BLΞ: leave out the words καὶ οἱ ἄνθρωποι; and in that mutilated form the modern critical editors are contented to exhibit St. Luke ii. 15. One would have supposed that Tischendorf's eyes would have been opened when he noticed that in his own Codex (א) one word more (οἱ) is dropped,—whereby nonsense is made of the passage (viz. of οἱ ἄγγελοι ποιμένες). Self-evident it is that a line with a 'like ending' has been omitted by the copyist of some very early codex of St. Luke's Gospel; which either read,—

ΟΙ ΑΓΓΕΛΟΙ		ΟΙ ΑΓΓΕΛΟΙ
[ΚΑΙ ΟΙ **ΑΝΟ**Ι ΟΙ]	} or else {	[ΚΑΙ ΟΙ **ΑΝΟ**Ι]
ΠΟΙΜΕΝΕΣ		ΟΙ ΠΟΙΜΕΝΕΣ

Another such place is found in St. John vi. 11. The Evangelist certainly described the act of our Saviour on a famous occasion in the well-known words,—καὶ εὐχαριστήσας διέδωκεν τοις [μαθηταις, οι δε μαθηται τοις] ανακειμενοις.

The one sufficient proof that St. John did so write, being the testimony of the MSS. Moreover, we are expressly assured by St. Matthew (xiv. 19), St. Mark (vi. 41), and St. Luke (ix. 16), that our Saviour's act was performed in this way. It is clear however that some scribe has suffered his eye to wander from τοις in l. 2 to τοις in l. 4,—whereby St. John is made to say that our Saviour himself distributed to the 5000. The blunder is a very ancient one; for it has crept into the Syriac, Bohairic, and Gothic versions, besides many copies of the. Old Latin; and has established itself in the Vulgate. Moreover some good Fathers (beginning with Origen) so quote the place. But such evidence is unavailing to support אABLΠ, the early reading of being also contradicted by the fourth hand in the seventh century against the great cloud of witnesses,—beginning with D and including twelve other uncials, beside the body of the cursives, the Ethiopic and two copies of the Old Latin, as well as Cyril Alex.

Indeed, there does not exist a source of error which has proved more fatal to the transcribers of MSS. than the proximity of identical, or nearly identical, combinations of letters. And because these are generally met with in the final syllables of words, the error referred to is familiarly known by a Greek name which denotes 'likeness of ending' (Homoeoteleuton). The eye of a scribe on reverting from his copy to the original before him is of necessity apt sometimes to alight on the same word, or what looks like the same word, a little lower down. The consequence is obvious. All that should have come in between gets omitted, or sometimes duplicated.

It is obvious, that however inconvenient it may prove to find oneself in this way defrauded of five, ten, twenty, perhaps thirty words, no very serious consequence for the most part ensues. Nevertheless, the result is often sheer nonsense. When this is the case, it is loyally admitted by all. A single example may stand for a hundred. [In St. John vi. 55, that most careless of careless transcripts, the Sinaitic א omits on a most sacred subject seven words, and the result hardly admits of being characterized. Let the reader judge for himself. The passage stands thus:—ἡ γὰρ σάρξ μου ἀληθῶς ἐστι βρῶσις, καὶ τὸ αἷμά μου ἀληθῶς ἐστιν πόσις The transcriber of א by a very easy mistake let his eye pass from one ἀληθῶς to another, and characteristically enough the various correctors allowed the error to remain till it was removed in the seventh century, though the error issued in nothing less than 'My Flesh is drink indeed.' Could that MS. have undergone the test of frequent use?]

But it requires very little familiarity with the subject to be aware that occasions must inevitably be even of frequent occurrence when the result is calamitous, and even perplexing, in the extreme. The writings of Apostles and Evangelists, the Discourses of our Divine Lord Himself, abound in short formulae; and the intervening matter on such occasions is constantly an integral sentence, which occasionally may be discovered from its context without evident injury to the general meaning of the place. Thus [ver. 14 in St. Matt. xxiii. was omitted in an early age, owing to the recurrence of οὐαὶ ὑμῖν at the beginning, by some copyists, and the error was repeated in the Old Latin versions. It passed to Egypt, as some of the Bohairic copies, the Sahidic, and Origen testify. The Vulgate is not quite consistent: and of course אBDLZ, a concord of bad witnesses especially in St. Matthew, follow suit, in company with the Armenian, the Lewis, and five or more cursives, enough to make the more emphatic the condemnation by the main body of them. Besides the verdict of the cursives, thirteen uncials (as against five) including Φ and Σ, the Peshitto, Harkleian, Ethiopic, Arabian, some MSS. of the Vulgate, with Origen (iii. 838 (only in Lat.)); Chrysostom (vii. 707 (*bis*); ix. 755); Opus Imperf. 185 (*bis*); 186 (*bis*); John Damascene (ii. 517); Theophylact (i. 124); Hilary (89; 725); Jerome (iv. 276; v. 52; vi. 138; vii. 185)].

Worst of all, it will sometimes of necessity happen that such an omission took place at an exceedingly remote period; (for there have been careless scribes in every age:) and in consequence the error is pretty sure to have propagated itself widely. It is observed to exist (suppose) in several of the known copies; and if,—as very often is the case,—it is discoverable in two or more of the 'old uncials,' all hope of its easy extirpation is at an end. Instead of being loyally recognized as a blunder,—which it clearly is,—it is forthwith charged upon the Apostle or Evangelist as the case may be. In other words, it is taken for granted that the clause in dispute can have had no place in the sacred autograph. It is henceforth treated as an unauthorized accretion to the text. Quite idle henceforth becomes the appeal to the ninety-nine copies out of a hundred which contain the missing words. I proceed to give an instance of my meaning.

Our Saviour, having declared (St. Matt. xix. 9) that whosoever putteth away his wife εἰ μὴ ἐπὶ πορνείᾳ καὶ γαμήσῃ ἄλλην, μοιχᾶται. Those five words are not found in Codd. אDLS, nor in several copies of the Old Latin nor in some copies of the Bohairic, and the Sahidic. Tischendorf and Tregelles accordingly reject them.

And yet it is perfectly certain that the words are genuine. Those thirty-one letters probably formed three lines in the oldest copies of all. Hence they are observed to exist in the Syriac (Peshitto, Harkleian and Jerusalem), the Vulgate, some copies of the Old Latin, the Armenian, and the Ethiopic, besides at least seventeen uncials (including BΦΣ), and the vast majority of the cursives. So that there can be no question of the genuineness of the clause.

A somewhat graver instance of omission resulting from precisely the same cause meets us a little further on in the same Gospel. The threefold recurrence of των in the expression **ΤῶΝ ψιχίων ΤῶΝ πιπτόν ΤωΝ** (St. Luke xvi. 20, has (naturally enough) resulted in the dropping of the words ψιχίων τῶν out of some copies. Unhappily the sense is not destroyed by the omission. We are not surprised therefore to discover that the words are wanting in—אBL: or to find that אBL are supported here by copies of the Old Latin, and (as usual) by the Egyptian versions, nor by Clemens Alex.[49] and the author of the Dialogus[50]. Jerome, on the other hand, condemns the Latin reading, and the Syriac Versions are observed to approve of Jerome's verdict, as well as the Gothic. But what settles the question is the fact that every known Greek MS., except those three, witnesses against the omission: besides Ambrose[51], Jerome[52], Eusebius[53] Alex., Gregory[54] Naz., Asterius[55], Basil[56], Ephraim[57] Syr., Chrysostom[58], and Cyril[59] of Alexandria. Perplexing it is notwithstanding to discover, and distressing to have to record, that all the recent Editors of the Gospels are more or less agreed in abolishing 'the crumbs which fell from the rich man's table.'

[The foregoing instances afford specimens of the influence of accidental causes upon the transmission from age to age of the Text of the Gospels. Before the sense of the exact expressions of the Written Word was impressed upon the mind of the Church,—when the Canon was not definitely acknowledged, and the halo of antiquity had not yet gathered round writings which had been recently composed,—severe accuracy was not to be expected. Errors would be sure to arise, especially from accident, and early ancestors would be certain to have a numerous progeny; besides that evil would increase, and slight deviations would give rise in the course of natural development to serious and perplexing corruptions.

In the next chapter, other kinds of accidental causes will come under consideration.]

[49] P. 232.
[50] *Ap.* Orig. i. 827.
[51] Ambrose i. 659, 1473, 1491:— places which shew how insecure would be an inference drawn from i. 543 and 665.
[52] Hieron. v. 966; vi. 969.
[53] *Ap.* Mai ii. 516, 520.
[54] i. 370.
[55] P. 12.
[56] ii. 169.
[57] ii. 142.
[58] i. 715, 720; ii. 662 (*bis*), 764; vii. 779.
[59] v[2]. 149 (luc. text, 524).

Chapter Four - Accidental Causes of Corruption - III. From Writing in Uncials

§ 1.

CORRUPT readings have occasionally resulted from the ancient practice of writing Scripture in the uncial character, without accents, punctuation, or indeed any division of the text. Especially are they found in places where there is something unusual in the structure of the sentence.

St. John iv. 35-6 (λευκαί εἰσι πρὸς θερισμόν ἤδη) has suffered in this way,—owing to the unusual position of ἤδη. Certain of the scribes who imagined that ἤδη might belong to ver. 36, rejected the καὶ as superfluous; though no Father is known to have been guilty of such a solecism. Others, aware that ἤδη can only belong to ver. 35, were not unwilling to part with the copula at the beginning of ver. 36. A few, considering both words of doubtful authority, retained neither[60]. In this way it has come to pass that there are four ways of exhibiting this place:—(a) πρὸς θερισμὸν ἤδη. Καὶ ὁ θερίζων:—(b) πρὸς θερισμόν Ἤδη ὁ θ.:—(c) πρὸς θερισμὸν ἤδη. Ὁ θερίζων:—(d) πρὸς θερισμόν. Ὁ θερίζων, κ.τ.λ..

The only point of importance however is the position of ἤδη: which is claimed for ver. 35 by the great mass of the copies: as well as by Origen[61], Eusebius[62], Chrysostom[63], Cyril[64], the Vulgate, Jerome of course, and the Syriac. The Italic copies are hopelessly divided here[65]: and Codd. אBMΠ do not help us. But ἤδη is claimed for ver. 36 by CDEL, 33, and by the Curetonian and Lewis (= καὶ ἤδη ὁ θερίζων): while Codex A is singular in beginning ver. 36, ἤδη καὶ—which shews that some early copyist, with the correct text before him, adopted a vicious punctuation. For there can be no manner of doubt that the commonly received text and the usual punctuation is the true one: as, on a careful review of the evidence, every unprejudiced reader will allow. But recent critics are for leaving out καὶ (with אBCDL): while Tischendorf, Westcott and Hort, Tregelles (*marg.*), are for putting the full stop after πρὸς θερισμόν and (with ACDL) making ἤδη begin the next sentence,—which (as Alford finds out) is clearly inadmissible.

§ 2.

Sometimes this affects the translation. Thus, the Revisers propose in the parable of the prodigal 'And I perish *here* with hunger!' But why '*here*?' Because I answer, whereas in the earliest copies of St. Luke the words stood thus,—ΕΓωΔΕΛΙΜωΑΠΟΛΛΥΜΑΙ, some careless scribe after writing ΕΓωΔΕ, reduplicated the three last letters (ωΔΕ): he mistook them for an independent word. Accordingly in the Codex Bezae, in R and U and about ten cursives, we encounter εγω δε ωδε. The inventive faculty having thus done its work it remained to superadd 'transposition,' as was done by אBL. From εγω δε ωδε λιμω the sentence has now developed into εγω δε λιμω ωδε: which approves itself to Griesbach and Schultz, to Lachmann and Tischendorf and Tregelles, to Alford and Westcott and Hort, and to the Revisers. A very ancient blunder, certainly, ἐγὼ δὲ ὧδε is: for it is found in the Latin[66] and the Syriac translations. It must therefore date from the second century. But it is a blunder notwithstanding: a blunder against which 16 uncials and the whole body of the cursives bear emphatic witness[67]. Having detected its origin, we have next to trace its progress.

The inventors of ὧδε or other scribes quickly saw that this word requires a correlative in the earlier part of the sentence. Accordingly, the same primitive authorities which advocate 'here,' are observed also to advocate, above, 'in my Father's house.' No extant Greek copy is known to contain the bracketed words in the sentence [ἐν τῷ οἴκῳ τοῦ πατρός μου: but such copies must have existed in the second century. The Peshitto, the Cureton and Lewis recognize the three words in question; as well as copies of the Latin with which Jerome[68], Augustine[69] and Cassian[70] were acquainted. The phrase '*in domo patris mei*' has accordingly established itself in the Vulgate. But surely we of the Church of England who have been hitherto spared this second blunder, may reasonably (at the end of 1700 years) refuse to take the first downward step. Our Lord intended no contrast whatever between two localities—but between two parties. The comfortable estate of the hired servants He set against the abject misery of the Son: not the house wherein the servants dwelt, and the spot where the poor prodigal was standing when he came to a better mind.—These are many words; but I know not how to be briefer. And,—what is worthy of discussion, if not the utterances of 'the Word made flesh?'

If hesitation to accept the foregoing verdict lingers in any quarter, it ought to be dispelled by a glance at the context in אBL. What else but the instinct of a trained understanding is it to survey the neighbourhood of a place like the present? Accordingly, we discover that in ver. 16, for γεμίσαι τὴν κοιλίαν αὐτοῦ ἀπὸ, אBDLR present us with χορτασθῆναι εκ: and in ver. 22, the prodigal, on very nearly the same authority (אBDUX), is made to say to his father,—Ποίησόν με ὡς ἕνα τῶν μισθίων σου:

Which certainly he did not say[71]. Moreover, אBLX and the Old Latin are for thrusting in ταχυ (D ταχεως) after ἐξενέγκατε. Are not these one and all confessedly fabricated readings? the infelicitous attempts of some well-meaning critic to improve upon the inspired original?

From the fact that three words in St. John v. 44 were in the oldest MSS. written thus,—ΜΟΝΟΥΘΥΟΥ (i.e. μόνου Θεοῦ οὐ), the middle word (θεοῦ) got omitted from some very early copies; whereby the sentence is made to run thus in English,—'And seek not the honour which cometh from the only One.' It is so that Origen[72], Eusebius[73], Didymus[74], besides the two best copies of the Old Latin, exhibit the place. As to Greek MSS., the error survives only in B at the present day, the preserver of an Alexandrian error.

§ 3.

St. Luke explains (Acts xxvii. 14) that it was the 'typhonic wind called Euroclydon' which caused the ship in which St. Paul and he sailed past Crete to incur the 'harm and loss' so graphically described in the last chapter but one of the Acts. That wind is mentioned nowhere but in this one place. Its name however is sufficiently intelligible; being compounded of Εὖρος, the 'south-east wind,' and κλύδων, 'a tempest:' a compound which happily survives intact in the Peshitto version. The Syriac translator, not knowing what the word meant, copied what he saw,—'the blast' (he says) 'of the tempest[75], which [blast] is called Tophonikos Euroklīdon.' Not so the licentious scribes of the West. They insisted on extracting out of the actual 'Euroclydon,' the imaginary name 'Euro-aquilo,' which accordingly stands to this day in the Vulgate. (Not that Jerome himself so read the name of the wind, or he would hardly have explained *'Eurielion'* or *'Euriclion'* to mean 'commiscens, sive deorsum ducens[76].') Of this feat of theirs, Codexes ℵ and A (in which ΕΥΡΟΚΛΥΔωΝ has been perverted into ΕΥΡΑΚΥΛωΝ) are at this day *the sole surviving Greek witnesses.* Well may the evidence for 'Euro-aquilo' be scanty! The fabricated word collapses the instant it is examined. Nautical men point out that it is inconsistent in its construction with the principles on which the names of the intermediate or compound winds are framed:'—

'*Euornotus* is so called as intervening immediately between *Eurus* and *Notus,* and as partaking, as was thought, of the qualities of both. The same holds true of *Libonotus,* as being interposed between *Libs* and *Notus.* Both these compound winds lie in the same quarter or quadrant of the circle with the winds of which they are composed, and no other wind intervenes. But *Eurus* and *Aquilo* are at 90° distance from one another; or according to some writers, at 105°; the former lying in the south-east quarter, and the latter in the north-east: and two winds, one of which is the East cardinal point, intervene, as Caecias and Subsolanus[77].'

Further, why should the wind be designated by an impossible *Latin* name? The ship was 'a ship of Alexandria' (ver. 6). The sailors were Greeks. What business has *'Aquilo'* here? Next, if the wind did bear the name of 'Euro-aquilo,' why is it introduced in this marked way (ἄνεμος τυφωνικὸς, ὁ καλούμενος) as if it were a kind of curiosity? Such a name would utterly miss the point, which is the violence of the wind as expressed in the term Euroclydon. But above all, if St. Luke wrote ΕΥΡΑΚ-, how has it come to pass that every copyist but three has written ΕΥΡΟΚ-? The testimony of B is memorable. The original scribe wrote ΕΥΡΑΚΥΔωΝ[78]: the *secunda manus* has corrected this into ΕΥΡΥΚΛΥΔωΝ,—which is also the reading of Euthalius[79]. The essential circumstance is, that *not* ΥΛωΝ but ΥΔωΝ has all along been the last half of the word in Codex B[80].

In St. John iv. 15, on the authority of ℵB, Tischendorf adopts διέρχεσθαι (in place of the uncompounded verb), assigning as his reason, that 'If St. John had written ἔρχεσθαι, no one would ever have substituted διέρχεσθαι for it.' But to construct the text of Scripture on such considerations, is to build a lighthouse on a quicksand. I could have referred the learned Critic to plenty of places where the thing he speaks of as incredible has been done. The proof that St. John used the uncompounded verb is the fact that it is found in all the copies except our two untrustworthy friends. The explanation of ΔΙερχωμαι is sufficiently accounted for by the final syllable (ΔΕ) of μηδὲ which immediately precedes. Similarly but without the same excuse,

St. Mark x. 16 ευλογει has	become	κατευλογει (ℵBC)
" xii. 17 θααυμασαν	"	εξεθαυμασαν (ℵB)
" xiv. 40 βεβαρημενοι	"	καταβεβαρημενοι (AℵB)

It is impossible to doubt that κα (in modern critical editions of St. Luke xvii. 37) is indebted for its existence to the same cause. In the phrase ἐκεῖ συναχθήσονται οἱ ἀετοί it might have been predicted that the last syllable of ἐκεῖ would some day be mistaken for the conjunction. And so it has actually come to pass. KAI οι αετοι is met with in many ancient authorities. But אLB also transposed the clauses, and substituted επισυναχθησονται for συναχθήσονται. The self-same casualty, viz. και elicited out of the insertion of εκει and the transposition of the clauses, is discoverable among the Cursives at St. Matt. xxiv. 28,—the parallel place: where by the way the old uncials distinguish themselves by yet graver eccentricities[81]. How can we as judicious critics ever think of disturbing the text of Scripture on evidence so precarious as this?

It is proposed that we should henceforth read St. Matt. xxii. 23 as follows:—'On that day there came to Him Sadducecs *saying* that there is no Resurrection.' A new incident would be in this way introduced into the Gospel narrative: resulting from a novel reading of the passage. Instead of οἱ λέγοντες, we are invited to read λέγοντες, on the authority of n אBDMSZP and several of the Cursives, besides Origen, Methodius, Epiphanius. This is a respectable array. There is nevertheless a vast preponderance of numbers in favour of the usual reading, which is also found in the Old Latin copies and in the Vulgate. But surely the discovery that in the parallel Gospels it is—

οἵτινες λέγουσιν ἀνάστασιν μὴ εἶναι (St. Mark xii. 18) and οἱ ἀντιλέγοντες ἀνάστασιν μὴ εἶναι (St. Luke xx. 27)

may be considered as decisive in a case like the present. Sure I am that it will be so regarded by any one who has paid close attention to the method of the Evangelists. Add that the origin of the mistake is seen, the instant the words are inspected as they must have stood in an uncial copy:

ΟΛΔΔΟΥΚΑΙΟΙΟΙΛΕΓΟΝΤΕΣ

and really nothing more requires to be said. The second OI was safe to be dropped in a collocation of letters like that. It might also have been anticipated, that there would be found copyists to be confused by the antecedent KAI. Accordingly the Peshitto, Lewis, and Curetonian render the place 'et dicentes;' shewing that they mistook KAI OI ΛΕΓΟΝΤΕΣ for a separate phrase.

§ 4.

The termination TO (in certain tenses of the verb), when followed by the neuter article, naturally leads to confusion; sometimes to uncertainty. In St. John v. 4 for instance, where we read in our copies καὶ ἐτάρασσε τὸ ὕδωρ but so many MSS. read ἐταράσσετο, that it becomes a perplexing question which reading to follow. The sense in either case is excellent: the only difference being whether the Evangelist actually says that the Angel 'troubled' the water, or leaves it to be inferred from the circumstance that after the Angel had descended, straightway the water 'was troubled.'

The question becomes less difficult of decision when (as in St. Luke vii. 21) we have to decide between two expressions ἐχαρίσατο βλέπειν (which is the reading of א*ABDEG and 11 other uncials) and ἐχαρίσατο τὸ βλέπειν which is only supported by אᵇELVA. The bulk of the Cursives faithfully maintain the former reading, and merge the article in the verb.

Akin to the foregoing are all those instances,—and they are literally without number—, where the proximity of a like ending has been the fruitful cause of error. Let me explain: for this is a matter which cannot be too thoroughly apprehended.

Such a collection of words as the following two instances exhibit will shew my meaning.

In the expression ἐσθῆτα λαμπρὰν ἀνέπεμψεν (St. Luke xxiii. 11), we are not surprised to find the first syllable of the verb (αν) absorbed by the last syllable of the immediately preceding λαμπρὰν. Accordingly, אLR supported by one copy of the Old Latin and a single cursive MS. concur in displaying ἔπεμψεν in this place.

The letters NAIKωNAIKAI in the expression (St. Luke xxiii. 27) γυναικῶν αἱ καὶ were safe to produce confusion. The first of these three words could of course take care of itself. (Though D, with some of the Versions, make it into γυναικες.) Not so however what follows. ABCDLX and the Old Latin (except c) drop the και: א and C drop the αι. The truth rests with the fourteen remaining uncials and with the cursives.

Thus also the reading εν ολη τη Γαλιλαια (B) in St. Matt. iv. 23, (adopted by Lachmann, Tischendorf, Tregelles, Alford, Westcott and Hort and the Revisers,) is due simply to the reduplication on the part of some inattentive scribe of the last two letters of the immediately preceding word,—περιηγεν. The received reading of the place is the correct one,—καὶ περιῆγεν ὅλην τῇ Γαλιλαίαν ὁ Ἰησοῦς because the first five words are so exhibited in all the Copies except BאC; and those three MSS. are observed to differ as usual from one another,—which ought to be deemed fatal to their evidence. Thus,

B reads καὶ περιῆγεν ἐν ὅλῃ τῇ Γαλιλαίᾳ.

א   ″   καὶ περιῆγεν ὁ ῑϛ̄ ἐν τῇ Γαλιλαίᾳ.

C   ″   καὶ περιῆγεν ὁ ῑϛ̄ ἐν ὅλῃ τῇ Γαλιλαίᾳ.

But—(I shall be asked)—what about the position of the Sacred Name? How comes it to pass that ὁ Ἰησοῦς, which comes after Γαλιλαίαν in almost every other known copy, should come after ριῆγεν ὁ in three of these venerable authorities (in D as well as in א and C), and in the Latin, Peshitto, Lewis, and Harkleian? Tischendorf, Alford, Westcott and Hort and the Revisers at all events (who simply follow B in leaving out ὁ Ἰησοῦς altogether) will not ask me this question: but a thoughtful inquirer is sure to ask it.

The phrase (I reply) is derived by אCD from the twin place in St. Matthew (ix. 35) which in all the MSS. begins καὶ περιῆ;γεν ὁ ῑϛ̄. So familiar had this order of the words become, that the scribe of א, (a circumstance by the way of which Tischendorf takes no notice,) has even introduced the expression into St. Mark vi. 6,—the parallel place in the second Gospel,—where ὁ ῑϛ̄ is clearly has no business. I enter into these minute details because only in this way is the subject before us to be thoroughly understood. This is another instance where 'the Old Uncials' shew their text to be corrupt; so for assurance in respect of accuracy of detail we must resort to the Cursive Copies.

§ 5.

The introduction of ἀπό in the place of ἅγιοι made by the 'Revisers' into the Greek Text of 2 Peter i. 27,—derives its origin from the same prolific source. [1] some very ancient scribe mistook the first four letters of αγιοι, for απο. It was but the mistaking of ΑΓΙΟ for ΑΠΟ. At the end of 1700 years, the only Copies which witness to this deformity are BP with four cursives,—in opposition to אAKL and the whole body of the cursives, the Vulgate[82] and the Harkleian. Euthalius knew nothing of it[83]. Obvious it was, next, for some one in perplexity,—[2] to introduce both readings (ἀπό and ἅγιοι) into the text. Accordingly ἀπὸ Θεοῦ ἅγιοι, is found in C, two cursives, and Didymus[84]. Then, [3], another variant crops up, (viz. ὑπό for ἀπό—but only because ὑπό went immediately before); of which fresh blunder ὑπό Θεοῦ ἅγιοι) Theophylact is the sole patron[85]. The consequence of all this might have been foreseen: [4] it came to pass that from a few Codexes, both απο and αγιοι were left out,—which accounts for the reading of certain copies of the Old Latin[86]. Unaware how the blunder began, Tischendorf and his followers claim '[1],' '[3],' and '[4],' as proofs that '[1]' is the right reading: and, by consequence, instead of 'holy men of God spake,' require us to read 'men spake from God,' which is wooden and vapid. Is it not clear that a reading attested by only BP and four cursive copies must stand self-condemned?

Another excellent specimen of this class of error is furnished by Heb. vii. 1. Instead of Ὁ συναντήσας Ἀβραάμ—said of Melchizedek,—אABD exhibit OC. The whole body of the copies, headed by CLP, are against them[87], — besides Chrysostom[88], Theodoret[89], Damascene[90]. It is needless to do more than state how this reading arose. The initial letter of συναντήσας has been reduplicated through careless transcription: OCCYN—instead of OCYN—. That is all. But the instructive feature of the case is that it is in the four oldest of the uncials that this palpable blunder is found.

§ 6.

I have reserved for the last a specimen which is second to none in suggestiveness. 'Whom will ye that I release unto you?' asked Pilate on a memorable occasion[91]: and we all remember how his enquiry proceeds. But the discovery is made that, in an early age there existed copies of the Gospel which proceeded thus,—'Jesus [who is called[92]] Barabbas, or Jesus who is called Christ?' Origen so quotes the place, but 'In many copies,' he proceeds, 'mention is not made that Barabbas was also called Jesus: and those copies may perhaps be right,—else would the name of Jesus belong to one of the wicked,—of which no instance occurs in any part of the Bible: nor is it fitting that the name of Jesus should like Judas have been borne by saint and sinner alike. 'I think,' Origen adds, 'something of this sort must have been an interpolation of the heretics[93].' From this we are clearly intended to infer that 'Jesus Barabbas' was the prevailing reading of St. Matt. xxvii. 17 in the time of Origen, a circumstance which—besides that a multitude of copies existed as well as those of Origen—for the best of reasons, we take leave to pronounce incredible[94].

The sum of the matter is probably this:—Some inattentive second century copyist [probably a Western Translator into Syriac who was an indifferent Greek scholar] mistook the final syllable of *'unto you'* (ΥΜΙΝ) for the word *'Jesus'* (ΙΝ̅): in other words, carelessly reduplicated the last two letters of ΥΜΙΝ,—from which, strange to say, results the form of inquiry noticed at the outset. Origen caught sight of the extravagance, and condemned it though he fancied it to be prevalent, and the thing slept for 1500 years. Then about just fifty years ago Drs. Lachmann, Tischendorf and Tregelles began to construct that 'fabric of Textual Criticism' which has been the cause of the present treatise [though indeed Tischendorf does not adopt the suggestion of those few aberrant cursives which is supported by no surviving uncial, and in fact advocates the very origin of the mischief which has been just described]. But, as every one must see, such things as these are not 'readings' at all, nor even the work of 'the heretics;' but simply transcriptional mistakes. How Dr. Hort, admitting the blunder, yet pleads that 'this remarkable reading is attractive by the new and interesting fact which it seems to attest, and by the antithetic force which it seems to add to the question in ver. 17,' [is more than we can understand. To us the expression seems most repulsive. No 'antithetic force' can outweigh our dislike to the idea that Barabbas was our Saviour'S namesake! We prefer Origen's account, though he mistook the cause, to that of the modern critic.]

60   It is clearly unsafe to draw any inference from the mere omission of ἤδη in ver. 35, by those Fathers who do not shew how they would have begun ver. 36—as Eusebius (see below, note 2), Theodoret (i. 1398: 233), and Hilary (78. 443. 941. 1041).
61   i. 219: iii. 158: iv. 248, 250 *bis*, 251 *bis*, 252, 253, 255 *bis*, 256, 257. Also iv. 440 note, which = cat^{ox} iv. 21.
62   *dem.* 440. But not *in cs.* 426: *theoph.* 262, 275.
63   vii. 488, 662: ix. 32.
64   i. 397. 98. (Palladius) 611: iii. 57. So also in iv. 199, ἕτοιμος ἤδη πρὸς τὸ πιστεύειν.
65   Ambrose, ii. 279, has *'Et qui metit.'* Iren.^{int} substitutes *'nam'* for *'et,'* and omits jam.' Jerome 9 times introduces *'jam'* before *'albae sunt.'* So Aug. (iii^2 417): but elsewhere (iv.

639: v. 531) he omits the word altogether.
66   *'Hic'* is not recognized in Ambrose. *Append.* ii. 367.
67   The Fathers render us very little help here. Ps.-Chrys. twice (viii. 34: x. 838) has ἐγὼ δὲ ὧδε: once (viii. 153) not. John Damascene (ii. 579) is without the ὧδε.
68   i. 76: vi. 16 (*not* vi. 484).
69   iii.^{2} 259 (*not* v. 511).
70   p. 405.
71   [The prodigal was prepared to say this; but his father's kindness stopped him:—a feature in the account which the Codexes in question ignore.]
72   iii. 687. But in i. 228 and 259 he recognizes θεοῦ.
73   *Ap.* Mai vii. 135.

[74] Praep. xiii. 6,—μόνου τοῦ ἑνός (vol. ii. 294).

[75] Same word occurs in St. Mark iv. 37.

[76] iii. 101.

[77] Falconer's Dissertation on St. Paul's Voyage, pp. 16 and 12.

[78] Let the learned Vercellone be heard on behalf of Codex B: 'Antequam manum de tabulâ amoveamus, e re fore videtur, si, ipso codice Vaticano inspecto, duos injectos scrupulos eximamus. Cl. Tischendorfius in nuperrimâ suâ editione scribit (Proleg. p. cclxxv), Maium ad Act. xxvii. 14, codici Vaticano tribuisse a primâ manu ευρακλυδων; nos vero ευρακυδων atque subjungit, "*utrumque, ut videtur, male.*" At, quidquid "videri" possit, certum nobis exploratumque est Vaticanum codicem primo habuisse ευρακυδων, prout expressum fait tum in tabellâ quâ Maius Birchianas lectiones notavit, tum in alterâ quâ nos errata corrigenda recensuimus.'—Praefatio to Mai's 2nd ed. of the Cod. Vaticanus, 1859 (8vo), p. v. vi. [Any one may now see this in the photographed copy.]

[79] *Ap.* Galland. x. 225.

[80] Remark that some vicious sections evidently owed their origin to the copyist *knowing more of Latin than of Greek.*

True, that the compounds euronotus euroauster exist in Latin. *That it the reason why* the Latin translator (not understanding the word) rendered it *Euroaquilo:* instead of writing *Euraquilo.*

I have no·doubt that it was some Latin copyist who began the mischief. Like the man who wrote ἐπ᾽ αὐτῷ τῷ φόρῳ for ἐπ᾽ αὐτοφώρῳ.

Readings of Euroclydon
ΕΥΡΑΚΥΔωΝ B (sic)
ΕΥΡΑΚΥΛωΝ ℵ A
ΕΥΡΑΚΗΛωΝ
ΕΥΤΡΑΚΗΛωΝ
ΕΥΡΑΚΛΗΔωΝ Peshitto.
ΕΥΡΑΚΥΚΛ;ωΝ
Euroaquilo Vulg.
ΕΥΡΟΚΛΥΔωΝ HLP
ΕΥΡΑΚΛΥΔωΝ Syr. Harkl.
ΕΥΡΥΚΛΥΔωΝ B[2 man.]

[81] Οπου (ου ℵ) γαρ (—γαρ ℵBDL) εαν (αν D) το πτωμα (σωμα ℵ).

[82] *Sancti Dei homines.*

[83] *Ap.* Galland. x. 236 a.

[84] Trin. 234.

[85] iii. 389.

[86] '*Locuti sunt homines D .*'

[87] Their only supporters seem to be K [i.e. Paul 117 (Matthaei's §)], 17, 59 [published in full by Cramer, vii. 202], 137 [Reiche, p. 60]. Why does Tischendorf quote besides E of Paul, which is nothing else but a copy of D of Paul?

[88] Chrys. xii. 120 b, 121 a.

[89] Theodoret, iii. 584.

[90] J. Damascene, ii. 240 c.

[91] St. Matt. xxvii. 17.

[92] Cf. ὁ λεγόμενος Βαραββᾶς. St. Mark xv. 7.

[93] *Int.* iii. 918 c d.

[94] On the two other occasions when Origen quotes St. Matt. xxvii. 17 (i. 316 a and ii. 245 a) nothing is said about 'Jesus Barabbas.'—Alluding to the place, he elsewhere (iii. 853 d) merely says that '*Secundum quosdam Barabbas dicebatter et Jesus.*'—-The author of a well-known scholion, ascribed to Anastasius, Bp. of Antioch, but query, for see Migne, vol. lxxxix. p. 1352 b c (= Galland. xii. 253 c), and 1604 a, declares that he had found

the same statement 'in very early copies.' The scholion in question is first cited by Birch (Varr. Lectt. p. 110) from the following MSS.:—S, 108, 129, 137, 138, 143, 146, 181, 186, 195, 197, 199 or 200, 209, 210, 221, 222: to which Scholz adds 41, 237, 238, 253, 259, 299: Tischendorf adds 1, 118. In Gallandius (Bibl. P. P. xiv. 81 d e, *Append.*), the scholion may be seen more fully given than by Birch,—from whom Tregelles and Tischendorf copy it. Theophylact (p. 156 a) must have seen the place as quoted by Gallandius. The only evidence, so far as I can find, for reading '*Jesus* Barabbas' (in St. Matt. xxvii. 16, 17) are five disreputable Evangelia 1, 118, 209, 241, 299,—the Armenian Version, the Jerusalem Syriac, [and the Sinai Syriac]; (see Adler, pp. 172-3).

Chapter Five - Accidental Causes of Corruption - IV. Itacism

[IT has been already shewn in the First Volume that the Art of Transcription on vellum did not reach perfection till after the lapse of many centuries in the life of the Church. Even in the minute elements of writing much uncertainty prevailed during a great number of successive ages. It by no means followed that, if a scribe possessed a correct auricular knowledge of the Text, he would therefore exhibit it correctly on parchment. Copies were largely disfigured with misspelt words. And vowels especially were interchanged; accordingly, such change became in many instances the cause of corruption, and is known in Textual Criticism under the name 'Itacism.']

§ 1.

It may seem to a casual reader that in what follows undue attention is being paid to minute particulars. But it constantly happens,—and this is a sufficient answer to the supposed objection,—that, from exceedingly minute and seemingly trivial mistakes, there result sometimes considerable and indeed serious misrepresentations of the Spirit's meaning. New incidents:— unheard-of statements:—facts as yet unknown to readers of Scripture:— perversions of our Lord's Divine sayings:—such phenomena are observed to follow upon the omission of the article,—the insertion of an expletive,—the change of a single letter. Thus παλιν, thrust in where it has no business, makes it appear that our Saviour promised to return the ass on which He rode in triumph into Jerusalem[95]. By writing ω for ο, many critics have transferred some words from the lips of Christ to those of His Evangelist, and made Him say what He never could have dreamed of saying[96]. By subjoining ς to a word in a place which it has no right to fill, the harmony of the heavenly choir has been marred effectually, and a sentence produced which defies translation[97]. By omitting τῷ and Κύριε, the repenting malefactor is made to say, 'Jesus! remember me, when Thou comest in Thy kingdom[98].'

Speaking of our Saviour's triumphal entry into Jerusalem, which took place 'the day after' 'they made Him a supper,' and Lazarus 'which had been dead, whom He raised from the dead,' sat at the table with Him' (St. John xii. 1, 2), St. John says that 'the multitude which had been with Him *when* He called Lazarus out of the tomb and raised Him from the dead bare testimony' (St. John xii. 17). The meaning of this is best understood by a reference to St. Luke xix. 37, 38, where it is explained that it was the sight of so many acts of Divine Power, the chiefest of all being the raising of Lazarus, which moved the crowds to yield the memorable testimony recorded by St. Luke in ver. 38,—by St. John in ver. 13[99]. But Tischendorf and Lachmann, who on the authority of D and four later uncials read ὅτι instead of ὅτε, import into the Gospel quite another meaning. According to their way of exhibiting the text, St. John is made to say that the multitude which was with Jesus, testified *that* He called Lazarus out of the tomb and raised him from the dead': which is not only an entirely different statement, but also the introduction of a highly improbable circumstance. That many copies of the Old Latin (not of the Vulgate) recognize On, besides the Peshitto and the two Egyptian versions, is not denied. This is in fact only one more proof of the insufficiency of such collective testimony. ℵAB with the rest of the uncials and, what is of more importance, *the whole body of the cursive*, exhibit ὅτε,—which, as every one must see, is certainly what St. John wrote in this place. Tischendorf's assertion that the prolixity of the expression ἐφώνησεν ἐκ τοῦ μνημείου καὶ ἤγειρεν αὐτὸν ἐκ νεκρῶν is inconsistent with ὅτε[100],—may surprise, but will never convince any one who is *even* moderately acquainted with St. John's peculiar manner.

The same mistake—of ὅτι for ὅτε—is met with at ver. 41 of the same chapter. These things said Isaiah *because* he saw His glory' (St. John xii. 41). And why not '*when* he saw His glory'? which is what the Evangelist wrote according to the strongest attestation. True, that eleven manuscripts (beginning with ℵABL) and the Egyptian versions exhibit ὅτι: also Nonnus, who lived in the Thebaid (A.D. 410): but all other MSS., the Latin, Peshitto, Gothic, Ethiopic, Georgian, and one Egyptian version:—Origen[101],— Eusebius in four places[102],—Basil[103],—Gregory of Nyssa twice[104], —Didymus three times[105],—Chrysostom twice[106],—Severianus of Gabala[107];—these twelve Versions and Fathers constitute a body of ancient evidence which is overwhelming. Cyril three times reads ὅτι[108], three times ὅτε[109], and once ἡνίκα[110], which proves at least how he understood the place.

§ 2.

[A suggestive example[111] of the corruption introduced by a petty Itacism may be found in Rev. i. 5, where the beautiful expression which has found its way into so many tender passages relating to Christian devotion, 'Who hath *washed*[112] us from our sins in His own blood' (A.V.), is replaced in many critical editions (R.V.) by, 'Who hath *loosed*[113] us from our sins by His blood.' In early times a purist scribe, who had a dislike of anything that savoured of provincial retention of Aeolian or Dorian pronunciations, wrote from uncon-

43

scious bias υ for ου, transcribing λύσαντι for λούσαντι (unless he were not Greek scholar enough to understand the difference): and he was followed by others, especially such as, whether from their own prejudices or owing to sympathy with the scruples of other people, but at all events under the influence of a slavish literalism, hesitated about a passage as to which they did not rise to the spiritual height of the precious meaning really conveyed therein. Accordingly the three uncials, which of those that give the Apocalypse date nearest to the period of corruption, adopt υ, followed by nine cursives, the Harkleian Syriac, and the Armenian versions. On the other side, two uncials—viz. B[2] of the eighth century and P of the ninth—the Vulgate, Bohairic, and Ethiopic, write λούσαντι; and—what is most important—all the other cursives except the handful just mentioned, so far as examination has yet gone, form a barrier which forbids intrusion.

An instance where an error from an Itacism has crept into the Textus Receptus may be seen in St. Luke xvi. 25. Some scribes needlessly changed ὧδε into ὅδε, misinterpreting the letter which served often for both the long and the short o, and thereby cast out some illustrative meaning, since Abraham meant to lay stress upon the enjoyment 'in his bosom' of comfort by Lazarus. The unanimity of the uncials, a majority of the cursives, the witness of the versions, that of the Fathers quote the place being uncertain, are sufficient to prove that ὧδε is the genuine word.

Again, in St. John xiii. 25, οὕτως has dropped out of many copies and so out of the Received Text because by an Itacism it was written οὗτος in many manuscripts. Therefore ἐκεῖνος οὗτος was thought to be a clear mistake, and the weaker word was accordingly omitted. No doubt Latins and others who did not understand Greek well considered also that οὕτως was redundant, and this was the cause of its being omitted in the Vulgate. But really οὕτως, being sufficiently authenticated[114], is exactly in consonance with Greek usage and St. John's style[115], and adds considerably to the graphic character of the sacred narrative. St. John was reclining (ἀνακείμενος) on his left arm over the bosom of the robe (ἐν τῷ κόλπῳ) of the Saviour. When St. Peter beckoned to him he turned his head for the moment and sank (ἐπιπεσών, not ἀναπεσών which has the testimony only of B and about twenty-five uncials, א and C being divided against themselves) on the breast of the Lord, being still in the general posture in which he was (οὕτως[116]), and asked Him in a whisper 'LORD, who is it?'

Another case of confusion between ω and o may be seen in St. Luke xv. 24, 32, where ἀπολωλώς has gained so strong a hold that it is found in the Received Text for ἀπολωλός, which last being the better attested appears to be the right reading[117]. But the instance which requires the most attention is καθάριζον in St. Mark vii. 19, and all the more because in *The Last Twelve Verses of St. Mark,* the alteration into καθάριζων is advocated as being 'no part of the Divine discourse, but the Evangelist's inspired comment on the Saviour's words[118]:' Such a question must be decided strictly by the testimony, not upon internal evidence—which in fact is in this case absolutely decisive neither way, for people must not be led by the attractive view opened by καθαρίζων, and καθάριζον bears a very intelligible meaning. When we find that the uncial evidence is divided, there being eight against the change (ΦΣΚΜΥΥΓΠ), and eleven for it (ℵABEFGHLSXΔ);—that not much is advanced by the versions, though the Peshitto, the Lewis Codex, the Harkleian (?), the Gothic, the Old Latin[119]. the Vulgate, favour καθάριζον;—nor by the Fathers:—since Aphraates[120], Augustine (?)[121], and Novatian[122] are contradicted by Origen[123], Theophylact[124], and Gregory Thaumaturgus[125]. we discover that we have not so far made much way towards a satisfactory conclusion. The only decided element of judgement, so far as present enquiries have reached, since suspicion is always aroused by the conjunction of ℵAB, is supplied by the cursives which with a large majority witness to the received reading. It is not therefore safe to alter it till a much larger examination of existing evidence is made than is now possible. If difficulty is felt in the meaning given by καθάριζον,—and that there is such difficulty cannot candidly be denied,—this is balanced by the grammatical difficulty introduced by καθαρίζων, which would be made to agree in the same clause with a verb separated from it by thirty-five parenthetic words, including two interrogations and the closing sentence. Those people who form their judgement from the Revised Version should bear in mind that the Revisers, in order to make intelligible sense, were obliged to introduce three fresh English words that have nothing to correspond to them in the Greek; being a repetition of what the mind of the reader would hardly bear in memory. Let any reader who doubts this leave out the words in italics and try the effect for himself. The fact is that to make this reading satisfactory, another alteration is required. Καθαρίζων πάντα τὰ βρώματα ought either to be transferred to the 20th verse or to the beginning of the 18th. Then all would be clear enough, though destitute of a balance of authority: as it is now proposed to read, the passage would have absolutely no parallel in the simple and transparent sentences of St. Mark. We must therefore be guided by the balance of evidence, and that is turned by the cursive testimony.]

§ 3.

Another minute but interesting indication of the accuracy and fidelity with which the cursive copies were made, is supplied by the constancy with which they witness to the preposition ἐν (*not the numeral* ἓν) in St. Mark iv. 8. Our Lord says that the seed which 'fell into the good ground' yielded by (ἐν) thirty, and by (ἐν) sixty, and by (ἐν) an hundred.' Tischendorf notes that besides all the uncials which are furnished with accents and breathings (viz. EFGHKMUVΠ) 'nearly 100 cursives' exhibit ἐν here and in ver. 20. But this is to misrepresent the case. All the cursives may be declared to exhibit ἐν, e.g. all Matthaei's and all Scrivener's. I have myself with this object examined a large number of Evangelia, and found ἐν in all. The Basle MS. from which Erasmus derived his text[126] exhibits ἐν,—though he printed ἓν out of respect for the Vulgate. The Complutensian having ἓν, the reading of the Textus Receptus follows in consequence: but the Traditional reading has been shewn to be ἐν,—which is doubtless intended by EN in Cod. A.

Codd. ℵCA (two ever licentious and Δ similarly so throughout St. Mark) substitute for the preposition ἐν the preposition εἰς,—(a sufficient proof to me that they understand EN to represent ἐν, not ἓν): and are followed by Tischendorf, Tregelles, and the Revisers. As for the chartered libertine B (and its servile henchman L), for the first ἐν (but not for the second and third) it substitutes the preposition EIC: while, in ver. 20, it retains the first ἐν, but omits the other two. In all these vagaries Cod. B is followed by Westcott and Hort[127].

§ 4.

St. Paul[128] in his Epistle to Titus [ii. 5] directs that young women shall be 'keepers at home,' οἰκουροὺς. So, (with five exceptions,) every known Codex[129], including the corrected ℵ and D,—HKLP; besides 17, 37, 47. So also Clemens Alex.[130] (A.D. 180),—Theodore of Mopsuestia[131],—Basil[132],—Chrysostom[133],—Theodoret[134],—Damascene[135]. So again the Old Latin (*domum custodientes*[136]),—the Vulgate (*domus curam habentes*[137]), — and Jerome (*habentes domus diligentiam*[138]): and so the Peshitto and the Harkleian versions,—besides the Bohairic. There evidently can be no doubt whatever about such a reading so supported. To be οἰκουροὺς was held to be a woman's chiefest praise[139]: κάλλιστον ἔργον γυνὴ οἰκουρός, writes Clemens Alex.[140]; assigning to the wife οἰκουρία as her proper province[141]. On the contrary, 'gadding about from house to house' is what the Apostle, writing to Timothy[142], expressly condemns. But of course the decisive consideration is not the support derived from internal evidence; but the plain fact that antiquity, variety, respectability, numbers, continuity of attestation, are all in favour of the Traditional reading.

Notwithstanding this, Lachmann, Tischendorf, Tregelles, Westcott and Hort, because they find οἰκουργούς in ℵ*ACD*F-G, are for thrusting that 'barbarous and scarcely intelligible' word, if it be not even a non-existent[143], into Titus ii. 5. The Revised Version in consequence exhibits 'workers at home,'—which Dr. Field may well call an 'unnecessary and most tasteless innovation.' But it is insufficiently attested as well, besides being a plain perversion of the Apostle's teaching. [And the error must have arisen from carelessness and ignorance, probably in the West where Greek was not properly understood.]

So again, in the cry of the demoniacs, τί ἡμῖν καὶ σοί, Ἰησοῦ, υἱὲ τοῦ Θεοῦ (St. Matt. viii. 29) the name Ἰησοῦ is omitted by Bℵ.

The reason is plain the instant an ancient MS. is inspected:—KAICOIΙΥΥΙΕΤΟΥΘΥ:—the recurrence of the same letters caused too great a strain to scribes, and the omission of two of them was the result of ordinary human infirmity.

Indeed, to this same source are to be attributed an extraordinary number of so-called 'various readings'; but which in reality, as has already been shewn, are nothing else but a collection of mistakes,—the surviving tokens that anciently, as now, copying clerks left out words; whether misled by the fatal proximity of a like ending, or by the speedy recurrence of the like letters, or by some other phenomenon with which most men's acquaintance with books have long since made them familiar.

95   St. Mark xi. 4. Sec Revision Revised, pp. 57-58.

96   St. Mark vii. 19, καθαρίζον for καθάριζον. See below, pp. 61-3.

97   St. Luke ii. 14.

98   St. Luke xxiii. 42.

99   St. Matt. xxi. 9. See also St. Mark xi. 9, 10.

100   'Quae quidem orationis prolixitas non conveniens esset si ὅτε legendum esset.'

101   iv. 577: 'quando.'

102   Dem. Ev. 310, 312, 454 *bis*.

103   i. 301.

104   ii. 488, and *ap*. Gall. vi. 580.

105   Trin. 59, 99, 242.

106   viii. 406, 407. Also ps.-Chrysost. v. 613. Note, that 'Apolinarius' in Cramer's Cat. 332 is Chrys. viii. 407.

107   *Ap*. Chrys. vi. 453.

108   iv. 505, 709, and *ap*. Mai iii. 85.

109   ii. 102: iv. 709, and *ap*. Mai iii. 118.

110   v¹. 642.

111   Unfortunately, though the Dean left several lists of instances of Itacism, he worked out none, except the substitution of ἐν for ἑν in St. Mark iv. 8, which as it is not strictly on all fours with the rest I have reserved till last. He mentioned all that I have introduced (besides a few others), on detached papers, some of them more than once, and λούσαντι and καθάριζον even more than the others. In the brief discussion of each instance which I have supplied, I have endeavoured whenever it was practicable to include any slight expressions of the Dean's that I could find, and to develop all surviving hints.

112   λούσαντι.

113   λύσαντι.

114   οὕτως. BCEFGHLMXΔ. Most cursives. Goth.
   οὗτος. KSUΓΛ. Ten cursives.
   Omit ℵADΠ Many cursives. Vulg. Pesh. Ethiop. Armen. Georg. Slavon. Bohair. Pers.

115   E. g. Thuc. vii. 15, St. John iv. 6.

116   See St. John iv. 6: Acts xx. 11, xxvii. 17. The beloved Apostle was therefore called ὁ ἐπιστήθιος. See Suicer. s.v. Westcott on St. John xiii. 25.

117   24. ἀπολωλώς. ℵᵃABD &c.
   ἀπολωλός. ℵ*GKMRSXΓΠ*. Most curs.
   32. ἀπολωλώς. ℵ*ABD &c.
   ἀπολωλός. ℵᶜKMRSXΓΠ*. Most curs.

118   Pp. 179, 1So. Since the Dean has not adopted καθαρίζων into his corrected text, and on account of other indications which caused me to doubt whether he retained the opinion of his earlier years, I applied to the Rev. W. F. Rose, who answered as follows:—'I am thankful to say that I can resolve all doubt as to my uncle's later views of St. Mark vii. 29. In his annotated copy of the *Twelve Verses* he deletes the words in his note p. 179, "This appears to be the true reading," and writes in the margin, "The old reading is doubtless the true one," and in the margin of the paragraph referring to καθαρίζων, on p. 180 he writes, "Alter the wording of this." This entirely agrees with my own recollection of many conversations with him on the subject. I think he felt that the weight of the cursive testimony to the old reading was conclusive,— at least that he was not justified in changing the text in spite of it.' These last words of Mr. Rose express exactly the inference that I had drawn.

119 'The majority of the Old Latin MSS. have "in secessum uadit (or exiit) purgans omnes escas"; *i* (Vindobonensis) and *r* (Usserianus) have "et purgat" for "purgans": and *a* has a conflation "in secessum exit purgans omnes escas et exit in rivum"—so they all point the same way.'—(Kindly communicated by Mr. H. J. White.)

120 Dem. xv. (Graffin)—'Vadit enim esca in ventrem, unde purgatione in secessum emittitur.' (Lat.)

121 iii. 764. 'Et in secessum exit, purgans omnes escas.'

122 Galland. 319. 'Cibis, quos Dominus dicit perire, et in secessu naturali lege purgari.'

123 iii. 494. ἔλεγε ταῦτα ὁ Σωτήρ, καθαρίζων πάντα τὰ βρώματα.

124 i. 206. ἐκκαθαρίζων πάντα τὰ βρώματα.

125 Galland. 400. ἀλλὰ καὶ ὁ Σωτήρ, πάντα καθαρίζων τὰ βρώματα.

126 Evan. 2. Sce Hoskier, Collation of Cod. Evan. 604, App. F. p. 4.

127 [The following specimens taken from the first hand of B may illustrate the kakigraphy, if I may use the expression, which is characteristic of that MS. and also of ℵ. The list might be easily increased.

I. *Proper Names.*

Ιωανης, generally: Ιωαννης, Luke i. 13*, 60, 63; Acts iii. 4; iv. 6, 13, 19; xii. 25; xiii. 5, 25; xv. 37; Rev. i. 1, 4, 9; xxii. 8.

Βεεζεβουλ, Matt. x. 25; xii. 24, 27; Mark iii. 22; Luke xi. 15, 18, 19.

Ναζαρετ, Matt. ii. 23; Luke i. 26; John i. 46, 47. Ναζαρα, Matt. iv. 13. Ναζαρεθ, Matt. xxi. 11; Luke ii. 51; iv. 16.

Μαρια for Μαριαμ, Matt. i. 20; Luke ii. 19. Μαριαμ for Μαρια, Matt. xxvii. 61; Mark xx. 40; Luke x. 42; xi. 32; John xi. 2; xii. 3; xx. 16, 18. See Traditional Text, p. 86.

Κουμ, Mark v. 41. Γολγοθ, Luke xix. 27.

Ιστραηλειται, Ιστραηλιται, Ισραηλειται, Ισραηλιται.

Ελεισαβετ, Ελισαβετ.

Μωσησ, Μωυσης.

Δαλμανουθα, Mark viii. 10.

Ιωση (Joseph of Arimathea), Mark xv. 45. Ιωσηφ, Matt. xxvii. 57, 59; Mark xv. 42; Luke xxiii. 50; John xix. 38.

II. *Mis-spelling of ordinary words.*

καθ' ἴδιαν, Matt. xvii. 1, 19; xxiv. 3; Mark iv. 34; vi. 31, &c. κατ' ιδιαν, Matt. xiv. 13, 23; Mark vi. 32; vii. 33, &c.

γενημα, Matt. xxvi. 29; Mark xiv. 25; Luke xxii. 18. γεννημα, Matt. iii. 7; xii. 34; xxiii. 33; Luke iii. 7 (the well-known γεννήματα ἐχιδνῶν).

A similar confusion between γένεσις and γέννησις, Matt. i, and between ἐγενήθην and ἐγεννήθην, and γεγένημαι and γεγέννημαι. See Kuenen and Cobet N. T. ad fid. Cod. Vaticani lxxvii.

III. *Itacisms.*

κρίνεω, John xii. 48 (κρινεῖ;). κρίνω, Matt. vii. 1; xix. 28; Luke vi. 37; vii. 43; xii. 57, &c.

τειμῶ, τιμῶ, Matt. xv. 4, 5, 8; xix. 19; xxvii. 9; Mark vii. 6, 10, &c.

ἐνεβριμήθη (Matt. ix. 30) for ἐνεβριμήσατο. ἀνακλειθῆναι (Mark vi. 39) for ἀνακλῖναι. σεῖτος for σῖτος (Mark iv. 28).

IV. *Bad Grammar.*

τῷ οἰκοδεσπότῃ ἐπεκάλεσαν or τὸν οἰκοδεσπότην ἐκάλ.. (Matt. x. 25). καταπατήσουσιν for -σωσιν, (Matt. vii. 6). ὃ ἂν αἰτήσεται (Matt. xiv. 7). ὅταν δὲ ἀκούετε (Mark xiii. 7).

V. *Impossible words.*

ἐμνηστευμένην (Luke i. 27). οὐρανοῦ for οὐρανίου (ii. 13). ἀνεζήτουν (Luke ii. 44). κοπιῦσιν (Matt. vi. 28). ἠρώτουν (Matt. xv. 23). κατασκηνοῖν (Mark iv. 32). ἡμεῖς for ὑμεῖς. ὑμεῖς for ἡμεῖς.]

128 This paper on Titus ii. 5 was marked by the Dean as being 'ready for

press.' It was evidently one of his later essays, and was left in one of his later portfolios.

[129] *All* Matthaei's 16,—*all* Rinek's 7,—*all* Reiche's 6,—*all* Scrivener's 13, &c., &c.

[130] 622.

[131] *Ed.* Swete, ii. 247 (*domos suas bene regentes*); 248 (*domus proprias optime regant*).

[132] ii. (*Eth.*) 291 a, 309 b.

[133] xi. 750 a, 751 b c d—ἡ οἰκουρὸς καὶ οἰκονομική.

[134] iii. 704.

[135] ii. 271.

[136] Cod. Clarom.

[137] Cod. Amiat., and August. iii¹. 804.

[138] vii. 716 c, 718 b (*Bene domum regere*, 718 c).

[139] κατ᾽ οἶκον οἰκουροῦσιν ὥστε παρθένοι (Soph. Oed. Col. 343).—᾽Οἰκουρός est quasi proprium vocabulum mulierum: οἰκουργός est scribarum commentum,'—as Matthaei, whose note is worth reading, truly states. Wetstein's collections here should by all means be consulted. See also Field's delightful Otium Norv., pp. 135-6.

[140] P. 293, *lin.* 4 (see *lin.* 2).

[141] P. 288, *lin.* 20.

[142] 1 Tim. v. 13.

[143] οἰκουργεῖν—which occurs in Clemens Rom. (ad Cor. c. 1)—is probably due to the scribe.

Chapter Six - Accidental Causes of Corruption - V. Liturgical Influence

§. 1.

THERE is one distinct class of evidence provided by Almighty God for the conservation of the deposit in its integrity[144] which calls for special notice in this place. The Lectionaries of the ancient Church have not yet nearly enjoyed the attention they deserve, or the laborious study which in order to render them practically available they absolutely require. Scarcely any persons, in fact, except professed critics, are at all acquainted with the contents of the very curious documents alluded to: while collations of any of them which have been hitherto effected are few indeed. I speak chiefly of the Books called Evangelistaria (or Evangeliaria), in other words, the proper lessons collected out of the Gospels, and transcribed into a separate volume. Let me freely admit that I subjoin a few observations on this subject with unfeigned diffidence; having had to teach myself throughout the little I know;— and discovering in the end how very insufficient for my purpose that little is. Properly handled, an adequate study of the Lectionaries of the ancient Church would become the labour of a life. We require exact collations of at least too of them. From such a practical acquaintance with about a tenth of the extant copies some very interesting results would infallibly be obtained[145].

As for the external appearance of these documents, it may be enough to say that they range, like the mass of uncial and cursive copies, over a space of about 700 years,—the oldest extant being of about the eighth century, and the latest dating in the fifteenth. Rarely are any so old as the former date,—or so recent as the last named. When they began to be executed is not known; but much older copies than any which at present exist must have perished through constant use: [for they are in perfect order when we first become acquainted with them, and as a whole they are remarkably consistent with one another]. They are almost invariably written in double columns, and not unfrequently are splendidly executed. The use of Uncial letters is observed to have been retained in documents of this class to a later period than in the case of the Evangelia, viz. down to the eleventh century. For the most part they are furnished with a kind of musical notation executed in vermilion; evidently intended to guide the reader in that peculiar recitative which is still customary in the oriental Church.

In these books the Gospels always stand in the following order: St. John: St. Matthew: St. Luke: St. Mark. The lessons are brief,—resembling the Epistles and Gospels in our Book of Common Prayer.

They seem to me to fall into two classes: (*a*) Those which contain a lesson for every day in the year: (*b*) Those which only contain [lessons for fixed Festivals and] the Saturday-Sunday lessons (σαββατοκυριακαί). We are reminded by this peculiarity that it was not till a very late period in her history that the Eastern Church was able to shake herself clear of the shadow of the old Jewish Sabbath[146]. [To these Lectionaries Tables of the Lessons were often added, of a similar character to those which we have in our Prayer-books. The Table of daily Lessons went under the title of Synaxarion (or Eclogadion); and the Table of the Lessons of immovable Festivals and Saints' days was styled Menologion[147].]

Liturgical use has proved a fruitful source of textual perturbation. Nothing less was to have been expected,—as every one must admit who has examined ancient Evangelia with any degree of attention. For a period before the custom arose of writing out the Ecclesiastical Lections in the 'Evangelistaries,' and 'Apostolos,' it may be regarded as certain that the practice generally prevailed of accommodating an ordinary copy, whether of the Gospels or of the Epistles, to the requirements of the Church. This continued to the last to be a favourite method with the ancients[148]. Not only was it the invariable liturgical practice to introduce an ecclesiastical lection with an ever-varying formula,—by which means the holy Name is often found in MSS. where it has no proper place,—but notes of time, &c., ['like the unique and indubitably genuine word δευτεροπρώτῳ[149],' are omitted as carrying no moral lesson, as well as longer passages like the case of the two verses recounting the ministering Angel with the Agony and the Bloody Sweat[150].

That Lessons from the New Testament were probably read in the assemblies of the faithful according to a definite scheme, and on an established system, at least as early as the fourth century, has been shewn to follow from plain historical fact in the tenth chapter of the Twelve Last Verses of St. Mark's Gospel, to which the reader is referred for more detailed information.

Cyril, at Jerusalem,—and by implication, his namesake at Alexandria,—Chrysostom, at Antioch and at Constantinople,—Augustine, in Africa,—all four expressly witness to the circumstance. In other words, there is found to have been at least at that time fully established throughout the Churches of Christendom a Lectionary, which seems to have been essentially one and the same in the West and in the East. That it must have been of even Apostolic antiquity may be inferred from several considerations[151]. For example, Marcion, in A. D. 140, would hardly have constructed an Evangelistarium and Apostolicon of his own, as we learn from Epiphanius[152], if he had not been induced by the Lectionary System prevailing around him to form a counter-plan of teaching upon the same model.]

§ 2.

Indeed, the high antiquity of the Church's Lectionary System is inferred with certainty from many a textual phenomenon with which students of Textual Science are familiar.

It may be helpful to a beginner if I introduce to his notice the class of readings to be discussed in the present chapter, by inviting his attention to the first words of the Gospel for St. Philip and St. James' Day in our own English Book of Common Prayer,—'And Jesus said unto His disciples.' Those words he sees at a glance are undeniably nothing else but an Ecclesiastical accretion to the Gospel,—words which breed offence in no quarter, and occasion error to none. They have nevertheless stood prefixed to St. John xiv. 1 from an exceedingly remote period; for, besides establishing themselves in every Lectionary of the ancient Church[153], they are found in Cod. D[154],—in copies of the Old Latin[155] as the Vercellensis, Corbeiensis, Aureus, Bezae,— and in copies of the Vulgate. They may be of the second or third, they must be as old as the fourth century. It is evident that it wants but a very little for those words to have established their claim to a permanent place in the Text. Readings just as slenderly supported have been actually adopted before now[156].

I proceed to cite another instance; and here the success of an ordinary case of Lectionary licence will be perceived to have been complete: for besides recommending itself to Lachmann, Tischendorf, Tregelles, and Westcott and Hort, the blunder in question has established itself in the pages of the Revised Version. Reference is made to an alteration of the Text occurring in certain copies of Acts iii. 1, which will be further discussed below[157]. When it has been stated that these copies are אABCG,—the Vulgate,—the two Egyptian versions,—besides the Armenian,—and the Ethiopic,—it will be admitted that the Ecclesiastical practice which has resulted in so widespread a reading, must be primitive indeed. To some persons such a formidable array of evidence may seem conclusive in favour of any reading: but it can only seem so to those who do not realize the weight of counter-testimony.

But by far the most considerable injury which has resulted to the Gospel from this cause is the suspicion which has alighted in certain quarters on the last twelve verses of the Gospel according to St. Mark. [Those verses made up by themselves a complete Lection. The preceding Lection, which was used on the Second Sunday after Easter, was closed with the Liturgical note 'The End,' or TO ΤΕΛΟC, occurring after the eighth verse. What more probable, nay, more certain result could there be, than that some scribe should mistake the end of the Lection for the end of St. Mark's Gospel, if the last leaf should chance to have been torn off, and should then transcribe no more[158]? How natural that St. Mark should express himself in a more condensed and abrupt style than usual. This of course is only put forward as an explanation, which leaves the notion of another writer and a later date unnecessary. If it can be improved upon, so much the better. Candid critics ought to study Dean Burgon's elaborate chapter already referred to before rejecting it.]

3.

And there probably does not exist, in the whole compass of the Gospel, a more interesting instance of this than is furnished by the words εἶπε δὲ ὁ Κύριος, in St. Luke vii. 31. This is certainly derived from the Lectionaries; being nothing else but the formula with which it was customary to introduce the lection that begins at this place. Accordingly, only one out of forty copies which have been consulted for the purpose contains them. But the circumstance of interest remains to be stated. When these four unauthorized words have been thus got rid of, the important discovery is made that the two preceding verses (verses 28 and 29) must needs form a part of our Lord's discourse,—which it is perceived flows on unbroken from v. 24 to v. 35. This has been seen already by some[159], though denied by others. But the fact does not admit of rational doubt; though it is certainly not as yet generally known. It is not generally known, I mean, that the Church has recovered a piece of knowledge with which she was once familiar[160], but which for many centuries she has forgotten, viz. that thirty-two words which she supposed to be those of the Evangelist are in reality those of her Lord.

Indeed, when the expressions are considered, it is perceived that this account of them must needs be the true one. Thus, we learn from the 24th verse that our Saviour was at this time addressing the 'crowds' or 'multitudes.' But the four classes specified in verses 29, 30, cannot reasonably be thought to be the Evangelist's analysis of those crowds. In fact what is said of the Pharisees and Lawyers' in ver. 30 is clearly not a remark made by the Evangelist on the reception which our Saviour's words were receiving at the hands of his auditory; but our Saviour's own statement of the reception which His Forerunner's preaching had met with at the hands of the common people and the publicans on the one hand,—the Pharisees and the Scribes on the other. Hence the inferential particle οὖν in the 31st verse; and the use in ver. 35 of the same verb (ἐδικαιώθη) which the Divine Speaker had employed in ver. 29: whereby He takes up His previous statement while He applies and enforces it.

Another specimen of unauthorized accretion originating in the same way is found a little farther on. In St. Luke ix. 1 ('And having called together His twelve Disciples'), the words μαθητὰς αὐτοῦ are confessedly spurious: being condemned by nearly every known cursive and uncial. Their presence in the meantime is fully accounted for by the adjacent rubrical direction how the lesson is to be introduced: viz. At that time Jesus having called together His twelve Disciples.' Accordingly we are not surprised to find the words ὁ Ἰησοῦς also thrust into a few of the MSS.: though we are hardly prepared to discover that the words of the Peshitto, besides the Latin and Cureton's Syriac, are disfigured in the same way. The admirers of the 'old uncials' will learn with interest that, instead of μαθητὰς αὐτοῦ, אC with LXAΞ and a choice assortment of cursives exhibit ἀποστόλους,—being supported in this manifestly spurious reading by the best copies of the Old Latin, the Vulgate, Gothic, Harkleian, Bohairic, and a few other translations.

Indeed, it is surprising what a fertile source of corruption Liturgical usage has proved. Every careful student of the Gospels remembers that St. Matthew describes our Lord's first and second missionary journey in very nearly the same words. The former place (iv. 23) ending καὶ πᾶσαν μαλακίαν ἐν τῷ λαῷ used to conclude the lesson for the second Sunday after Pentecost,—the latter (ix. 35) ending καὶ πᾶσαν μαλακίαν occupies the same position in the Gospel for the seventh Sunday. It will not seem strange to any one who considers the matter, that ἐν τῷ λαῷ has in consequence not only found its way into ix. 35, but has established itself there very firmly: and that from a very early time. The spurious words are first met with in the Codex Sinaiticus[161].

But sometimes corruptions of this class are really perplexing. Thus א testifies to the existence of a short additional clause (καὶ πολλοὶ ἠκολούθησαν αὐτῷ) at the end, as some critics say, of the same 35th verse. Are we not rather to regard the words as the beginning of ver. 36, and as being nothing else but the liturgical introduction to the lection for the Twelve Apostles, which follows (ix. 36–x. 8), and whose Festival falls on the 30th June? Whatever its origin, this confessedly spurious accretion to the Text, which exists besides only in L and six cursive copies, must needs be of extraordinary antiquity, being found in the two oldest copies of the Old Latin:—a sufficient indication, by the way, of the utter insufficiency of such an amount of evidence for the genuineness of any reading.

This is the reason why, in certain of the oldest documents accessible, such a strange amount of discrepancy is discoverable in the text of the first words of St. Luke x. 25 (καὶ ἰδοὺ νομικός τις ἀνέστη, ἐκπειράζων αὐτὸν, καὶ λέγων). Many of the Latin copies preface this with et haec eo dicente. Now, the established formula of the lectionaries here is,—νομικός τις προσῆλθεν τῷ Ἰ. which explains why the Curetonian, the Lewis, with 33, 'the queen of the cursives,' as their usual leader in aberrant readings is absurdly styled. so read the place: while D, with one copy of the Old Latin, stands alone in exhibiting,—ἀνέστη δέ τις νομικός. Four Codexes (אBLΞ) with the Curetonian omit the second καὶ which is illegible in the Lewis. To read this place in its purity you have to take up any ordinary cursive copy.

4.

Take another instance. St. Mark xv. 28 has been hitherto read in all Churches as follows And the Scripture was fulfilled, which saith, "And He was numbered with the transgressors.'" In these last days however the discovery is announced that every word of this is an unauthorized addition to the in-spired text. Griesbach indeed only marks the verse as probably spurious; while Tregelles is content to enclose it in brackets. But Alford, Tischendorf, Westcott and Hort, and the Revisers eject the words καὶ ἐπληρώθη ἡ γραφὴ ἡ λέγουσα, καὶ μετὰ ἀνόμων ἐλογίσθη from the text altogether. What can be the reason for so extraordinary a proceeding?

Let us not be told by Schulz (Griesbach's latest editor) that 'the quotation is not in Mark's manner; that the formula which introduces it is John's: and that it seems to be a gloss taken from Luke xxii. 37.' This is not criticism but dicta-tion,—imagination, not argument. Men who so write forget that they are as-suming the very point which they are called upon to prove.

Now it happens that all the Uncials but six and an immense majority of the Cursive copies contain the words before us:—that besides these, the Old Lat-in, the Syriac, the Vulgate, the Gothic and the Bohairic versions, all concur in exhibiting them:—that the same words are expressly recognized by the Sec-tional System of Eusebius;—having a section (σις/η i.e. 216/8) to them-selves—which is the weightiest sanction that Father had it in his power to give to words of Scripture. So are they also recognized by the Syriac sectional system (260/8), which is diverse from that of Eusebius and independent of it. What then is to be set against such a weight of ancient evidence? The fact that the following six Codexes are without this 28th verse, אABCDX, together with the Sahidic and Lewis. The notorious Codex k (Bobiensis) is the only other ancient testimony producible; to which Tischendorf adds 'about forty-five cursive copies.' Will it be seriously pretended that this evidence for omit-ting ver. 28 from St. Mark's Gospel can compete with the evidence for retain-ing it?

Let it not be once more insinuated that we set numbers before antiquity. Codex D is of the sixth century; Cod. X not older than the ninth: and not one of the four Codexes which remain is so old, within perhaps two centuries, as either the Old Latin or the Peshitto versions. We have Eusebius and Jerome's Vulgate as witnesses on the same side, besides the Gothic version, which rep-resents a Codex probably as old as either. To these witnesses must be added Victor of Antioch, who commented on St. Mark's Gospel before either A or C were written[162].

It will be not unreasonably asked by those who have learned to regard whatever is found in B or א as oracular,— 'But is it credible that on a point like this such authorities as אABCD should all be in error?'

It is not only credible, I answer, but a circumstance of which we meet with so many undeniable examples that it ceases to be even a matter of surprise. On the other hand, what is to be thought of the credibility that on a point like this all the ancient versions (except the Sahidic) should have conspired to mislead mankind? And further, on what intelligible principle is the consent of all the other uncials, and the whole mass of cursives, to be explained, if this verse of Scripture be indeed spurious?

54

I know that the rejoinder will be as follows:—'Yes, but if the ten words in dispute really are part of the inspired verity, how is their absence from the earliest Codexes to be accounted for?' Now it happens that for once I am able to assign the reason. But I do so under protest, for I insist that to point out the source of the mistakes in our oldest Codexes is no part of a critic's business. It would not only prove an endless, but also a hopeless task. This time, however, I am able to explain.

If the reader will take the trouble to inquire at the Bibliotheque at Paris for a Greek Codex numbered '71,' an Evangelium will be put into his hands which differs from any that I ever met with in giving singularly minute and full rubrical directions. At the end of St. Mark xv. 27, he will read as follows:—'When thou readest the sixth Gospel of the Passion,—also when thou readest the second Gospel of the Vigil of Good Friday,—stop here: skip verse 28: then go on at verse 29.' The inference from this is so obvious, that it would be to abuse the reader's patience if I were to enlarge upon it, or even to draw it out in detail. Very ancient indeed must the Lectionary practice in this particular have been that it should leave so fatal a trace of its operation in our four oldest Codexes: but *it has left it*[163]. The explanation is evident, the verse is plainly genuine, and the Codexes which leave it out are corrupt.

One word about the evidence of the cursive copies on this occasion. Tischendorf says that 'about forty-five' of them are without this precious verse of Scripture. I venture to say that the learned critic would be puzzled to produce forty-five copies of the Gospels in which this verse has no place. But in fact his very next statement (viz. that about half of these are Lectionaries),—satisfactorily explains the matter. Just so. From every Lectionary in the world, for the reason already assigned, these words are away; as well as in every MS. which, like B and ℵ, has been depraved by the influence of the Lectionary practice.

And now I venture to ask,—What is to be thought of that Revision of our Authorized Version which omits ver. 28 altogether; with a marginal intimation that many ancient authorities insert it'? Would it not have been the course of ordinary reverence,—I was going to say of truth and fairness,—to leave the text unmolested: with a marginal memorandum that just 'a very few ancient authorities leave it out'?

5.

A gross depravation of the Text resulting from this cause, which nevertheless has imposed on several critics, as has been already said, is furnished by the first words of Acts iii. The most ancient witness accessible, namely the Peshitto, confirms the usual reading of the place, which is also the text of the cursives: viz. Ἐπὶ τὸ αὐτό δὲ Πέτρος καὶ Ἰωάννης κ.τ.λ.So the Harkleian and Bede. So Codex E.

The four oldest of the six available uncials conspire however in representing the words which immediately precede in the following unintelligible fashion:—ὁ δὲ Κύριος προσετίθει τοὺς σωζομένους καθ᾽ ἡμέραν

Chapter Seven - Causes of Corruption Chiefly Intentional - I. Harmonistic Influence

[IT must not be imagined that all the causes of the depravation of the text of Holy Scripture were instinctive, and that mistakes arose solely because scribes were overcome by personal infirmity, or were unconsciously the victims of surrounding circumstances. There was often more design and method in their error. They, or those who directed them, wished sometimes to correct and improve the copy or copies before them. And indeed occasionally they desired to make the Holy Scriptures witness to their own peculiar belief. Or they had their ideas of taste, and did not scruple to alter passages to suit what they fancied was their enlightened judgement.

Thus we can trace a tendency to bring the Four Records into one harmonious narrative, or at least to excise or vary statements in one Gospel which appeared to conflict with parallel statements in another. Or else, some Evangelical Diatessaron, or Harmony, or combined narrative now forgotten, exercised an influence over them, and whether consciously or not,—since it is difficult always to keep designed and unintentional mistakes apart, and we must not be supposed to aim at scientific exactness in the arrangement adopted in this analysis,—induced them to adopt alterations of the pure Text.

We now advance to some instances which will severally and conjointly explain themselves.]

§ 1.

Nothing can be more exquisitely precise than St. John's way of describing an incident to which St. Mark (xvi. 9) only refers; viz. our Lord's appearance to Mary Magdalene,—the first of His appearances after His Resurrection. The reason is discoverable for every word the Evangelist uses:—its form and collocation. Both St. Luke (xxiv. 3) and previously St. Mark (xvi. 5) expressly stated that the women who visited the Sepulchre on the first Easter morning, 'after they had entered in' (εἰσελθοῦσαι), saw the Angels. St John explains that at that time Mary was not with them. She had separated herself from their company;—had gone in quest of Simon Peter and 'the other disciple.' When the women, their visit ended, had in turn departed from the Sepulchre, she was left in the garden alone. 'Mary was standing [with her face] *towards the sepulchre* weeping,—*outside*[172] .'

All this, singular to relate, was completely misunderstood by the critics of the two first centuries. Not only did they identify the incident recorded in St. John xx. 12 with St. Mark xv. 5 and St. Luke xxiv. 3, 4, from which, as we have seen, the first-named Evangelist is careful to distinguish it;—not only did they further identify both places with St. Matt. xxviii. 2, 3[173], from which they are clearly separate;—but they considered themselves at liberty to tamper with the inspired text in order to bring it into harmony with their own convictions. Some of them accordingly altered πρὸς τὸ μνημεῖον into πρὸς τῷ μνημείῳ (which is just as ambiguous in Greek as 'at the sepulchre' in English[174]), and ἔξω they boldly erased. It is thus that Codex A exhibits the text. But in fact this depravation must have begun at a very remote period and prevailed to an extraordinary extent: for it disfigures the best copies of the Old Latin, (the Syriac being doubtful): a memorable circumstance truly, and in a high degree suggestive. Codex B, to be sure, reads εἰστήκει πρὸς τῷ μνημείῳ ἔξω κλαίουσα,—merely transposing (with many other authorities) the last two words. But then Codex B substitutes ἐλθοῦσαι for for εἰσελθοῦσαι in St. Mark xvi. 5, in order that the second Evangelist may not seem to contradict St. Matt. xxviii. 2, 3. So that, according to this view of the matter, the Angelic appearance was outside the sepulchre[175]. Codex ℵ, on the contrary, is thorough. Not content with omitting ἔξω,—(as in the next verse it leaves out δύο, in order to prevent St. John xx. 12 from seeming to contradict St. Matt. xxviii. 2, 3, and St. Mark xvi. 5),—it stands alone in reading 'ΕΝ τῷ μνημείῳ. (C and D are lost here.) When will men learn that these 'old uncials' are *ignes fatui*,— not beacon lights; and admit that the texts which they exhibit are not only inconsistent but corrupt?

There is no reason for distrusting the received reading of the present place in any particular. True, that most of the uncials and many of the cursives read πρὸς τῷ μνημείῳ: but so did neither Chrysostom[176] nor Cyril[177] read the place. And if the Evangelist himself had so written, is it credible that a majority of the copies would have forsaken the easier and more obvious, in order to exhibit the less usual and even slightly difficult expression? Many, by writing πρὸς τῷ μνημείῳ, betray themselves; for they retain a sure token that the accusative ought to end the sentence. I am not concerned however just now to discuss these matters of detail. I am only bent on illustrating how fatal to the purity of the Text of the Gospels has been the desire of critics, who did not understand those divine compositions, to bring them into enforced agreement with one another. The sectional system of Eusebius, I suspect, is not so much the cause as the consequence of the ancient and inveterate misapprehensions which prevailed in respect of the history of the Resurrection. It is time however to proceed.

§ 2.

Those writers who overlook the corruptions which the text has actually experienced through a mistaken solicitude on the part of ancient critics to reconcile what seemed to them the conflicting statements of different Evangelists, are frequently observed to attribute to this kind of officiousness expressions which are unquestionably portions of the genuine text. Thus, there is a general consensus amongst critics of the destructive school to omit the words καὶ τινες σὺν αὐταῖς from St. Luke xxiv. 1. Their only plea is the testimony of ℵBCL and certain of the Latin copies,—a conjunction of authorities which, when they stand alone, we have already observed to bear invariably false witness. Indeed, before we proceed to examine the evidence, we discover that those four words of St. Luke are even required in this place. For St.

Matthew (xxvii. 61), and St. Mark after him (xv. 47), had distinctly specified two women as witnesses of how and where our Lord's body was laid. Now they were the same women apparently who prepared the spices and ointment and hastened therewith at break of day to the sepulchre. Had we therefore only St. Matthew's. Gospel we should have assumed that 'the ointment-bearers,' for so the ancients called them, were but two (St. Matt. xxviii. 1). That they were at least three, even St. Mark shews by adding to their number Salome (xvi. 1). But in fact their company consisted of more than four; as St. Luke explains when he states that it was the same little band of holy women who had accompanied our Saviour out of Galilee (xxiii. 55, cf. viii. 2). In anticipation therefore of what he will have to relate in ver. 10, he says in ver. 1, 'and certain with them.'

But how, I shall be asked, would you explain the omission of these words which to yourself seem necessary? And after insisting that one is never bound to explain how the text of any particular passage came to be corrupted, I answer, that these words were originally ejected from the text in order to bring St. Luke's statement into harmony with that of the first Evangelist, who mentions none but Mary Magdalene and Mary the mother of James and Joses. The proof is that four of the same Latin copies which are for the omission of καὶ τινες σὺν αὐταῖς are observed to begin St. Luke xxiii. 55 as follows,—κατακολουθήσασαι δὲ ΔΥΟ γυναῖκες. The same fabricated reading is found in D. It exists also in the Codex which Eusebius employed when he wrote his Demonstratio Evangelica. Instead therefore of wearying the reader with the evidence, which is simply overwhelming, for letting the text alone, I shall content myself with inviting him to notice that the tables have been unexpectedly turned on our opponents. There is indeed found to have been a corruption of the text hereabouts, and of the words just now under discussion; but it belongs to an exceedingly remote age; and happily the record of it survives at this day only in ℵBCDL and certain of the Old Latin copies. Calamitous however it is, that what the Church has long since deliberately refused to part with should, at the end of so many centuries, by Lachmann and Tregelles and Tischendorf, by Alford and Westcott and Hort, be resolutely thrust out of place; and indeed excluded from the Sacred Text by a majority of the Revisers.

[A very interesting instance of such Harmonistic Influence may be found in the substitution of 'wine' (οἶνον) for vinegar (ὄξος), respecting which the details are given in the second Appendix to the Traditional Text.]

[Observe yet another instance of harmonizing propensities in the Ancient Church.]

In St. Luke's Gospel iv. 1-13, no less than six copies of the Old Latin versions (b c f g^1 l q) besides Ambrose (Com. St. Luke, 1340), are observed to transpose the second and third temptations; introducing verses 9-12 between verses 4 and 5; in order to make the history of the Temptation as given by St. Luke correspond with the account given by St. Matthew.

The scribe of the Vercelli Codex (a) was about to do the same thing; but he checked himself when he had got as far as 'the pinnacle of the temple,'—which he seems to have thought as good a scene for the third temptation as 'a high mountain,' and so left it.

§ 3.

A favourite, and certainly a plausible, method of accounting for the presence of unauthorized matter in MSS. is to suggest that, in the first instance, it probably existed only in the shape of a marginal gloss, which through the inadvertence of the scribes, in process of time, found its way into the sacred text. That in this way some depravations of Scripture may possibly have arisen, would hardly I presume be doubted. But I suspect that the hypothesis is generally a wholly mistaken one; having been imported into this subject-matter (like many other notions which are quite out of place here), from the region of the Classics,—where (as we know) the phenomenon is even common. Especially is this hypothesis resorted to (I believe) in order to explain those instances of assimilation which are so frequently to be met with in Codd. B and ℵ.

Another favourite way of accounting for instances of assimilation, is by taking for granted that the scribe was thinking of the parallel or the cognate place. And certainly (as before) there is no denying that just as the familiar language of a parallel place in another Gospel presents itself unbidden to the memory of a reader, so may it have struck a copyist also with sufficient vividness to persuade him to write, not the words which he saw before him, but the words which he remembered. All this is certainly possible.

But I strongly incline to the suspicion that this is not by any means .the right way to explain the phenomena under discussion. I am of opinion that such depravations of the text were in the first instance intentional. I do not mean that they were introduced with any sinister motive. My meaning is that [there was a desire to remove obscurities, or to reconcile incongruous passages, or generally to improve the style of the authors, and thus to add to the merits of the sacred writings, instead of detracting from them. Such a mode of dealing with the holy deposit evinced no doubt a failure in the part of those who adopted it to understand the nature of the trust committed to the Church, just as similar action at the present day does in the case of such as load the New Testament with 'various readings,' and illustrate it as they imagine with what are really insinuations of doubt, in the way that they prepare an edition of the classics for the purpose of enlarging and sharpening the minds of youthful students. There was intention, and the intention was good: but it was none the less productive of corruption.]

I suspect that if we ever obtain access to a specimen of those connected Gospel narratives called Diatessarons, which are known to have existed anciently in the Church, we shall be furnished with a clue to a problem which at present is shrouded in obscurity,—and concerning the solution of which, with such instruments of criticism as we at present possess, we can do little else but conjecture. I allude to those many occasions on which the oldest documents extant, in narrating some incident which really presents no special difficulty, are observed to diverge into hopeless variety of expression. An example of the thing referred to will best explain my meaning. Take then the incident of our Lord's paying tribute,—set down in St. Matt. xvii. 25, 26.

The received text exhibits,—'And when he [Peter] had entered (ὅτε εἰσῆλθεν) into the house, Jesus was beforehand with him, saying, What thinkest thou, Simon? Of whom do earthly kings take toll or tribute? of their sons or of strangers?' Here, for ὅτε εἰσῆλθεν, Codex B (but no other uncial) substitutes ἐλθόντα: Codex ℵ (but no other) εἰσελθόντα Codex D (but no other) εἰσελθόντι: Codex C (but no other) ὅτε ἦλθον: while a fifth lost copy certainly contained εἰσελθόντων; and a sixth, ἐλθόντων αὐτῶν. A very fair specimen this, be it remarked in passing, of the *concordia discors* which prevails in the most ancient uncial copies[178]. How is all this discrepancy to be accounted for?

The Evangelist proceeds,—'Peter saith unto Him (Λέγει αὐτῷ ὁ Πέτρος), Of strangers.' These four words C retains, but continues—'Now when he had said, Of strangers' (Εἰπόντος δὲ αὐτοῦ, ἀπὸ τῶν ἀλλοτρίων);—which unauthorized clause, all but the word αὐτοῦ, is found also in ℵ, but in no other uncial. On the other hand, for Λέγει αὐτῷ ὁ Πέτρος, ℵ (alone of uncials) substitutes Ὁ δὲ ἔφη: and B (also alone of uncials) substitutes Εἰπόντος δέ,—and then proceeds exactly like the received text: while D merely omits ὁ Πέτρος. Again I ask,—How is all this discrepancy to be explained[179]?

As already hinted, I suspect that it was occasioned in the first instance by the prevalence of harmonized Gospel narratives. In no more loyal way can I account for the perplexing phenomenon already described, which is of perpetual recurrence in such documents as Codexes BℵD, Cureton's Syriac, and copies of the Old Latin version. It is well known that at a very remote period some eminent persons occupied themselves in constructing such exhibitions of the Evangelical history: and further, that these productions enjoyed great favour, and were in general use. As for their contents,—the notion we form to ourselves of a Diatessaron, is that it aspired to be a weaving of the fourfold Gospel into one continuous narrative: and we suspect that in accomplishing this object, the writer was by no means scrupulous about retaining the precise words of the inspired original. He held himself at liberty, on the contrary, (a) to omit what seemed to himself superfluous clauses: (b) to introduce new incidents: (c) to supply picturesque details: (d) to give a new turn to the expression: (e) to vary the construction at pleasure: (f) even slightly to paraphrase. Compiled after some such fashion as I have been describing, at a time too when the preciousness of the inspired documents seems to have been but imperfectly apprehended,—the works I speak of, recommended by their graphic interest, and sanctioned by a mighty name, must have imposed upon ordinary readers. Incautious owners of Codexes must have transferred without scruple certain unauthorized readings to the margins of their own copies. A calamitous partiality for the fabricated document may have prevailed with some for whom copies were executed. Above all, it is to be inferred that licentious and rash Editors of Scripture,—among whom Origen may be regarded as a prime offender,—must have deliberately introduced into their recensions many an unauthorized gloss, and so given it an extended circulation.

Not that we would imply that permanent mischief has resulted to the Deposit from the vagaries of individuals in the earliest age. The Divine Author of Scripture hath abundantly provided for the safety of His Word written. In the multitude of copies,—in Lectionaries,—in Versions,—in citations by the Fathers, a sufficient safeguard against error hath been erected. But then, of these multitudinous sources of protection we must not be slow to avail ourselves impartially. The prejudice which would erect Codexes B and ℵ into an authority for the text of the New Testament from which there shall be no appeal:—the superstitious reverence which has grown up for one little cluster of authorities, to the disparagement of all other evidence wheresoever found; this, which is for ever landing critics in results which are simply irrational and untenable, must be unconditionally abandoned, if any real progress is to be made in this department of inquiry. But when this has been done, men will begin to open their eyes to the fact that the little handful of documents recently so much in favour, are, on the contrary, the only surviving witnesses to corruptions of the Text which the Church in her corporate capacity has long since deliberately rejected. But to proceed.

[From the Diatessaron of Tatian and similar attempts to harmonize the Gospels, corruption of a serious nature has ensued in some well-known places, such as the transference of the piercing of the Lord's side from St. John xix. 34 to St. Matt. xxvii. 49[180], and the omission of the words 'and of an honeycomb' (καὶ ἀπὸ τοῦ μελισσίου κηρίου[181]).]

Hence also, in Cureton's Syriac[182], the *patch-work* supplement to St. Matt. xxi. 9: viz.:—πολλοὶ δὲ (St. Mark xi. 8) ἐξῆλθον εἰς ὑπάντησιν αὐτῦ. καὶ (St. John xii. 13) ἤρξαντο . . . χαίροντες αἰνεῖν τὸν Θεὸν . . . περὶ πασῶν ὧν εἶδον (St. Luke xix. 37). This self-evident fabrication, 'if it be not a part of the original Aramaic of St. Matthew,' remarks Dr. Cureton, 'would appear to have been supplied from the parallel passages of Luke and John conjointly.' How is it that even a sense of humour did not preserve that eminent scholar from hazarding the conjecture, that such a self-evident deflection of his corrupt Syriac Codex from the course all but universally pursued is a recovery of one more genuine utterance of the Holy Ghost?

172 Μαρία δὲ εἱστήκει πρὸς τὸ μνημεῖον κλαίουσα ἔξω, (St. John xx. 11). Comp. the expression πρὸς τὸ φῶς in St. Luke xxii. 56. Note, that the above is not offered as a revised translation; but only to shew unlearned readers what the words of the original exactly mean.

173 Note, that in the sectional system of Eusebius *according to the Greek*, the following places are brought together:— (St. Matt. xxviii)1-4. (St. Mark xvi)2-5. (St. Luke xxiv)1-4. (St. John

xx)1, 11, 12. According to the Syriac:—
3, 4. 5. 3, 4, 5(½). 11, 12.

174 Consider ὁ δὲ Πέτρος εἰστήκει
πρὸς τῇ θύρᾳ ἔξω (St. John xviii. 16).
Has not this place, by the way, exerted
an assimilating influence over St. John
xx. 11?

175 Hesychius, qu. 51 (apud Cotelerii
Eccl. Gr. Mon. iii. 43), explains St.
Mark's phrase ἐν τοῖς δεξιοῖς as follows:—δηλονότι τοῦ ἐξωτέρου
σπηλαίου.

176 viii. 513.

177 iv. 1079.

178 Traditional Text, pp. 81-8.

179 I am tempted to inquire,—By virtue of what verifying faculty do Lachmann and Tregelles on the former occasion adopt the reading of א; Tischendorf, Alford, W. and I fort, the reading
of B? On the second occasion, I venture
to ask,—What enabled the Revisers,
with Lachmann, Tischendorf, Tregelles,
Westcott and Hort, to recognize in a
reading, which is the peculiar property
of B, the genuine language of the Holy
Ghost? Is not a superstitious reverence
for B and א betraying for ever people
into error?

180 Revision Revised, p. 33.

181 Traditional Text, Appendix I, pp.
244-252.

182 The Lewis MS. is defective here.

Chapter Eight - Causes of Corruption Chiefly Intentional - II. Assimilation

§ 1.

THERE results inevitably from the fourfold structure of the Gospel,.—
from the very fact that the story of Redemption is set forth in four narratives,
three of which often ran parallel,—this practical inconvenience: namely, that
sometimes the expressions of one Evangelist get improperly transferred to
another. This is a large and important subject which calls for great attention,
and requires to be separately handled. The phenomena alluded to, which are
similar to some of those which have been treated in the last chapter, may be
comprised under the special head of Assimilation.

It will I think promote clearness in the ensuing discussion if we determine
to consider separately those instances of Assimilation which may rather be
regarded as deliberate attempts to reconcile one Gospel with another: indications of a fixed determination to establish harmony between place and
place. I am saying that between ordinary cases of Assimilation such as occur
in every page, and extraordinary instances where *per fas et nefas* an enforced
Harmony has been established,—which abound indeed, but are by no means
common,—I am disposed to draw a line.

This whole province is beset with difficulties: and the matter is in itself
wondrously obscure. I do not suppose, in the absence of any evidence direct
or indirect on the subject,—at all events I am not aware—that at any time
has there been one definite authoritative attempt made by the Universal

Church in her corporate capacity to remodel or revise the Text of the Gospels. An attentive study of the phenomena leads me, on the contrary, to believe that the several corruptions of the text were effected at different times, and took their beginning in widely different ways. I suspect that Accident was the parent of many; and well-meant critical assiduity of more. Zeal for the Truth is accountable for not a few depravations: and the Church's Liturgical and Lectionary practice must insensibly have produced others. Systematic villainy I am persuaded has had no part or lot in the matter. The decrees of such an one as Origen, if there ever was another like him, will account for a strange number of aberrations from the Truth: and if the Diatessaron of Tatian could be recovered[183], I suspect that we should behold there the germs at least of as many more. But, I repeat my conviction that, however they may have originated, the causes [are not to be found in bad principle, but either in infirmities or influences which actuated scribes unconsciously, or in a want of understanding as to what is the Church's duty in the transmission from generation to generation of the sacred deposit committed to her enlightened care.]

§ 2.

1. When we speak of Assimilation, we do not mean that a writer while engaged in transcribing one Gospel was so completely beguiled and overmastered by his recollections of the parallel place in another Gospel,—that, forsaking the expressions proper to the passage before him, he unconsciously adopted the language which properly belongs to a different Evangelist. That to a very limited extent this may have occasionally taken place, I am not concerned to deny: but it would argue incredible inattention to what he was professing to copy, on the one hand,—astonishing familiarity with what he was not professing to copy, on the other,—that a scribe should have been capable of offending largely in this way. But in fact a moderate acquaintance with the subject is enough to convince any thoughtful person that the corruptions in MSS. which have resulted from accidental Assimilation must needs be inconsiderable in bulk, as well as few in number. At all events, the phenomenon referred to, when we speak of 'Assimilation,' is not to be so accounted for: it must needs be explained in some entirely different way. Let me make my meaning plain:

(*a*) We shall probably be agreed that when the scribe of Cod. ℵ, in place of βασανίσαι ἡμᾶς (in St. Matt. viii. 29), writes ἡμᾶς ἀπολέσαι,—it may have been his memory which misled him. He may have been merely thinking of St. Mark i. 24, or of St. Luke iv. 34.

(*b*) Again, when in Codd. ℵB we find τασσόμενος thrust without warrant into St. Matt. viii. 9, we see that the word has lost its way from St. Luke vii. 8; and we are prone to suspect that only by accident has it crept into the parallel narrative of the earlier Evangelist.

(*c*) In the same way I make no doubt that ποταμῷ (St. Matt. iii. 6) is indebted for its place in ℵBC, &c., to the influence of the parallel place in St. Mark's

Gospel (i. 5); and I am only astonished that critics should have been beguiled into adopting so clear a corruption of the text as part of the genuine Gospel.

(d) To be brief:—the insertion by ℵ of ἀδελφέ (in St. Matt. vii. 4) is confessedly the result of the parallel passage in St. Luke vi. 42. The same scribe may be thought to have written τῷ ἀνέμῳ instead of τοῖς ἀνέμοις in St. Matt. viii. 26, only because he was so familiar with τῷ ἀνέμῳ in St. Luke viii. 24 and in St. Mark iv. 39.—The author of the prototype of ℵBD (with whom by the way are some of the Latin versions) may have written ἔχετε in St. Matt. xvi. 8, only because he was thinking of the parallel place in St. Mark viii. 17.—Ἤρξαντο ἀγανακτεῖν (St. Matt. xx. 24) can only have been introduced into ℵ from the parallel place in St. Mark x. 41, and *may* have been supplied *memoriter*.— St. Luke xix. 21 is clearly not parallel to St. Matt. xxv. 24; yet it evidently furnished the scribe of ℵ with the epithet αὐστηρός; in place of σκληρός.—The substitution by ℵ of ὃν παρητοῦντο in St. Matt. xxvii. 15 for ὃν ἤθελον may seem to be the result of inconvenient familiarity with the parallel place in St. Mark xv. 6; where, as has been shewn[184], instead of ὅνπερ ᾐτοῦντο, ℵAB viciously exhibit ὃν παρητοῦντο, which Tischendorf besides Westcott and Hort mistake for the genuine Gospel. Who will hesitate to admit that, when ℵL exhibit in St. Matt. xix. 16,—instead of the words ποιήσω ἵνα ἔχω ζωὴν αἰώνιον,—the formula which is found in the parallel place of St. Luke xviii. 18, viz. ποιήσας ζωὴν αἰώνιον κληρονομήσω,—those unauthorized words must have been derived from this latter place? Every ordinary reader will be further prone to assume that the scribe who first inserted them into St. Matthew's Gospel did so because, for whatever reason, he was more familiar with the latter formula than with the former.

(e) But I should have been willing to go further. I might have been disposed to admit that when ℵDL introduce into St. Matt. x. 12 the clause λέγοντες, εἰρήνη τῷ οἴκῳ τούτῳ (which last four words confessedly belong exclusively to St. Luke x. 5), the author of the depraved original from which ℵDL were derived may have been only yielding to the suggestions of an inconveniently good memory:—may have succeeded in convincing himself from what follows in verse 13 that St. Matthew must have written, 'Peace be to this house;' though he found no such words in St. Matthew's text. And so, with the best intentions, he may most probably have inserted them.

(f) Again. When ℵ and Evan. 61 thrust into St. Matt. ix. 24 (from the parallel place in St. Luke viii. 53) the clause εἰδότες ὅτι ἀπέθανεν, it is of course conceivable that the authors of those copies were merely the victims of excessive familiarity with the third Gospel. But then,—although we are ready to make every allowance that we possibly can for memories so singularly constituted, and to imagine a set of inattentive scribes open to inducements to recollect or imagine instead of copying, and possessed of an inconvenient familiarity with one particular Gospel,—it is clear that our complaisance must stop somewhere. Instances of this kind of licence at last breed suspicion. Systematic 'assimilation' cannot be the effect of accident. Considerable interpolations must of course be intentional. The discovery that Cod. D, for example, introduces at the end of St. Luke v. 14 thirty-two words from St. Mark's Gospel (i. 45-ii. 1, ὁ δὲ ἐξελθών down to Καφαρναούμ), opens our eyes. This wholesale importation suggests the inquiry,—How did it come about? We look further, and we find that Cod. D abounds in instances of 'Assimilation' so unmistakably intentional, that this speedily becomes the only question, How may all these depravations of the sacred text be most satisfactorily accounted for? [And the answer is evidently found in the existence of extreme licentiousness in the scribe or scribes responsible for Codex D, being the product of ignorance and carelessness combined with such looseness of principle, as permitted the exercise of direct attempts to improve the sacred Text by the introduction of passages from the three remaining Gospels and by other alterations.]

§ 3.

Sometimes indeed the true Text bears witness to itself, as may be seen in the next example.

The little handful of well-known authorities (אBDL, with a few copies of the Old Latin, and one of the Egyptian Versions[185]), conspire in omitting from St. John xvi. 16 the clause ὅτι ἐγὼ ὑπάγω πρὸς τὸν Πατέρα: for which reason Tischendorf, Tregelles, Alford, Westcott and Hort omit those six words, and Lachmann puts them into brackets. And yet, let the context be considered. Our Saviour had said (ver. 16),—'A little while, and ye shall not see Me: and again, a little while, and ye shall see Me, because I go to the Father; It follows (ver. 17),—'Then said some of His disciples among themselves, What is this that He saith unto us, A little while, and ye shall not see Me: and again, a little while, and ye shall see Me: and, *Because I go to the* Father?'—Now, the context here,—the general sequence of words and ideas—in and by itself, creates a high degree of probability that the clause is genuine. It must at all events be permitted to retain its place in the Gospel, unless there is found to exist an overwhelming amount of authority for its exclusion. What then are the facts? All the other uncials, headed by A and Iᵇ (*both* of the fourth century),— every known Cursive—all the Versions, (Latin, Syriac, Gothic, Coptic, &c.)—are for retaining the clause. Add, that Nonnus[186] (A.D. 400) recognizes it: that the texts of Chrysostom[187] and of Cyril[188] do the same; and that both those Fathers (to say nothing of Euthymius and Theophylact) in their Commentaries expressly bear witness to its genuineness:—and, With what shew of reason can it any longer be pretended that some Critics, including the Revisers, are warranted in leaving out the words? . . . It were to trifle with the reader to pursue this subject further. But how did the words ever come to be omitted? Some early critic, I answer, who was unable to see the exquisite proprieties of the entire passage, thought it desirable to bring ver. 16 into conformity with ver. 19, where our Lord seems at first sight to resyllable the matter. That is all !

Let it be observed—and then I will dismiss the matter—that the selfsame thing has happened in the next verse but one (ver. 18), as Tischendorf candidly acknowledges. The τοῦτο τί ἐστιν of the Evangelist has been tastelessly assimilated by BDLY to the τί ἐστιν τοῦτο, which went immediately before.

§ 4.

Were I invited to point to a beautifully described incident in the Gospel, I should find it difficult to lay my finger on anything more apt for my purpose than the transaction described in St. John xiii. 21-25. It belongs to the closing scene of our Saviour's Ministry. 'Verily, verily, I say unto you,' (the words were spoken at the Last Supper), one of you will betray Me. The disciples therefore looked one at another, wondering of whom He spake. Now there was reclining in the bosom of Jesus (ἦν δὲ ἀνακείμενος ἐν τῷ κόλπῳ τοῦ Ἰ..) one of His disciples whom Jesus loved. To him therefore Simon Peter motioneth to inquire who it may be concerning whom He speaketh. He then, just sinking on the breast of Jesus (ἐπιπεσὼν δὲ ἐκεῖνος οὕτως ἐπὶ τὸ στῆθος τοῦ Ἰ.) [i.e. otherwise keeping his position, see above, p. 60], saith unto Him, Lord, who is it?'

The Greek is exquisite. At first, St. John has been simply 'reclining (ἀνακείμενος) in the bosom' of his Divine Master: that is, his place at the Supper is the next adjoining His,—for the phrase really means little more. But the proximity is of course excessive, as the sequel shews. Understanding from St. Peter's gesture what is required of him, St. John merely sinks back, and having thus let his head fall (ἐπιπεσών) on (or close to) His Master's chest (ἐπὶ τὸ στῆθος), he says softly,—'Lord, who is it?' . . . The moment is perhaps the most memorable in the Evangelist's life: the position, one of unutterable privilege. Time, place, posture, action,—all settle so deep into his soul, that when, in his old age, he would identify himself, he describes himself as 'the disciple whom Jesus loved; who also at the Supper' (*that* memorable Supper !) 'lay (ἀνέπεσεν[189]) on Jesus' breast,' (literally, 'upon His chest,'—ἐπὶ τὸ στῆθος αὐτοῦ;), and said, 'Lord, who is it that is to betray Thee?' (ch. xxi. 20). . . . Yes, and the Church was not slow to take the beautiful hint. His language so kindled her imagination that the early Fathers learned to speak of St. John the Divine, as ὁ ἐπιστήθιος,—'the (recliner) on the chest[190].'

Now, every delicate discriminating touch in this sublime picture is faithfully retained throughout by the cursive copies in the proportion of about eighty to one. The great bulk of the MSS., as usual, uncial and cursive alike, establish the undoubted text of the Evangelist, which is here the Received Text. Thus, a vast majority of the MSS., with אAD at their head, read ἐπιπεσών in St. John xiii. 25. Chrysostom[191] and probably Cyril[192] confirm the same reading. So also Nonnus[193]. Not so B and C with four other uncials and about twenty cursives (the vicious Evan. 33 being at their head), besides Origen[194] in two places and apparently Theodorus of Mopsuestia[195]. These by mischievously assimilating the place in ch. xiii to the later place in ch. xxi in which such affecting reference is made to it, hopelessly obscure the Evangelist's meaning. For they substitute ἀναπεσὼν οὖν ἐκεῖνος κ.τ.λ. It is exactly as when children, by way of improving the sketch of a great Master, go over his matchless outlines with a clumsy pencil of their own.

That this is the true history of the substitution of ἀναπεσών in St. John xiii. 25 for the less obvious ἐπιπεσών is certain. Origen, who was probably the author of all the mischief, twice sets the two places side by side and elaborately compares them; in the course of which operation, by the way, he betrays the viciousness of the text which he himself employed. But what further helps to explain how easily ἀναπεσών might usurp the place of ἐπιπεσών[196], is the discovery just noticed, that the ancients from the earliest period were in the habit of identifying St. John, as St. John had identified himself, by calling him '*the one that lay* (ὁ ἀναπεσών) *upon the* Lord's *chest.*' The expression, derived from St. John xxi. 20, is employed by Irenaeus[197] (A.D. 178) and by Polycrates[198] (Bp. of Ephesus A.D. 196); by Origen[199] and by Ephraim Syrus[200]: by Epiphanius[201] and by Palladius[202]: by Gregory of Nazianzus[203] and by his namesake of Nyssa[204]: by pseudo-Eusebius[205], by pseudo-Caesarius[206], and by pseudo-Chrysostom[207]. The only wonder is, that in spite of such influences all the MSS. in the world except about twenty-six have retained the true reading.

Instructive in the meantime it is to note the fate which this word has experienced at the hands of some Critics. Lachmann, Tischendorf, Tregelles, Alford, Westcott and Hort, have all in turn bowed to the authority of Cod. B and Origen. Bishop Lightfoot mistranslates[208] and contends on the same side. Alford informs us that ἐπιπεσών has surreptitiously crept in 'from St. Luke xv. 20': (why should it? how could it?) 'ἀναπεσών not seeming appropriate.' Whereas, on the contrary, ἀναπεσών is the invariable and obvious expression,—ἐπιπεσών the unusual, and, till it has been explained, the unintelligible word. Tischendorf,—who had read ἐπιπεσών in 1848 and ἀναπεσών in 1859,—in 1869 reverts to his first opinion advocating with parental partiality what he had since met with in Cod. ℵ. Is then the truth of Scripture aptly represented by that fitful beacon-light somewhere on the French coast,— now visible, now eclipsed, now visible again,—which benighted travellers amuse themselves by watching from the deck of the Calais packet?

It would be time to pass on. But because in this department of study men are observed never to abandon a position until they are fairly shelled out and left without a pretext for remaining, I proceed to shew that ἀναπεσών (for ἐπιπεσών) is only one corrupt reading out of many others hereabouts. The proof of this statement follows. Might it not have been expected that the 'old uncials' (ℵABCD) would exhibit the entire context of such a passage as the present with tolerable accuracy? The reader is invited to attend to the results of collation:—

xiii. 21. —ο ℵB: υμιν λεγω *tr.* B.

22. —ουν BC: + οι Ιουδαιοι ℵ: απορουντει D.

23. —δε B: + εκ ℵABCD: — ο B: + και D.

(for πυθεσθαι τις αν ειη + ουτος D) και λεγει αυτω, ειπε τις εστιν

24. BC: (for λεγει) ελεγεν ℵ: + και λεγει αυτω ειπε τις εστιν περι ου λεγει ℵ.

25. (for επιπεσων) αναπεσων BC: —δε BC: (for δε) ουν ℵD: —ουτος ℵAD.

26. + ουν BC: + αυτω D: —ο B: + και λεγει ℵBD: + αν D: (for βαψας) εμβαψας AD: βαψω . . . και δωσω αυτω BC: + ψωμου (after ψωμιον) C: (for εμβαψας) βαψας D: (for και εμβαψας) βαψας ουν ℵBC: —το B: + λαμβανει και BC: Ισκαριωτου ℵBC: απο Καρυωτου D.

27. —τοτε ℵ: —μετα το ψωμιον τοτε D: (for λεγει ουν και λενει D: —ο B.

In these seven verses therefore, (which present no special difficulty to a transcriber,) the Codexes in question are found to exhibit at least thirty-five varieties,—for twenty-eight of which (jointly or singly) B is responsible: ℵ for twenty-two: C for twenty-one: D for nineteen: A for three. It is found that twenty-three words have been added to the text: fifteen substituted: fourteen taken away; and the construction has been four times changed. One case there has been of senseless transposition. Simon, the father of Judas, (not Judas the traitor), is declared by ℵBCD to have been called 'Iscariot.' Even this is not all. What St. John relates concerning himself is hopelessly obscured; and a speech is put into St. Peter's mouth which he certainly never uttered. It is not too much to say that every delicate lineament has vanished from the picture. What are we to think of guides like ℵBCD, which are proved to be utterly untrustworthy?

§ 5.

The first two verses of St. Mark's Gospel have fared badly. Easy of transcription and presenting no special difficulty, they ought to have come down to us undisfigured by any serious variety of reading. On the contrary. Owing to entirely different causes, either verse has experienced calamitous treatment. I have elsewhere[209] proved that the clause υἱοῦ τοῦ Θεοῦ; in verse 1 is beyond suspicion. Its removal from certain copies of the Gospel was originally due to heretical influence. But because Origen gave currency to the text so mutilated, it re-appears mechanically in several Fathers who are intent only on reproducing a certain argument of Origen's against the Manichees in which the mutilated text occurs. The same Origen is responsible to, some extent, and in the same way, for the frequent introduction of 'Isaiah's' name into verse 21—whereas 'in the prophets' is what St. Mark certainly wrote; but the appearance of 'Isaiah' there in the first instance was due to quite a different cause. In the meantime, it is witnessed to by the Latin, Syriac[210], Gothic, and Egyptian versions, as well as by ℵBDLA, and (according to Tischendorf) by nearly twenty-five cursives; besides the following ancient writers: Irenaeus, Origen, Porphyry, Titus, Basil, Serapion, Epiphanius, Severianus, Victor, Eusebius, Victorinus, Jerome, Augustine. I proceed to shew that this imposing array of authorities for reading ἐν τῷ Ἡσαΐᾳ τῷ προφήτῃ instead of ἐν τοῖς προφήταις in St. Mark i. 2, which has certainly imposed upon every recent editor and critic[211],—has been either overestimated or else misunderstood.

1. The testimony of the oldest versions, when attention is paid to their contents, is discovered to be of inferior moment in minuter matters of this nature. Thus, copies of the Old Latin version thrust Isaiah's name into St. Matt. i. 22, and Zechariah's name into xxi. 4: as well as thrust out Jeremiah's name from xxvii. 9:—the first, with Curetonian, Lewis, Harkleian, Palestinian, and D,—the second, with Chrysostom and Hilary,—the third, with the Peshitto. The Latin and the Syriac further substitute τοῦ προφήτου for τῶν προφητῶν in St. Matt. ii. 23,—through misapprehension of the Evangelist's meaning. What is to be thought of Cod. ℵ for introducing the name of 'Isaiah' into St. Matt. xiii. 35,—where it clearly cannot stand, the quotation being confessedly from Ps. lxxviii. 2; but where nevertheless Porphyry[212], Eusebius[213], and pseudo-Jerome[214] certainly found it in many ancient copies?

2. Next, for the testimony of the Uncial Codexes ℵBDLΔ:—If any one will be at the pains to tabulate the 900[215] new 'readings' adopted by Tischendorf in editing St. Mark's Gospel, he will discover that for 450, or just half of them,— all the 450, as I believe, being corruptions of the text,—ℵBL are responsible: and further, that their responsibility is shared on about 200 occasions by D: on about 265 by C: on about 350 by Δ[216]. some very remote period therefore there must have grown up a vicious general reading of this Gospel which remains in the few bad copies: but of which the largest traces (and very discreditable traces they are) at present survive in ℵBCDLA. After this discovery the avowal will not be thought extraordinary that I regard with unmingled suspicion readings which are exclusively vouched for by five of the same Codexes: e. g. by ℵBDLΔ.

3. The cursive copies which exhibit 'Isaiah' in place of 'the prophet,' reckoned by Tischendorf at 'nearly twenty-five,' are probably less than fifteen[217], and those, almost all of suspicious character. High time it is that the inevitable consequence of an appeal to such evidence were better understood.

4. From Tischendorf's list of thirteen Fathers, serious deductions have to be made. Irenaeus and Victor of Antioch are clearly with the Textus Receptus. Serapion, Titus, Basil do but borrow from Origen; and, with his argument, reproduce his corrupt text of St. Mark i. 2. The last-named Father however saves his reputation by leaving out the quotation from Malachi; so, passing directly from the mention of Isaiah to the actual words of that prophet. Epiphanius (and Jerome too on one occasion[218]) does the same thing. Victorinus and Augustine, being Latin writers, merely quote the Latin version ('sicut scriptum est in Isaiâ propheta'), which is without variety of reading. There remain Origen (the faulty character of whose Codexes has been remarked upon already), Porphyry[219] the heretic (who wrote a book to convict the Evangelists of mis-statements[220], and who is therefore scarcely a trust-

worthy witness), Eusebius, Jerome and Severianus. Of these, Eusebius[221] and Jerome[222] deliver it as their opinion that the name of 'Isaiah' had obtained admission into the text through the inadvertency of copyists. Is it reasonable, on the slender residuum of evidence, to insist that St. Mark has ascribed to Isaiah words confessedly written by Malachi? 'The fact,' writes a recent editor in the true spirit of modern criticism, 'will not fail to be observed by the careful and honest student of the Gospels.' But what if 'the fact' should prove to be 'a fiction' only? And (I venture to ask) would not 'carefulness' be better employed in scrutinizing the adverse testimony? 'honesty' in admitting that on grounds precarious as the present no indictment against an Evangelist can be seriously maintained? This proposal to revive a blunder which the Church in her corporate capacity has from the first refused to sanction (for the Evangelistaria know nothing of it) carries in fact on its front its own sufficient condemnation. Why, in the face of all the copies in the world (except a little handful of suspicious character), will men insist on imputing to an inspired writer a foolish mis-statement, instead of frankly admitting that the text must needs have been corrupted in that little handful of copies through the officiousness of incompetent criticism?

And do any inquire,—How then did this perversion of the truth arise? In the easiest way possible, I answer. Refer to the Eusebian tables, and note that the foremost of his sectional parallels is as follows:—

St. Matt.	St. Mark.	St. Luke.	St. John.
η′ (i.e. 3).	β′ (i.e. 3).	ζ′ (i.e. iii. 3-6).	ι′ (i.e. 23)[223].

Now, since the name of Isaiah occurs in the first, the third and the fourth of these places in connexion with the quotation from Is. xl. 3, *what* more obvious than that some critic with harmonistic proclivities should have insisted on supplying *the second also,* i.e. the parallel place in St. Mark's Gospel, with the name of the evangelical prophet, elsewhere so familiarly connected with the passage quoted? This is nothing else in short but an ordinary instance of Assimilation, so unskilfully effected however as to betray itself. It might have been passed by with fewer words, for the fraud is indeed transparent, but that it has so largely imposed upon learned men, and established itself so firmly in books. Let me hope that we shall not hear it advocated any more.

Regarded as an instrument of criticism, Assimilation requires to be very delicately as well as very skilfully handled. If it is to be applied to determining the text of Scripture, it must be employed, I take leave to say, in a very different spirit from what is met with in Dr. Tischendorf's notes, or it will only mislead. Is a word—a clause—a sentence—omitted by his favourite authorities אBDL? It is enough if that learned critic finds nearly the same word,—a very similar clause,— a sentence of the same general import,—in an account of the same occurrence by another Evangelist, for him straightway to insist that the sentence, the clause, the word, has been imported into the commonly received Text from such parallel place; and to reject it accordingly.

But, as the thoughtful reader must see, this is not allowable, except under peculiar circumstances. For first, whatever *a priori* improbability might be supposed to attach to the existence of identical expressions in two Evangelical records of the same transaction, is effectually disposed of by the discovery that very often identity of expression actually does occur. And (2), the only condition which could warrant the belief that there has been assimilation, is observed to be invariably away from Dr. Tischendorf's instances,—viz. a sufficient number of respectable attesting witnesses: it being a fundamental principle in the law of Evidence, that the very few are rather to be suspected than the many. But further (3), if there be some marked diversity of expression discoverable in the two parallel places; and if that diversity has been carefully maintained all down the ages in either place;—then it may be regarded as certain, on the contrary, that there has not been assimilation; but that this is only one more instance of two Evangelists saying similar things or the same thing in slightly different language. Take for example the following case:—Whereas St. Matt. (xxiv. 15) speaks of 'the abomination of desolation τὸ ῥηθὲν ΔΙΑ Δανιὴλ τοῦ προφήτου, standing (ἑστώς) in the holy place'; St. Mark (xiii. 14) speaks of it as 'τὸ ῥηθὲν ΥΠΟ Δανιὴλ τοῦ προφήτου. standing (ἑστός) where it ought not.' Now, because אBDL with copies of the Italic, the Vulgate, and the Egyptian versions omit from St. Mark's Gospel the six words written above in Greek, Tischendorf and his school are for expunging those six words from St. Mark's text, on the plea that they are probably an importation from St. Matthew. But the little note of variety which the Holy Spirit has set on the place in the second Gospel (indicated above in capital letters) suggests that these learned men are mistaken. Accordingly, the other fourteen uncials and all the cursives,—besides the Peshitto, Harkleian, and copies of the Old Latin—a much more weighty body of evidence—are certainly right in retaining the words in St. Mark xiii. 14.

Take two more instances of misuse in criticism of Assimilation.

St. Matthew (xii. 10), and St. Luke in the parallel place of his Gospel (xiv. 3), describe our Lord as asking,—'Is it lawful to heal on the sabbath day?' Tischendorf finding that his favourite authorities in this latter place continue the sentence with the words 'or *not*?' assumes that those two words must have fallen out of the great bulk of the copies of St. Luke, which, according to him, have here assimilated their phraseology to that of St. Matthew. But the hypothesis is clearly inadmissible,—though it is admitted by most modern critics. Do not these learned persons see that the supposition is just as lawful, and the probability infinitely greater, that it is on the contrary the few copies which have here undergone the process of assimilation; and that the type to which they have been conformed, is to be found in St. Matt. xxii. 17; St. Mark xii. 14; St. Luke xx. 22?

It is in fact surprising how often a familiar place of Scripture has exerted this kind of assimilating influence over a little handful of copies. Thus, some critics are happily agreed in rejecting the proposal of אBDLR, (backed scantily by their usual retinue of evidence) to substitute for γεμίσαι τὴν κοιλίαν αὐτοῦ ἀπό, in St. Luke xv. 16, the words χορτασθῆναι ἐκ. But editors have omitted to point out that the words ἐπεθύμει χορτασθῆναι, introduced in defiance of the best authorities into the parable of Lazarus (xvi. 20), have simply been transplanted thither out of the parable of the prodigal son.

The reader has now been presented with several examples of Assimilation. Tischendorf, who habitually overlooks the phenomenon where it seems to be sufficiently conspicuous, is observed constantly to discover cases of Assimilation where none exist. This is in fact his habitual way of accounting for not a few of the omissions in Cod. ℵ. And because he has deservedly enjoyed a great reputation, it becomes the more necessary to set the reader on his guard against receiving such statements without a thorough examination of the evidence on which they rest.

§ 6.

The value—may I not say, the use?—of these delicate differences of detail becomes apparent whenever the genuineness of the text is called in question. Take an example. The following fifteen words are deliberately excluded from St. Mark's Gospel (vi. 11) by some critics on the authority of ℵBCDLΔ,—a most suspicious company, and three cursives; besides a few copies of the Old Latin, including the Vulgate:—ἀμὴν λέγω ὑμῖν, ἀνεκτότερον ἔσται Σοδόμοις ἢ Γομόρροις ἐν ἡμέρᾳ κρίσεως, ἢ τῇ πόλει ἐκείνῃ. It is pretended that this is nothing else but an importation from the parallel place of St. Matthew's Gospel (x. 15). But that is impossible: for, as the reader sees at a glance, a delicate but decisive note of discrimination has been set on the two places. St. Mark writes, ΣοδόμΟΙΣ Ἤ ΓομόρρΟΙΣ: St. Matthew, ΓΗ ΣοδόμΩΝ ΚΑΊ ΓομόρρΩΝ. And this threefold, or rather fourfold, diversity of expression has existed from the beginning; for it has been faithfully retained all down the ages: it exists to this hour in every known copy of the Gospel,—except of course those nine which omit the sentence altogether. There can be therefore no doubt about its genuineness. The critics of the modern school (Lachmann, Tischendorf, Tregelles, Alford, Westcott and Hort) seek in vain to put upon us a mutilated text by omitting those fifteen words. The two places are clearly independent of each other.

It does but remain to point out that the exclusion of these fifteen words from the text of St. Mark, has merely resulted from the influence of the parallel place in St. Luke's Gospel (ix. 5),—where nothing whatever is found[224] corresponding with St. Matt. x. 5—St. Mark vi. 11. The process of Assimilation therefore has been actively at work here, although not in the way which some critics suppose. It has resulted, not in the insertion of the words in dispute in the case of the very many copies; but on the contrary in their omission from the very few. And thus, one more brand is set on ℵBCDLA and their Latin allies,—which will be found *never* to conspire together exclusively except to mislead.

§ 7.

Because a certain clause (e.g. καὶ ἡ λαλιά σου ὁμοιάζει in St. Mark xiv. 70) is absent from Codd. אBCDL, Lachmann, Tischendorf, Tregelles, Alford, Westcott and Hort entirely eject these five precious words from St. Mark's Gospel, Griesbach having already voted them 'probably spurious.' When it has been added that many copies of the Old Latin also, together with the Vulgate and the Egyptian versions, besides Eusebius, ignore their existence, the present writer scarcely expects to be listened to if he insists that the words are perfectly genuine notwithstanding. The thing is certain however, and the Revisers are to blame for having surrendered five precious words of genuine Scripture, as I am going to shew.

1. Now, even if the whole of the case were already before the reader, although to some there might seem to exist a *prima facie* probability that the clause is spurious, yet even so,—it would not be difficult to convince a thoughtful man that the reverse must be nearer the truth. For let the parallel places in the first two Gospels be set down side by side:—

St. Matt. xxvi. 73.	St. Mark xiv. 70.
(1) Ἀληθῶς καὶ σὺ	(1) Ἀληθῶς
(2) ἐξ αὐτῶν εἶ·	(2) ἐξ αὐτῶν εἶ·
(3) καὶ γὰρ	(3) καὶ γὰρ Γαλιλαῖος εἶ,
(4) ἡ λαλιά σου δῆλόν σε ποιεῖ.	(4) καὶ ἡ λαλιά σου ὁμοιάζει

What more clear than that the later Evangelist is explaining what his predecessor meant by 'thy speech bewrayeth thee' [or else is giving an independent account of the same transaction derived from the common source]? To St. Matthew,—a Jew addressing Jews,—it seemed superfluous to state that it was the peculiar accent of Galilee which betrayed Simon Peter. To St. Mark,—or rather to the readers whom St. Mark specially addressed,—the point was by, no means so obvious. Accordingly, he paraphrases,—'for thou art a Galilean and thy speech correspondeth.' Let me be shewn that all down the ages, in ninety-nine copies out of every hundred, this peculiar diversity of expression has been faithfully retained, and instead of assenting to the proposal to suppress St. Mark's (fourth) explanatory clause with its unique verb ὁμοιάζει, I straightway betake myself to the far more pertinent inquiry,—What is the state of the text hereabouts? What, in fact, the context? This at least is not a matter of opinion, but a matter of fact.

1. And first, I discover that Cod. D, in concert with several copies of the Old Latin (a b c ff² h q, &c.), only removes clause (4) from its proper place in St. Mark's Gospel, in order to thrust it into the parallel place in St. Matthew,—where it supplants the ἡ λαλιά σου δῆλόν σε ποιεῖ of the earlier Evangelist; and where it clearly has no business to be.

Indeed the object of D is found to have been to assimilate St. Matthew's Gospel to St. Mark,—for D also omits καὶ συ in clause (1).

2. The Ethiopic version, on the contrary, is for assimilating St. Mark to St. Matthew, for it transfers the same clause (4) as it stands in St. Matthew's Gospel (καὶ ἡ λαλιά σου δῆλόν σε ποιεῖ) to St. Mark.

3. Evan. 33 (which, because it exhibits an ancient text of a type like B, has been styled [with grim irony] 'the Queen of the Cursives') is more brilliant here than usual; exhibiting St. Mark's clause (4) thus,—καὶ γὰρ ἡ λαλιά σου δῆλόν σε ὁμοιάζει.

4. In C (and the Harkleian) the process of Assimilation is as conspicuous as in D, for St. Mark's third clause (3) is imported bodily into St. Matthew's Gospel. C further omits from St. Mark clause (4).

5. In the Vercelli Codex (a) however, the converse process is conspicuous. St. Mark's Gospel has been assimilated to St. Matthew's by the unauthorized insertion into clause (1) of καὶ συ, (which by the way is also found in M), and (in concert with the Gothic and Evann. 73, 131, 142*) by the entire suppression of clause (3).

6. Cod. L goes beyond all. [True to the craze of omission], it further obliterates as well from St. Matthew's Gospel as from St. Mark's all trace of clause (4).

7. ℵ and B alone of Codexes, though in agreement with the Vulgate and the Egyptian version, do but eliminate the final clause (4) of St. Mark's Gospel. But note, lastly, that—

8. Cod. A, together with the Syriac versions, the Gothic, and the whole body of the cursives, recognizes none of these irregularities: but exhibits the commonly received text with entire fidelity.

On a survey of the premises, will any candid person seriously contend that καὶ ἡ λαλιά σου ὁμοιάζει is no part of the genuine text of St. Mark xiv. 70? The words are found in what are virtually the most ancient authorities extant: the Syriac versions (besides the Gothic and Cod. A), the Old Latin (besides Cod. D)—retain them;—those in their usual place,—these, in their unusual. Idle it clearly is in the face of such evidence to pretend that St. Mark cannot have written the words in question[225]. It is too late to insist that a man cannot have lost his watch when his watch is proved to have been in his own pocket at eight in the morning, and is found in another man's pocket at nine. As for C and L, their handling of the Text hereabouts clearly disqualifies them from being cited in evidence. They are condemned under the note of Context. Adverse testimony is borne by B and ℵ: and by them only. They omit the words in dispute,—the ordinary habit of theirs, and most easily accounted for. But how is the punctual insertion of the words in every other known copy to be explained? In the meantime, it remains to be stated,—and with this I shall take leave of the discussion,—that hereabouts 'we have a set of passages which bear clear marks of wilful and critical correction, thoroughly carried out in Cod. ℵ, and only partially in Cod. B and some of its compeers; the object being so far to assimilate the narrative of Peter's denials with those of the other Evangelists, as to suppress the fact, vouched for by St. Mark only, that the cock crowed twice[226].' *That* incident shall be treated of separately. Can those principles stand, which in the face of the foregoing statement, and the evidence which preceded it, justify the disturbance of the text in St. Mark xiv. 70?

[We now pass on to a kindred cause of adulteration of the text of the New Testament.]

183 This paper bears the date 1877: but I have thought best to keep the words with this caution to the reader.
184 Above, p. 32.
185 The alleged evidence of Origen (iv. 453) is *nil*; the sum of it being that he takes no notice whatever of the forty words between ὄψεσθέ με (in ver. 16), and τοῦτο τί ἐστιν, (in ver. 18).
186 Nonnus,—ἵξομαι εἰς γεννητῆρα.
187 viii. 465 a and c.
188 iv. 932 and 933 c.
189 =ἀνα-κείμενος + ἐπι-πεσών. [Used not to suggest over-familiarity (?).
190 Beginning with Anatolius Laodicenus, A.D. 270 (*ap.* Galland. iii. 548). Cf. Routh, Rell. i. 42.
191 Οὐκ ἀνάκειται μόνον, ἀλλὰ καὶ τῷ στήθει ἐπιπίπτει (Opp. viii. 423 a).—Τὶ δὲ καὶ ἐπιπίπτει τῷ στήθει (ibid. d). Note that the passage ascribed to 'Apolinarius' in Cord. Cat. p. 342 (which includes the second of these two references) is in reality part of Chrysostom's Commentary on St. John (ubi supra, c d).
192 Cord. Cat. p. 341. But it is only in the κείμενον (or text) that the verb is found,—Opp. iv. 735.
193 ὁ δὲ θρασὺς ὀξέϊ παλμῷ | στήθεσιν ἀχράντοισι πεσὼν πεφιλημένος ἀνήρ.
194 iv. 437 c: 440 d.
195 Ibid. p. 342.
196 Even Chrysostom, who certainly read the place as we do, is observed twice to glide into the more ordinary expression, viz. viii. 423, line 13 from the bottom, and p. 424, line 18 from the top.
197 ὁ ἐπὶ τὸ στῆθος αὐτοῦ ἀναπεσών (iii. 2, § 1).
198 ὁ ἐπὶ τὸ στῆθος τοῦ Κυρίου ἀναπεσών (*ap.* Euseb. 31).
199 Τί δεῖ περὶ τοῦ ἀναπεσόντος ἐπὶ τὸ στῆθος λέγειν τοῦ Ἰησοῦ (ibid. vi. 25. Opp. iv. 95).
200 ὁ ἐπὶ τῷ στήθει τοῦ φλογὸς ἀναπεσών (Opp. ii. 49 a. Cf. 133 c).
201 (As quoted by Polycrates): Opp. i. 1062: ii. 8.
202 τοῦ εἰς τὸ τῆς σοφίας στῆθος πιστῶς ἐπαναπεσόντος (*ap.* Chrys. xiii. 55).
203 ὁ ἐπὶ τὸ στῆθος τοῦ Ἰησοῦ ἀναπαύεται (Opp. i. 591).
204 (As quoted by Polycrates): Opp. i. 488.
205 Wright's Apocryphal Acts (fourth century), translated from the Syriac, p. 3.
206 (Fourth or fifth century) *ap.* Galland. vi. 132.
207 *Ap.* Chrys. viii. 296.
208 On a fresh Revision, &c., p. 73.—'Ἀναπίπτειν, (which occurs eleven times in the N. T.', when said of guests (ἀνακείμενοι) at a repast, denotes nothing whatever but *the preliminary act* of each in taking his place at the table; being the Greek equivalent for our "*sitting down*" to dinner. So far only does it signify "change of posture." The notion of "falling *backward*" quite disappears in the notion of "reclining" or "lying down."'—In St. John xxi. 20, the language of the Evangelist is the very mirror of his thought; which evidently passed directly from the moment when he assumed his place at the table (ἀνέπεσεν), to that later moment when (ἐπὶ τὸ στῆθος αὐτοῦ) he interrogated his Divine Master concerning Judas. It

75

is a *general* description of an incident,—for the details of which we have to refer to the circumstantial and authoritative narrative which went before.

209 Traditional Text, Appendix IV.

210 Pesh. and Harkl.: Cur. and Lew. are defective.

211 Thus Griesbach, Scholz, Lachmann, Tischendorf, Tregelles, Alford, Wordsworth, Green, Scrivener, McClellan, Westcott and Hort, and the Revisers.

212 In pseudo-Jerome's Brev. in Psalm., Opp. vii. (ad calc.) 198.

213 Mont. i. 462.

214 Ubi supra.

215 Omitting trifling variants.

216 אBL are *exclusively* responsible on 45 occasions: +C (i.e. אBCL), on 27: + D, on 35: + Δ on 73: + CD, on 19: + CΔ, on 118: + DΔ (i.e. אBDLΔ), on 42: + CDΔ, on 66.

217 In the text of Evan. 72 the reading in dispute is *not* found: 205, 206 are duplicates of 209: and 222, 255 are only fragments. There remain 1, 22, 33, 62, 63, 115, 131, 151, 152, 161, 184, 209, 253, 372, 391:—of which the six at Rome require to be re-examined.

218 v. 20.

219 *Ap.* Hieron. vii. 17.

220 Evangelistas arguere falsitatis, hoc impiorum est, Celsi, Porphyrii, Juliani.' Hieron. 311.

221 γραφέως τοίνυν ἐστὶ σφάλμα. Quoted (from the lost work of Eusebius ad Marinum) in Victor of Ant.'s Catena, ed. Cramer, p. 267. (See Simon, iii. 89; Mai, iv. 299; Matthaei's N. T. ii. 20, &c.)

222 'Nos autem nomen Isaiae putamus *additum Scriptorum vitio*, quod et in aliis locis probare possumus.' vii. 17 (I suspect he got it from Eusebius).

223 See Studia Biblica, p. 249. Syrian Form of Ammonian sections and Eusebian Canons by Rev. G. H. Gwilliam, B.D. Mr. Gwilliam gives St. Luke iii. 4-6, according to the Syrian form.

224 Compare St. Mark vi. 7-13 with St. Luke ix. 1-6.

225 Schulz,—'et λαλια et ομοιαζει aliena a Marco.' Tischendorf—'omnino e Matthaeo fluxit: ipsum ομοιαζει glossatoris est.' This is foolishness,— not criticism.

226 Scrivener's Full Collation of the Cod. Sin., &c., 2nd ed., p. xlvii.

Chapter Nine - Causes of Corruption Chiefly Intentional - III. Attraction

§ 1.

THERE exist not a few corrupt Readings,—and they have imposed largely on many critics,—which, strange to relate, have arisen from nothing else but the proneness of words standing side by side in a sentence to be attracted into a likeness of ending,—whether in respect of grammatical form or of sound; whereby sometimes the sense is made to suffer grievously,— sometimes entirely to disappear. Let this be called the error of Attraction. The phenomena of 'Assimilation' are entirely distinct. A somewhat gross instance, which however has imposed on learned critics, is furnished by the Revised Text and Version of St. John vi. 71 and xiii. 26.

'Judas Iscariot' is a combination of appellatives with which every Christian ear is even awfully familiar. The expression Ἰούδας Ἰσκαριώτης is found in St. Matt. x. 4 and xxvi. 14: in St. Mark iii. 19 and xiv. 10: in St. Luke vi. 16, and in xxii. 31 with the express statement added that Judas was so 'surnamed.' So far happily we are all agreed. St. John's invariable practice is to designate the traitor, whom he names four times, as 'Judas Iscariot, the son of Simon;'—jealous doubtless for the honour of his brother Apostle, 'Jude (Ἰούδας) the brother of James[227]': and resolved that there shall be no mistake about the traitor's identity. Who does not at once recall the Evangelist's striking parenthesis in St. John xiv. 22,—'Judas (not Iscariot)'? Accordingly, in St. John xiii. 2 the Revisers present us with 'Judas Iscariot, Simon's son': and even in St. John xii. 4 they are content to read 'Judas Iscariot.'

But in the two places of St. John's Gospel which remain to be noticed, viz. vi. 71 and xiii. 26, instead of 'Judas Iscariot the son of Simon,' the Revisers require us henceforth to read, 'Judas the son of Simon Iscariot.' And *why*? Only, I answer, because—in place of Ἰούδαν Σίμωνος ἸσκαριώTHN (in vi. 71) and Ἰούδα Σίμωνος ἸσκαριώTH (in xiii. 26)—a little handful of copies substitute on both occasions ἸσκαριώTOY. Need I go on? Nothing else has evidently happened but that, through the oscitancy of some very early scribe, the ἸσκαριώTHN, ἸσκαριώTH, have been attracted into concord with the immediately preceding genitive ΣΙμωNOC . . . So transparent a blunder would have scarcely deserved a passing remark at our hands had it been suffered to remain,—where such *bêtises* are the rule and not the exception,—viz. in the columns of Codexes B and ℵ. But strange to say, not only have the Revisers adopted this corrupt reading in the two passages already mentioned, but they have not let so much as a hint fall that any alteration whatsoever has been made by them in the inspired Text.

§ 2.

Another and a far graver case of 'Attraction' is found in Acts xx. 24. St. Paul, in his address to the elders of Ephesus, refers to the discouragements he has had to encounter. 'But none of these things move me,' he grandly exclaims, 'neither count I my life dear unto myself, so that I might finish my course with joy.' The Greek for this begins ἀλλ' οὐδενὸς λόγον ποιοῦμαι where some second or third century copyist (misled by the preceding genitive) in place of λόγοN writes λόγοY with what calamitous consequence, has been found largely explained elsewhere[228]. Happily, the error survives only in Codd. B and C: and their character is already known by the readers of this book and the Companion Volume. So much has been elsewhere offered on this subject that I shall say no more about it here: but proceed to present my reader with another and more famous instance of attraction.

St. Paul in a certain place (2 Cor. iii. 3) tells the Corinthians, in allusion to the language of Exodus xxxi. 12, xxxiv. 1, that they are an epistle not written on '*stony tables* (ἐν πλαξὶ λιθίναις),' but on '*fleshy tables* of the heart (ἐν πλαξὶν καρδίας σαρκίναις).' The one proper proof that this is what St. Paul actually wrote, is not only (1) That the Copies largely preponderate in favour

77

of so exhibiting the place: but (2) That the Versions, with the single exception of 'that abject slave of manuscripts the Philoxenian [or Harkleian] Syriac,' are all on the same side: and lastly (3) That the Fathers are as nearly as possible unanimous. Let the evidence for καρδίας (unknown to Tischendorf and the rest) be produced in detail:—

In the second century, Irenaeus[229],—the Old Latin,—the Peshitto.

In the third century, Orison seven times[230],—the Coptic version.

In the fourth century, the Dialogus[231],—Didymus[232],—Basil[233],—Gregory Nyss.[234],—Marcus the Monk[235],—Chrysostom 126in two places[236],—Nilus[237],—the Vulgate,—and the Gothic versions.

In the fifth century, Cyril[238],—Isidorus[239],—Theodoret[240], —the Armenian—and the Ethiopic versions.

In the seventh century, Victor, Bp. of Carthage addressing Theodorus P.[241]

In the eighth century, J. Damascene[242] . . . Besides, of the Latins, Hilary[243],—Ambrose[244],—Optatus[245],—Jerome[246],—Tichonius[247],—Augustine thirteen times[248],—Fulgentius[249], and others[250] . . . If this be not overwhelming evidence, may I be told what *is*[251]?

But then it so happens that—attracted by the two datives between which καρδίας stands, and tempted by the consequent jingle, a surprising number of copies are found to exhibit the 'perfectly absurd' and 'wholly unnatural reading[252],' πλαξὶν καρδίAIC σαρκίνAIC. And because (as might have been expected from their character) A[253] BℵCD[254]are all five of the number,—Lachmann, Tischendorf, Tregelles, Alford, Westcott and Hort, one and all adopt and advocate the awkward blunder[255]. Καρδίαις is also adopted by the Revisers of 1881 without so much as a hint let fall in the margin that the evidence is overwhelmingly against themselves and in favour of the traditional Text of the Authorized Version[256].

---

[227] St. Luke vi. 16; Acts i. 13; St. Jude 1.

[228] Above, pp. 28-31.

[229] 753 int.

[230] ii. 843 e. Also *int*. ii. 96, 303; iv. 419, 489, 529, 558.

[231] *Ap*. Orig. i. 866 a,—interesting and emphatic testimony.

[232] Cord. Cat. in Ps. i. 272.

[233] i. 161 e. Cord. Cat. in Ps. i. 844.

[234] i. 683 (οὐκ ἐν πλαξὶ λιθίναις . . . ἀλλ᾽ ἐν τῷ τῆς καρδίας πυξίῳ).

[235] Galland. viii. 40 b.

[236] vii. 2: x. 475.

[237] i. 29.

[238] i. 8: 504: v². 65. (Aubert prints καρδίας σαρκίνης. The published Concilia (iii. 240) exhibits καρδίας σαρκίναις. Pusey, finding in one of his MSS. ἀλλ᾽ ἐν πλαξὶ καρδίαις λιθίναις (*sic*), prints καρδίαις σαρκίναις.) *Ap*. Mai, iii. 89, 90.

[239] 299.

[240] iii. 302.

[241] Concil. 154.

[242] ii. 129.

[243] 344.

[244] i. 762: ii. 668, 1380.

[245] Galland. v. 505.

[246] vi. 609.

[247] Galland. viii. 742 dis.

[248] i. 672: ii. 49: iii¹. 472, 560: iv. 1302: v. 743-4: viii. 311: x. 98, 101, 104, 107, 110.

[249] Galland. xi. 248.

[250] Ps.-Ambrose, ii. 176.

251 Yet strange to say, Tischendorf claims the support of Didymus and Theodoret for καρδίαις, on the ground that in the course of their expository remarks they contrast καρδίαι σαρκίναι (or λογικαί) with πλάκες λίθιναι: as if it were not the word πλαξί which alone occasions difficulty. Again, Tischendorf enumerates Cod. E (Paul) among his authorities. Had he then forgotten that E is *nothing better than a transcript of Cod. D* (Claromontanus), made by some ignorant person'? that 'the Greek *is manifestly worthless*, and that it should long since have been removed from the list of authorities'? (Scrivener's Introd., 4th edit., i. 177. See also Traditional Text, p. 65, and note. Tischendorf is frequently inaccurate in his references to the Fathers.]

252 Scrivener's Introd. 254.

253 A in the Epistles differs from A in the Gospels.

254 Besides GLP and the following cursivcs,—29, 30, 44, 45, 46, 47. 48, 55, 74, 104, 106, 109, 112, 113, 115, 137, 219, 221, 238, 252, 255, 257, 262, 277.

255 That I may not be accused of suppressing what is to be said on the other side, let it be here added that the sum of the adverse evidence (besides the testimony of many MSS.) is the Harkleian version:—the doubtful testimony of Eusebius (for, though Valerius reads καρδίας, the MSS. largely preponderate which read καρδίαιςin H. E. Mart. Pal. cxiii. § 6. See Burton's ed. p. 637):—Cyril in one place, as explained above:—and lastly, a quotation from Chrysostom on the Maccabees, given in Cramer's Catena, vii. 595 (ἐν πλαξὶ καρδίαις σαρκίναις), which reappears at the end of eight lines without the word πλαξί.

256 [The papers on Assimilation and Attraction were left by the Dean in the same portfolio. No doubt he would have separated them, if he had lived to complete his work, and amplified his treatment of the latter, for the materials under that head were scanty.—For 2 Cor. iii. 3, see also a note of my own to p. 65 of The Traditional Text.]

Chapter Ten - Causes of Corruption Chiefly Intentional - IV. Omission

[WE have now to consider the largest of all classes of corrupt variations from the genuine Text[257],—the omission of words and clauses and sentences,—a truly fertile province of inquiry. Omissions are much in favour with a particular school of critics; though a habit of admitting them whether in ancient or modern times cannot but be symptomatic of a tendency to scepticism.]

§ 1.

Omissions are often treated as 'Various Readings.' Yet only by an Hibernian licence can words omitted be so reckoned: for in truth the very essence of the matter is that on such occasions nothing is read. It is to the case of words omitted however that this chapter is to be exclusively devoted. And it will be borne in mind that I speak now of those words alone where the words are observed to exist in ninety-nine MSS. out of a hundred, so to speak;—being away only from that hundredth copy.

Now it becomes evident, as soon as attention has been called to the circumstance, that such a phenomenon requires separate treatment. Words so omitted labour *prima facie* under a disadvantage which is all their own. My meaning will be best illustrated if I may be allowed to adduce and briefly discuss a few examples. And I will begin with a crucial case;—the most conspicuous doubtless within the whole compass of the New Testament. I mean the last twelve verses of St. Mark's Gospel; which verses are either bracketed off, or else entirely severed from the rest of the Gospel, by Tischendorf, Tregelles, Alford and others.

The warrant of those critics for dealing thus unceremoniously with a portion of the sacred deposit is the fact that whereas Eusebius, for the statement rests solely with him, declares that anciently many copies were without the verses in question, our two oldest extant MSS. conspire in omitting them. But, I reply, the latter circumstance does not conduct to the inference that those verses are spurious. It only proves that the statement of Eusebius was correct. The Father cited did not, as is evident from his words[258], himself doubt the genuineness of the verses in question; but admitted them to be genuine. [He quotes two opinions; —the opinion of an advocate who questions their genuineness, and an opposing opinion which he evidently considers the better of the two, since he rests upon the latter and casts a slur upon the former as being an off-hand expedient; besides that he quotes several words out of the twelve verses, and argues at great length upon the second hypothesis.

On the other hand, one and that the least faulty of the two MSS. witnessing for the omission confesses mutely its error by leaving a vacant space where the omitted verses should have come in; whilst the other was apparently copied from an exemplar containing the verses[259]. And all the other copies insert them, except L and a few cursives which propose a manifestly spurious substitute for the verses,—together with all the versions, except one Old Latin (k), the Lewis Codex, two Armenian MSS. and an Arabic Lectionary,— besides more than ninety testimonies in their favour from more than 'forty-four' ancient witnesses[260]; —such is the evidence which weighs down the conflicting testimony over and over and over again. Beyond all this, the cause of the error is patent. Some scribe mistook the Τέλος occurring at the end of an Ecclesiastical Lection at the close of chapter xvi. 8 for the 'End' of St. Mark's Gospel[261].

That is the simple truth: and the question will now be asked by an intelligent reader, 'If such is the balance of evidence, how is it that learned critics still doubt the genuineness of those verses?'

To this question there can be but one answer, viz. 'Because those critics are blinded by invincible prejudice in favour of two unsafe guides, and on behalf of Omission.'

We have already seen enough of the character of those guides, and are now anxious to learn what there can be in omissions which render them so acceptable to minds of the present day. And we can imagine nothing except the halo which has gathered round the detection of spurious passages in modern times, and has extended to a supposed detection of passages which in fact are not spurious. Some people appear to feel delight if they can prove any charge against people who claim to be orthodox; others without any such feeling delight in superior criticism; and the flavour of scepticism especially commends itself to the taste of many. To the votaries of such criticism, omissions of passages which they style 'interpolations,' offer temptingly spacious hunting-fields.

Yet the experience of copyists would pronounce that Omission is the besetting fault of transcribers. It is so easy under the influence of the desire of accomplishing a task, or at least of anxiety for making progress, to pass over a word, a line, or even more lines than one. As has been explained before, the eye readily moves from one ending to a similar ending with a surprising tendency to pursue the course which would lighten labour instead of increasing it. The cumulative result of such abridgement by omission on the part of successive scribes may be easily imagined, and in fact is just what is presented in Codex B[262]. Besides these considerations, the passages which are omitted, and which we claim to be genuine, bear in themselves the character belonging to the rest of the Gospels, indeed—in Dr. Hort's expressive phrase—'have the true ring of genuineness.' They are not like some which some critics of the same school would fain force upon us[263]. But beyond all,—and this is the real source and ground of attestation, —they enjoy superior evidence from copies, generally beyond comparison with the opposing testimony, from Versions, and from Fathers.]

§ 2.

The fact seems to be all but overlooked that a very much larger amount of proof than usual is required at the hands of those who would persuade us to cancel words which have been hitherto by all persons,—in all ages,—in all countries,—regarded as inspired Scripture. They have (1) to account for the fact of those words' existence: and next (2), to demonstrate that they have no right to their place in the sacred page. The discovery that from a few copies they are away, clearly has very little to do with the question. We may be able to account for the omission from those few copies: and the instant we have done this, the negative evidence—the argument *e silentio*—has been effectually disposed of. A very different task—a far graver responsibility—is imposed upon the adverse party, as may be easily shewn. [They must establish many modes of accounting for many classes and groups of evidence. Broad and sweeping measures are now out of date. The burden of proof lies with them.]

§ 3.

The force of what I am saying will be best understood if a few actual specimens of omission may he adduced, and individually considered. And first, let us take the case of an omitted word. In St. Luke vi. 1 δευτεροπρώτῳ is omitted from some MSS. Westcott and Hort and the Revisers accordingly exhibit the text of that place as follows:—Ἐγένετο δὲ ἐν σαββάτῳ διαπορεύεσθαι αὐτὸν διὰ σπορίμων

Now I desire to be informed how it is credible that so very difficult and peculiar a word as this,—for indeed the expression has never yet been satisfactorily explained,—should have found its way into every known Evangelium except אBL and a few cursives, if it be spurious? How it came to be here and there omitted, is intelligible enough. (a) One has but to glance at the Cod. א,

ΤΟ εΝ CΑΒΒΑΤω

ΔεΥΤΡΟΠΡωΤω

in order to see that the like ending (Τω) in the superior line, fully accounts for the omission of the second line. (b) A proper lesson begins at this place; which by itself would explain the phenomenon. (c) Words which the copyists were at a loss to understand, are often observed to be dropped: and there is no harder word in the Gospels than δευτερόπρωτος. But I repeat,—will you tell us how it is conceivable that [a word nowhere else found, and known to be a *crux* to commentators and others, should have crept into all the copies except a small handful?]

In reply to all this, I shall of course be told that really I must yield to what is after all the weight of external evidence: that Codd. אBL are not ordinary MSS. but first-class authorities, of sufficient importance to outweigh any number of the later cursive MSS.

My rejoinder is plain:—Not only am I of course willing to yield to external evidence, but it is precisely 'external evidence' which makes me insist on retaining δευτεροπρώτῳ—ἀπὸ μελισσίου κηρίου—ἄρας τὸν στ9αυρόν—καὶ ἀνεφέρετο εἰς τὸν οὐρανόν—ὅταν \ἐκλίπητε—the 14th verse of St. Matthew's xxiiird chapter—and the last twelve verses of St. Mark's Gospel. For *my* own part, I entirely deny the cogency of the proposed proof, and I have clearly already established the grounds of my refusal. Who then is to be the daysman between us? We are driven back on first principles, in order to ascertain if it may not be possible to meet on some common ground, and by the application of ordinary logical principles of reasoning to clear our *view.* [As to these we must refer the reader to the first volume of this work. Various cases of omission have been just quoted, and many have been discussed elsewhere. Accordingly, it will not be necessary to exhibit this large class of corruptions at the length which it would otherwise demand. But a few more instances are required, in order that the reader may see in this connexion that many passages at least which the opposing school designate as Interpolations are really genuine, and that students may be placed upon their guard against the source of error that we are discussing.]

§ 4.

And first as to the rejection of an entire verse.

The 44th verse of St. Matt. xxi, consisting of the fifteen words printed at foot[264], is marked as doubtful by Tregelles, Westcott and Hort, and the Revisers:—by Tischendorf it is rejected as spurious. We insist that, on the contrary, it is indubitably genuine; reasoning from the antiquity, the variety, the respectability, the largeness, or rather, the general unanimity of its attestation.

For the verse is found in the Old Latin, and in the Vulgate,—in the Peshitto, Curetonian, and Harkleian Syriac,—besides in the Coptic, Armenian, and Ethiopic versions. It is found also in Origen[265],—ps.-Tatian[266]— Aphraates[267],—Chrysostom[268],—Cyril Alex.[269],—the Opus Imperfectum[270],— Jerome[271],—Augustine[272]:—in Codexes BאCΦΣΧΖΔΠEFGHKLMSUV,—in short, it is attested by every known Codex except two of bad character, viz.— D, 33; together with five copies of the Old Latin, viz.—a b e ff¹ ff². There have therefore been adduced for the verse in dispute at least five witnesses of the second or third century:—at least eight of the fourth:—at least seven if not eight of the fifth: after which date the testimony in favour of this verse is overwhelming. How could we be justified in opposing to such a mass of first-rate testimony the solitary evidence of Cod. D (concerning which see above, Vol. I. c. viii.) supported only by a single errant Cursive and a little handful of copies of the Old Latin versions, [even although the Lewis Codex has joined this petty band?]

But, says Tischendorf,—the verse is omitted by Origen and by Eusebius,— by Irenaeus and by Lucifer of Cagliari,—as well as by Cyril of Alexandria. I answer, this most insecure of arguments for mutilating the traditional text is plainly inadmissible on the present occasion. The critic refers to the fact that Irenaeus[273], Origen[274], Eusebius[275] and Cyril[276] having quoted 'the parable of the wicked husband-men' *in extenso* (viz. from verse 33 to verse 43). *leave off at verse* 43. Why may they not leave off where the parable leaves off? Why should they quote any further? Verse 44 is nothing to their purpose. And since the Gospel for Monday morning in Holy Week [verses 18-43], in every known copy of, the Lectionary actually ends at verse 43,—why should not their quotation of it end at the same verse? But, unfortunately for the critic, Origen and Cyril (as we have seen,—the latter expressly,) elsewhere actually quote the verse in dispute. And how can Tischendorf maintain that Lucifer yields adverse testimony[277]? That Father quotes *nothing but* verse 43, which is all he requires for his purpose[278]. Why should he have also quoted verse 44, which he does not require? As well might it be maintained that Macarius Egyptius[279] and Philo of Carpasus[280] omit verse 44, because (like Lucifer) they only quote verse 43.

I have elsewhere explained what I suspect occasioned the omission of St. Matt.xxi. 44 from a few Western copies of the Gospels[281]. Tischendorf's opinion that this verse is a fabricated imitation of the parallel verse in St. Luke's Gospel[282] (xx. 18) is clearly untenable. Either place has its distinctive type, which either has maintained all down the ages. The single fact that St. Matt. xxi. 44 in the Peshitto version has a sectional number to itself[283] is far too weighty to be set aside on nothing better than suspicion. If a verse so elaborately attested as the present be not genuine, we must abandon all hope of ever attaining to any certainty concerning the Text of Scripture.

In the meantime there emerges from the treatment which St. Matt. xxi. 44 has experienced at the hands of Tischendorf, the discovery that, in the estimation of Tischendorf, Cod. D [is a document of so much importance as occasionally to outweigh almost by itself the other copies of all ages and countries in Christendom.]

§ 5.

I am guided to my next example, viz. the text of St. Matt. xv. 8, by the choice deliberately made of that place by Dr. Tregelles in order to establish the peculiar theory of Textual Revision which he advocates so strenuously; and which, ever since the days of Griesbach, has it must be confessed enjoyed the absolute confidence of most of the illustrious editors of the New Testament. This is, in fact, the second example on Tregelles' list. In approaching it, I take leave to point out that that learned critic unintentionally hoodwinks his readers by not setting before them in full the problem which he proposes to discuss. Thoroughly to understand this matter, the student should be reminded that there is found in St. Matt. xv. 8,—and parallel to it in St. Mark vii. 6,—

ST. MATT.

ST. MARK

'Ye hypocrites, well did Isaiah prophesy of you saying, "This people draweth nigh unto Me with their mouth and honoureth me with their lips (ἐγγίζει μοι ὁ λαὸς οὗτος τῷ στόματι αὐτῶν, καὶ τοῖς χείλεσί με τιμᾷ·), but their

'Well did Isaiah prophesy of you, hypocrites, as it is written, "This people honoureth Me with their lips (οὗτος ὁ λαὸς τοῖς χείλεσί με τιμᾷ, but their heart is far from Me."'

heart is far from Me."'

The place of Isaiah referred to, viz. ch. xxix. 13, reads as follows in the ordinary editions of the LXX:—καὶ εἶπε Κύριος, ἐγγίζει μοι ὁ λαὸς οὗτος ἐν τῷ στόματι αὐτοῦ, καὶ ἐν τοῖς χείλεσιν αὐτῶν τιμῶσίν με.

Now, about the text of St. Mark in this place no question is raised. Neither is there any various reading worth speaking of in ninety-nine MSS. out of a hundred in respect of the text in St. Matthew. But when reference is made to the two oldest copies in existence, B and ℵ, we are presented with what, but for the parallel place in St. Mark, would have appeared to us a strangely abbreviated reading. Both MSS. conspire in exhibiting St. Matt. xv. 8, as follows:—ὁ λαὸς οὗτος τοῖς χείλεσίν με τιμᾷ. So that six words (ἐγγίζει μοι and τῷ στόματι αὐτῶν, καὶ) are not recognized by them: in which peculiarity they are countenanced by DLT[c], two cursive copies, and the following versions:—Old Latin except f, Vulgate, Curetonian, Lewis, Peshitto, and Bohairic, (Cod. A, the Sahidic and Gothic versions, being imperfect here.) To this evidence, Tischendorf adds a phalanx of Fathers:—Clemens Romanus (A.D. 70),

Ptolemaeus the Gnostic (A.D. 150), Clemens Alexandrinus (A.D. 190), Origen in three places (A.D. 210), Eusebius (A.D. 325), Basil, Cyril of Alexandria, Chrysostom: and Alford supplies also Justin Martyr (A.D. 150). The testimony of Didymus (A.D. 350), which has been hitherto overlooked, is express. Tertullian, Cyprian, Hilary, are naturally found to follow the Latin copies. Such a weight of evidence may not unreasonably inspire Dr. Tregelles with an exceeding amount of confidence. Accordingly he declares 'that this one passage might be relied upon as an important proof that it is the few MSS. and not the many which accord with ancient testimony.' Availing himself of Dr. Scrivener's admission of 'the possibility that the disputed words in the great bulk of the MSS. were inserted from the Septuagint of Isaiah xxix. 13[284],' Dr. Tregelles insists 'that on every true principle of textual criticism, the words must be regarded as an amplification borrowed from the Prophet. This naturally explains their introduction,' (he adds); 'and when once they had gained a footing in the text, it is certain that they would be multiplied by copyists, who almost always preferred to make passages as full and complete as possible' (p. 139). Dr. Tregelles therefore relies upon this one passage,—not so much as 'a proof that it is the few MSS. and not the many which accord with ancient testimony';—for one instance cannot possibly prove that; and that is after all beside the real question;—but, as a proof that we are to regard the text of Codd. Bℵ in this place as genuine, and the text of all the other Codexes in the world as corrupt.

The reader has now the hypothesis fully before him by which from the days of Griesbach it has been proposed to account for the discrepancy between 'the few copies' on the one hand, and the whole torrent of manuscript evidence on the other.

Now, as I am writing a book on the principles of Textual Criticism, I must be allowed to set my reader on his guard against all such unsupported dicta as the preceding, though enforced with emphasis and recommended by a deservedly respected name. I venture to think that the exact reverse will be found to be a vast deal nearer the truth: viz. that undoubtedly spurious readings, although they may at one time or other have succeeded in obtaining a footing in MSS., and to some extent may be observed even to have propagated themselves, are yet discovered to die out speedily; seldom indeed to leave any considerable number of descendants. There has always in fact been a process of elimination going on, as well as of self-propagation: a corrective force at work, as well as one of deterioration. How else are we to account for the utter disappearance of the many *monstra potius quam variae lectiones* which the ancients nevertheless insist were prevalent in their times? It is enough to appeal to a single place in Jerome, in illustration of what I have been saying[285]. To return however from this digression.

We are invited then to believe,—for it is well to know at the outset exactly what is required of us,—that from the fifth century downwards *every extant copy of the Gospels except five* (DLT[c], 33, 124) exhibits a text arbitrarily interpolated in order to bring it into conformity with the Greek version of Isa.

85

xxix. 13. On this wild hypothesis I have the following observations to make:—

1. It is altogether unaccountable, if this be indeed a true account of the matter, how it has come to pass that in no single MS. in the world, so far as I am aware, has this conformity been successfully achieved: for whereas the Septuagintal reading is ἐγγίζει μοι ὁ λαὸς οὗτος ΕΝ τῷ στόματι ΑΥΤΟΥ, καὶ ΕΝ τοῖς χείλεσιν ΑΥΤΩΝ ΤΙΜΩΣΙ με,—the Evangelical Text is observed to differ therefrom in no less than six particulars.

2. Further,—If there really did exist this strange determination on the part of the ancients in general to assimilate the text of St. Matthew to the text of Isaiah, how does it happen that not one of them ever conceived the like design in respect of the parallel place in St. Mark?

3. It naturally follows to inquire,—Why are we to suspect the mass of MSS. of having experienced such wholesale depravation in respect of the text of St. Matthew in this place, while yet we recognize in them such a marked constancy to their own peculiar type; which however, as already explained, is *not* the text of Isaiah?

4. Further,—I discover in this place a minute illustration of the general fidelity of the ancient copyists: for whereas in St. Matthew it is invariably ὁ λαὸς οὗτος, I observe that in the copies of St. Mark,—except to be sure in (a) Codd. B and D, (b) copies of the Old Latin, (c) the Vulgate, and (d) the Peshitto (all of which are confessedly corrupt in this particular,)—it is invariably οὗτος ὁ λαός. But now,—Is it reasonable that the very copies which have been in this way convicted of licentiousness in respect of St. Mark vii. 6 should be permitted to dictate to us against the great heap of copies in respect of their exhibition of St. Matt. xv. 8?

And yet, if the discrepancy between Codd. B and א and the great bulk of the copies in this place did not originate in the way insisted on by the critics, how is it to be accounted for? Now, on ordinary occasions, we do not feel ourselves called upon to institute any such inquiry,—as indeed very seldom would it be practicable to do. Unbounded licence of transcription, flagrant carelessness, arbitrary interpolations, omissions without number, disfigure those two ancient MSS. in every page. We seldom trouble ourselves to inquire into the history of their obliquities. But the case is of course materially changed when so many of the oldest of the Fathers and all the oldest Versions seem to be at one with Codexes B and א. Let then the student favour me with his undivided attention for a few moments, and I will explain to him how the misapprehension of Griesbach, Tischendorf, Tregelles and the rest, has arisen. About the MSS. and the Versions these critics are sufficiently accurate: but they have fatally misapprehended the import of the Patristic evidence; as I proceed to explain.

The established Septuagintal rendering of Isa. xxix. 13 in the Apostolic age proves to have been this,—Ἐγγίζει μοι ὁ λαὸς οὗτος τοῖς χείλεσιν αὐτῶν τιμῶσί με: the words ἐν τῷ στόματι αὐτῶν, καὶ ἐν being omitted. This is certain. Justin Martyr[286] and Cyril of Alexandria in two places[287] so quote the passage. Procopius Gazaeus in his Commentary on Origen's Hexapla of Isaiah says expressly that the six words in question were introduced into the text of the Septuagint by Aquila, Symmachus, and Theodotion. Accordingly they are often observed to be absent from MSS.[288] They are not found, for example, in the Codex Alexandrinus.

But the asyndeton resulting from the suppression of these words was felt to be intolerable. In fact, without a colon point between οὗτος and τοῖς, the result is without meaning. When once the complementary words have been withdrawn, ἐγγίζει μοι at the beginning of the sentence is worse than superfluous. It fatally encumbers the sense. To drop those two words, after the example of the parallel place in St. Mark's Gospel, became thus an obvious proceeding. Accordingly the author of the (so-called) second Epistle of Clemens Romanus (§ 3), professing to quote the place in the prophet Isaiah, exhibits it thus,—Ὁ λαὸς οὗτος τοῖς χείλεσιν με τιμᾷ. Clemens Alexandrinus certainly does the same thing on at least two occasions[289]. So does Chrysostom[290]. So does Theodoret[291].

Two facts have thus emerged, which entirely change the aspect of the problem: the first, (a) That the words ἐν τῷ στόματι αὐτῶν, καὶ ἐν, were anciently absent from the Septuagintal rendering of Isaiah xxix. 13: the second, (b) that the place of Isaiah was freely quoted by the ancients without the initial words ἐγγίζει μοι.

And after this discovery will any one be so perverse as to deny that on the contrary it must needs be Codexes B and ℵ, and not the great bulk of the MSS., which exhibit a text corrupted by the influence of the Septuagint rendering of Isaiah xxix. 13? The precise extent to which the assimilating influence of the parallel place in St. Mark's Gospel has been felt by the copyists, I presume not to determine. The essential point is that the omission from St. Matthew xv. 8 of the words Τῷ στόματι αὐτῶν, καὶ is certainly due in the first instance to the ascertained Septuagint omission of those very words in Isaiah xxix. 13.

But that the text of St. Mark vii. 6 has exercised an assimilating influence on the quotation from Isaiah is demonstrable. For there can be no doubt that Isaiah's phrase (retained by St. Matthew) is ὁ λαὸς οὗτος,—St. Mark's οὗτος ὁ λαός. And yet, when Clemens Romanus quotes Isaiah, he begins—οὗτος ὁ λαός[292]; and so twice does Theodoret[293].

The reader is now in a position to judge how much attention is due to Dr. Tregelles' dictum 'that this one passage may be relied upon' in support of the peculiar views he advocates: as well as to his confident claim that the fuller text which is found in ninety-nine MSS. out of a hundred 'must be regarded as an amplification borrowed from the prophet.' It has been shewn in answer to the learned critic that in the ancient Greek text of the prophet the 'amplification' he speaks of did not exist: it was the abbreviated text which was found there. So that the very converse of the phenomenon he supposes has taken place. Freely accepting his hypothesis that we have here a process of assimilation, occasioned by the Septuagintal text of Isaiah, we differ from him only as to the direction in which that process has manifested itself. He assumes that the bulk of the MSS. have been conformed to the generally received reading of Isaiah xxix. 13. But it has been shewn that, on the contrary, it is the two oldest MSS. which have experienced assimilation. Their prototypes were depraved in this way at an exceedingly remote period.

To state this matter somewhat differently.—In all the extant uncials but five, and in almost every known cursive copy of the Gospels, the words τῷ στόματι αὐτῶν, καί are found to belong to St. Matt. xv. 8. How is the presence of those words to be accounted for? The reply is obvious:—By the fact that they must have existed in the original autograph of the Evangelist. Such however is not the reply of Griesbach and his followers. They insist that beyond all doubt those words must have been imported into the Gospel from Isaiah xxix. But I have shewn that this is impossible because, at the time spoken of, the words in question had no place in the Greek text of the prophet. And this discovery exactly reverses the problem, and brings out the directly opposite result. For now we discover that we have rather to inquire how is the absence of the words in question from those few MSS. out of the mass to be accounted for? The two oldest Codexes are convicted of exhibiting a text which has been corrupted by the influence of the oldest Septuagint reading of Isaiah xxix. 13.

I freely admit that it is in a high degree remarkable that five ancient Versions, and all the following early writers,—Ptolemaeus[294], Clemens Alexandrinus[295], Origen[296], Didymus[297], Cyril[298], Chrysostom[299], and possibly three others of like antiquity[300],—should all quote St. Matthew in this place from a faulty text. But this does but prove at how extremely remote a period the corruption must have begun. It probably dates from the first century. Especially does it seem to shew how distrustful we should be of our oldest authorities when, as here, they are plainly at variance with the whole torrent of manuscript authority. This is indeed no ordinary case. There are elements of distrust here, such as are not commonly encountered.

§ 6.

What I have been saying is aptly illustrated by a place in our Lord's Sermon on the Mount: viz. St. Matt. v. 44; which in almost every MS. in existence stands as follows:

(1) ἀγαπᾶτε τοὺς ἐχθροὺς ὑμῶν

(2) εὐλογεῖτε τοὺς καταρωμένους ὑμᾶς

(3) καλῶς ποιεῖτε τοῖς μισοῦσιν[301]ὑμᾶς

(4) καὶ προσεύχεσθε ὑπὲρ τῶν ἐπηρεαζόντων ὑμᾶς

(5) καὶ διωκόντων ὑμᾶς[302].

On the other hand, it is not to be denied that there exists an appreciable body of evidence for exhibiting the passage in a shorter form. The fact that Origen six times[303] reads the place thus:

ἀγαπᾶτε τοὺς ἐχθροὺς ὑμῶν

καὶ προσεύχεσθε ὑπὲρ τῶν διωκόντων ὑμᾶς

(which amounts to a rejection of the second, third, and fourth clauses;)—and that he is supported therein by Bℵ, (besides a few cursives) the Curetonian, the Lewis, several Old Latin MSS., and the Bohairic[304], seems to critics of a certain school a circumstance fatal to the credit of those clauses. They are aware that Cyprian[305], and they are welcome to the information that Tertullian[306] once and Theodoret once[307] [besides Irenaeus[308], Eusebius[309], and Gregory of Nyssa[310]] exhibit the place in the same way. So does the author of the Dialogus contra Marcionitas[311],—whom however I take to be Origen. Griesbach, on far slenderer evidence, was for obelizing all the three clauses. But Lachmann, Tregelles, Tischendorf and the Revisers reject them entirely. I am persuaded that they are grievously mistaken in so doing, and that the received text represents what St. Matthew actually wrote. It is the text of all the uncials but two, of all the cursives but six or seven; and this alone ought to be decisive. But it is besides the reading of the Peshitto, the Harkleian, and the Gothic; as well as of three copies of the Old Latin.

Let us however inquire more curiously for the evidence of Versions and Fathers on this subject; remembering that the point in dispute is nothing else but the genuineness of clauses 2, 3, 4. And here, at starting, we make the notable discovery that Origen, whose practice was relied on for retaining none but the first and the fifth clauses,—himself twice[312] quotes the first clause in connexion with the fourth: while Theodoret, on two occasions[313], connects with clause 1 what he evidently means for clause 2; and Tertullian once if not twice connects closely clauses 1, 2; and once, clauses 1, 2, 5[314]. From which it is plain that neither Origen nor Theodoret, least of all Tertullian, can be held to disallow the clauses in question. They recognize them on the contrary, which is simply a fatal circumstance, and effectively disposes of their supposed hostile evidence.

But in fact the Western Church yields unfaltering testimony. Besides the three copies of the Old Latin which exhibit all the five clauses, the Vulgate retains the first, third, fifth and fourth. Augustine[315] quotes consecutively clauses I, 3, 5: Ambrose[316] clauses 1, 3, 4, 5—1, 4, 5: Hilary[317], clauses 1, 4, 5, and (apparently) 2, 4, 5: Lucifer[318], clauses I, 2, 3 (apparently), 5: pseudo-Epiphanius[319] a connects clauses 1, 3,—1, 3, 5: and Pacian[320], clauses 5, 2. Next we have to ascertain what is the testimony of the Greek Fathers.

And first we turn to Chrysostom [321] who (besides quoting the fourth clause from St. Matthew's Gospel by itself five times) quotes consecutively clauses 1, 3—iii. 167; 1, 4—iv. 619; 2, 4—v. 436; 4, 3—ii. 340, v. 56, xii. 654; 4, 5—ii. 258, iii. 341; 1, 2, 4—iv. 267; 1, 3, 4, 5—xii. 425; thus recognizing them *all*.

Gregory Nyss.[322] quotes connectedly clauses 3, 4, 5.

Eusebius[323], clauses 4, 5—2, 4, 5—1, 3, 4, 5.

The Apostolic Constitutions[324] (third century), clauses 1, 3, 4, 5 (having immediately before quoted clause 2,)—also clauses 2, 4, 1.

Clemens Alex.[325] (A.D. 192), clauses 1, 2, 4.

Athenagoras[326] (A.D. 177), clauses 1, 2, 5.

Theophilus[327] (A.D. 168), clauses 1, 4.

While Justin M.[328] (A. D. 140) having paraphrased clause 1, connects therewith clauses 2 and 4.

And Polycarp[329] (A.D. 108) apparently connects clauses 4 and 5.

Didache[330] (A.D. 100?) quotes 2, 4, 5 and combines 1 and 3 (pp. 5, 6).

In the face of all this evidence, no one it is presumed will any more be found to dispute the genuineness of the generally received reading in St. Matt. v. 44. All must see that if the text familiarly known in the age immediately after that of the Apostles had been indeed the bald, curt thing which the critics imagine, viz.

ἀγαπᾶτε τοὺς ἐχθροὺς ὑμῶν

καὶ προσεύχεσθε ὑπὲρ τῶν διωκόντων ὑμᾶς.—

by no possibility could the men of that age in referring to St. Matt. v. 44 have freely mentioned blessing those who curse,—doing good to those who hate,—and praying for those who despitefully use.' Since there are but two alternative readings of the passage,—one longer, one briefer,—every clear acknowledgement of a single disputed clause in the larger reading necessarily carries with it all the rest.

This result of 'comparative criticism' is therefore respectfully recommended to the notice of the learned. If it be not decisive of the point at issue to find such a torrent of primitive testimony at one with the bulk of the Uncials and Cursives extant, it is clear that there can be no Science of Textual Criticism. The Law of Evidence must be held to be inoperative in this subject-matter. Nothing deserving of the name of 'proof' will ever be attainable in this department of investigation.

But if men admit that the ordinarily received text of St. Matt. v. 44 has been clearly established, then let the legitimate results of the foregoing discussion be loyally recognized. The unique value of Manuscripts in declaring the exact text of Scripture—the conspicuous inadequacy of Patristic evidence by themselves,—have been made apparent: and yet it has been shewn that Patristic quotations are abundantly sufficient for their proper purpose,—which is, to enable us to decide between conflicting readings. One more indication has been obtained of the corruptness of the text which Origen employed,—concerning which he is so strangely communicative,—and of which Bℵ are the chief surviving examples; and the probability has been strengthened that when these are the sole, or even the principal witnesses, for any particular reading, that reading will prove to be corrupt.

Mill was of opinion, (and of course his opinion finds favour with Griesbach, Tischendorf, and the rest,) that these three clauses have been imported hither from St. Luke vi. 27, 28. But, besides that this is mere unsupported conjecture, how comes it then to pass that the order of the second and third clauses in St. Matthew's Gospel is the reverse of the order in St. Luke's? No. I believe that there has been excision here: for I hold with Griesbach that it cannot have been the result of accident[331].

[I take this opportunity to reply to a reviewer in the *Guardian* newspaper, who thought that he had reduced the authorities quoted from before A.D.

400 on page 103 of The Traditional Text to two on our side against seven, or rather six[332], on the other. Let me first say that on this perilous field I am not surprised at being obliged to re-judge or withdraw some authorities. I admit that in the middle of a long catena of passages, I did not lay sufficient stress, as I now find, upon the parallel passage in St. Luke vi. 27, 28. After fresh examination, I withdraw entirely Clemens Alex., Paed. i. 8,—Philo of Carpasus, I. 7,—Ambrose, De Abrahamo ii. 30, Ps. cxviii. 12. 51, and the two referred to Athanasius. Also I do not quote Origen, Cels. viii. 41,—Eusebius in Ps. iii.,—Apost. Const. vii. 4,—Greg. Nyss., In S. Stephanum, because they may be regarded as doubtful, although for reasons which I proceed to give they appear to witness in favour of our contention. It is necessary to add some remarks before dealing with the rest of the passages.

1. It must be borne in mind, that this is a question both negative and positive:—negative on the side of our opponents, with all the difficulties involved in establishing a negative conclusion as to the non-existence in St. Matthew's Gospel of clauses 2, 3, and 5,—and positive for us, in the establishment of those clauses as part of the genuine text in the passage which we are considering. If we can so establish the clauses, or indeed any one of them, the case against us fails: but unless we can establish all, we have not proved everything that we seek to demonstrate. Our first object is to make the adverse position untenable: when we have done that, we fortify our own. Therefore both the Dean and myself have drawn attention to the fact that our authorities are summoned as witnesses to the early existence in each case of 'some of the clauses,' if they do not depose to all of them. We are quite aware of the reply: but we have with us the advantage of positive as against negative evidence. This advantage especially rules in such an instance as the present, because alien circumstances govern the quotation, and regulate particularly the length of it. Such quotation is always liable to shortening, whether by leaving out intermediate clauses, or by sudden curtailment in the midst of the passage. Therefore, actual citation of separate clauses, being undesigned and fortuitous, is much more valuable than omission arising from what cause soever.

2. The reviewer says that 'all four clauses are read by both texts,' i.e. in St. Matthew and St. Luke, and appears to have been unaware as regards the present purpose of the existence of the fifth clause, or half-clause, in St. Matthew. Yet the words—ὑπὲρ . . . τῶ διωκόντων ὑμᾶς are a very label, telling incontestibly the origin of many of the quotations. Sentences so distinguished with St. Matthew's label cannot have come from St. Luke's Gospel. The reviewer has often gone wrong here. The ὑπὲρ—instead of the περί after אBLΞ in St. Luke—should be to our opponents a sign betraying the origin, though when it stands by itself—as in Eusebius, In Ps. iii.—I do not press the passage.

3. Nor again does the reviewer seem to have noticed the effects of the context in shewing to which source a quotation is to be referred. It is a common custom for Fathers to quote v. 45 in St. Matthew, which is hardly conceivable if they had St. Luke vi. 27, 28 before them, or even if they were quoting from

memory. Other points in the context of greater or less importance are often found in the sentence or sentences preceding or following the words quoted, and are decisive of the reference.

The references as corrected are given in the note[333]. It will be seen by any one who compares the verifications with the reviewer's list, how his failure to observe the points just explained has led him astray. The effect upon the list given in The Traditional Text will be that before the era of St. Chrysostom twenty-five testimonies are given in favour of the Traditional Text of St. Matt. v. 44, and adding Tertullian from the Dean nine against it. And the totals on page 102, lines 2 and 3 will be 522 and 171 respectively.]

§ 7.

Especially have we need to be on our guard against conniving at the ejection of short clauses consisting of from twelve to fourteen letters,—which proves to have been the exact length of a line in the earliest copies. When such omissions leave the sense manifestly imperfect, no evil consequence can result. Critics then either take no notice of the circumstance, or simply remark in passing that the omission has been the result of accident. In this way, [οἱ πατέρες αὐτῶν, though it is omitted by Cod. B in St. Luke vi. 26, is retained by all the Editors: and the strange reading of Cod. ℵ in St. John vi. 55, omitting two lines, was corrected on the manuscript in the seventh century, and has met with no assent in modern times].

ΗΓΑΡ
ϹΑΡΞΜΟΥΑΛΗΘωϹ
[εϹΤΙΒΡωϹΙϹΚΑΙ
ΤΟΑΙΜΑΜΟΥΑΛΗΘωϹ]
εϹΤΙΠΟϹΙϹ

But when, notwithstanding the omission of two or three words, the sense of the context remains unimpaired,—the clause being of independent signification,—then great danger arises lest an attempt should be made through the officiousness of modern Criticism to defraud the Church of a part of her inheritance. Thus [καὶ οἱ σὺν αὐτῷ (St. Luke viii. 45) is omitted by Westcott and Hort, and is placed in the margin by the Revisers and included in brackets by Tregelles as if the words were of doubtful authority, solely because some scribe omitted a line and was followed by B, a few cursives, the Sahidic, Curetonian, Lewis, and Jerusalem Versions].

When indeed the omission dates from an exceedingly remote period; took place, I mean, in the third, or more likely still in the second century; then the fate of such omitted words may be predicted with certainty. Their doom is sealed. Every copy made from that defective original of necessity reproduced the defects of its prototype: and if (as often happens) some of those copies have descended to our times, they become quoted henceforward as if they were independent witnesses[334]. Nor is this all. Let the taint have been communicated to certain copies of the Old Latin, and we find ourselves confronted with formidable because very venerable foes. And according to the recently approved method of editing the New Testament, the clause is allowed no quarter. It is declared without hesitation to be a spurious accretion to the Text. Take, as an instance of this, the following passage in St. Luke xii. 39. 'If' (says our Lord) 'the master of the house had known in what hour

ΟΚΛεΠΤΗС
εΡΧεΤΑΙ [εΓΡΗΓΟΡ
ΗСεΝΚΑΙ] ΟΥΚΑΝΑ
ΦΗΚεΝ

his house to be broken through.' Here, the clause within brackets, which has fallen out for an obvious reason, does not appear in Codd. א and D. But the omission did not begin with א. Two copies of the Old Latin are also without the words ἐγρηγόρησεν καὶ,—which are wanting besides in Cureton's Syriac. Tischendorf accordingly omits them. And yet, who sees not that such an amount of evidence as this is wholly insufficient to warrant the ejection of the clause as spurious? What is the 'Science' worth which cannot preserve to the body a healthy limb like this?

[The instances of omission which have now been examined at some length must by no means be regarded as the only specimens of this class of corrupt passages[335]. Many more will occur to the minds of the readers of the present volume and of the earlier volume of this work. In fact, omissions are much more common than Additions, or Transpositions, or Substitutions: and this fact, that omissions, or what seem to be omissions, are apparently so common,—to say nothing of the very strong evidence wherewith they are attested—when taken in conjunction with the natural tendency of copyists to omit words and passages, cannot but confirm the general soundness of the position. How indeed can it possibly be more true to the infirmities of copyists, to the verdict of evidence on the several passages, and to the origin of the New Testament in the infancy of the Church and amidst associations which were not literary, to suppose that a terse production was first produced and afterwards was amplified in a later age with a view to 'lucidity and completeness[336],' rather than that words and clauses and sentences were omitted upon definitely understood principles in a small class of documents by careless or ignorant or prejudiced scribes? The reply to this question must now be left for candid and thoughtful students to determine].

[257] It will be observed that these are empirical, not logical, classes. Omissions are found in many of the rest.
[258] Last Twelve Verses of St. Mark's Gospel, chapter v, and Appendix B.
[259] See Dr. Gwynn's remarks in Appendix VII of The Traditional Text, pp. 298-301.
[260] The Revision Revised, pp. 42-45, 422-424: Traditional Text, p. 109,

where thirty-eight testimonies are quoted before 400 A.D.
[261] The expression of Jerome, that almost all the Greek MSS. omit this passage, is only a translation of Eusebius. It cannot express his own opinion, for he admitted the twelve verses into the Vulgate, and quoted parts of them twice, i.e. ver. 9, 744-5, ver. 14, i. 327 c.
[262] Dr. Dobbin has calculated 330 omissions in St. Matthew, 365 in St.

Mark, 439 in St. Luke, 357 in St. John, 384 in the Acts, and 681 in the Epistles—2,556 in all as far as Heb. ix. 14, where it terminates. Dublin University Magazine, 1859, p. 620.

263   Such as in Cod. D after St. Luke vi. 4. 'On the same day He beheld a certain man working on the sabbath, and said unto him, "Man, blessed art thou if thou knowest what thou doest; but if thou knowest not, thou art cursed and a transgressor of the law"' (Scrivener's translation, Introduction, p. 8). So also a longer interpolation from the Curetonian after St. Matt. xx. 28. These are condemned by internal evidence as well as external.

264   καὶ ὁ πεσὼν ἐπὶ τὸν λίθον τοῦτον συνθλασθήσεται· ἐφ' ὃν δ' ἂν πέσῃ, λικμήσει αὐτόν.

265   iv. 25 d, 343 d.—What proves these two quotations to be from St. Matt. xxi. 44, and not from St. Luke xx. 18, is, that they alike exhibit expressions which are peculiar to the earlier Gospel. The first is introduced by the formula οὐδέποτε ἀνέγνωτε (ver. 42: comp. Orig. ii. 794 c), and both exhibit the expression ἐπὶ τὸν λίθον τοῦτον (ver. 44), not ἐπ' ἐκεῖνον τὸν λίθον. Vainly is it urged on the opposite side, that war πᾶς ὁ πεσὼν belongs to St. Luke,—whereas καὶ ὁ πεσών, is the phrase found in St. Matthew's Gospel. Chrysostom (vii. 672) writes πᾶς ὁ πίπτων while professing to quote from St. Matthew; and the author of Cureton's Syriac, who had this reading in his original, does the same.

266   P. 193.

267   P. 11.

268   vii. 672 a [freely quoted as Greg. Naz. in the Catena of Nicetas, p. 669] xii. 27 d.

269   *Ap.* Mai, ii. 401 dis.

270   *Ap.* Chrys. vi. 171 c.

271   vii. 171 d.

272   iii². 86, 245: v. 500 e, 598 d.

273   682-3 (Massuet 277).

274   iii. 786.

275   Theoph. 235-6 (=Mai, iv. 122).

276   ii. 660 a, b, c.

277   'Praeterit et Lucifer.'

278   *Ap.* Galland. vi. 191 d.

279   Ibid. vii. 20 c.

280   Ibid. ix. 768 a.

281   [I am unable to find any place in the Dean's writings where he has made this explanation. The following note, however, is appended here]:—

With verse 43, the long lesson for the Monday in Holy-week (ver. 18-43) comes to an end.

Verse 44 has a number all to itself (in other words, is sect. 265) in the fifth of the Syrian Canons,—which contains whatever is found exclusively in St. Matthew and St. Luke.

282   'Omnino ex Lc. assumpta videntur.'

283   The section in St. Matthew is numbered 265,—in St. Luke, 274: both being referred to Canon V, in which St. Matthew and St. Luke are exclusively compared.

284   Vol. i. 13.

285   Letter to Pope Damasus. See my book on St. Mark, p. 28.

286   Dial. § 78, *ad fin.* (p. 272).

287   Opp. ii. 215 a: v. part ii. 118 c.

288   See Holmes and Parsons' ed. of the LXX,—vol. iv. *in loc.*

289   Opp. pp. 143 and 206. P. 577 is allusive only.

290   Opp. vii. 158 c: ix. 638 b.

291   Opp. ii. 1345: iii. 763-4.

292   § xv:—on which his learned editor (Bp. Jacobson) pertinently remarks,— 'Hunc locum Prophetae Clemens exhibuisset sicut a Christo laudatum, S. Marc. vii. 6, si pro ἄπεστιν dedissct ἀπέχει.'

293   Opp. i. 1502: iii. 1114.

294   *Ap.* Epiphanium, Opp. i. 218 d.

295   Opp. p. 461.

296 Opp. iii. 49² (a remarkable place): ii. 723: iv. 121.

297 De Trinitate, p. 242.

298 Opp. ii. 413 b. [Observe how this evidence leads us to Alexandria.]

299 Opp. vii. 522 d. The other place, ix. 638 b, is uncertain.

300 It is uncertain whether Eusebius and Basil quote St. Matthew or Isaiah: but a contemporary of Chrysostom certainly quotes the Gospel,—Chrys. Opp. vi. 425 d (cf. p. 417, line 10).

301 But Eus.ᴱˢ 589 τοὺς μ.

302 I have numbered the clauses for convenience.—It will perhaps facilitate the study of this place, if (on my own responsibility) I subjoin a representation of the same words in Latin:— (1) Diligite inimicos vestros,
　(2) benedicite maledicentes vos,
　(3) benefacite odientibus vos,
　(4) et orate pro calumniantibus vos,
　(5) et persequentibus vos.

303 Opp. iv. 324 *bis*, 329 *bis*, 355. Gall. xiv. App. 106.

304 'A large majority, all but five, omit it. Some add it in the margin.' Traditional Text, p. 549.

305 Opp. p. 79, cf. 146.

306 Scap. c. 1.

307 Opp. iv. 946.

308 Haer. III. xviii. 5.

309 Dem. Evan. xiii. 7.

310 In Bapt. Christ.

311 Orig. Opp. i. 812.

312 Opp. i. 768: iv. 353.

313 Opp. i. 827: 399.

314 Spect. c. 16: (Anim. c. 35): Pat. c. 6.

315 [In Ep. Joh. IV. Tract. ix. 3 (1, 3 (ver. 45 &c.)); In Ps. cxxxviii. 27 (1, 3); Serm. XV. 8 (1, 3, 5); Serm. LXII. *in loc.* (1, 3, 4, 5).]

316 In Ps. xxxviii. 2.

317 Opp. pp. 303, 297.

318 Pro S. Athanas. ii.

319 Ps. cxviii. 10. 16; 9. 9.

320 Ep. ii.

321 Opp. iii. 167: iv. 619: v. 436:—ii. 340: v. 56: xii. 654:—ii. 258: iii. 41:—iv. 267: xii. 425.

322 Opp. iii. 379.

323 Praep. 654: Ps. 137, 699: Es. 589.

324 Pp. 3. 198.

325 Opp. p. 605 and 307.

326 Leg. pro Christian. 11.

327 Ad Autolycum, iii. 14.

328 Opp. i. 40.

329 Ad Philipp. c. 12.

330 § 1.

331 'Theodoret once (iv. 946) gives the verse as Tischendorf gives it: but on two other occasions (i. 827: ii. 399) the same Theodoret exhibits the second member of the sentence thus,—
εὐλογεῖτε τοὺς διώκοντας ὑμᾶς (so pseud.-Athan. ii. 95), which shews how little stress is to be laid on such evidence as the first-named place furnishes.

Origen also (iv. 324 bis, 329 bis, 351) repeatedly gives the place as Tischendorf gives it—but on one occasion, which it will be observed is *fatal* to his evidence (i. 768), he gives the second member thus,—iv. 353:
καὶ προσεύχεσθε ὑπὲρ τῶν ἐπηρεαζόντων ὑμᾶς.
∴ 1. 4.

Next observe how Clemens Al. (605) handles the same place:—
ἀγαπᾶτε τοὺς ἐχθροὺς ὑμῶν, εὐλογεῖτε τοὺς καταρωμένους ὑμᾶς, καὶ προσεύχεσθε ὑπὲρ τῶν ἐπηρεαζόντων ὑμῖν, καὶ τὰ ὅμοια
∴ 1, 2, 4.—3, 5.

Justin M. (i. 40) quoting the same place from memory (and with exceeding licence), yet is observed to recognize in part *both* the clauses which labour under suspicion:
∴ 1, 2, 4.—3, 5.

εὔχεσθε ὑπὲρ τῶν ἐχθρῶν ὑμῶν καὶ ἀγαπᾶτε τοὺς ὑμᾶς, which roughly represents καὶ εὐλογεῖτε τοὺς καταρωμένους ὑμῖν, καὶ εὔχεσθε ὑπὲρ τῶν ἐπηρεαζόντων ὑμᾶς.

The clause which hitherto lacks support is that which regards τοὺς μισοῦντας ὑμᾶς. But the required help is supplied by Irenaeus (i. 521), who (loosely enough) quotes the place thus,—

Diligite inimicos vestros, et orate pro eis, qui vos oderunt.

∴ (made up of 3, 4).—2, 5.

And yet more by the most venerable witness of all, Polycarp, who writes:—ad Philipp. c. 12:—

Orate pro persequentibus et odientibus vos.

∴ 4, 5.—1, 2, 3.

I have examined [Didaché] *Justin, Irenaeus, Eusebius, Hippolytus, Cyril Al., Greg. Naz., Basil, Athan., Didymus, Cyril Hier., Chrys., Greg. Nyss., Epiph., Theod., Clemens.*

And the following are the results:—

Didache. Εὐλογεῖτε τοὺς καταρωμένους ὑμῖν, καὶ προσεύχεσθε ὑπὲρ τῶν ἐχθρῶν ὑμῶν, νηστεύετε δὲ ὑπὲρ τῶν διωκότων ὑμᾶς· . . . ὑμεῖς δὲ ἀγαπᾶτε τοὺς μισοῦντας ὑμᾶς

∴ 2, 3, 4, 5.

Aphraates, Dem. ii. The Latin Translation runs:—Diligite inimicos vestros, benedicite ei qui vobis maledicit, orate pro eis qui vos vexunt et persequuntur.

Eusebius ^{Prae} 654. ∴ 2, 4, 5, omitting I, 3.

^{Ps} 699. ∴ 4, 5, omitting 1, 2, 3.

^{Es} 589. ∴ 2, 3, 4, 5, omitting 2.

Clemens Al. 605. ∴ 1, 2, 4, omitting 3, 5.

Greg. Nyss. iii. 379. ∴ 3, 4, 5, omitting 2.

Vulg. Diligite inimicos vestros, benefacite his qui oderunt vos, et orate pro persequentibus et calumniantibus vos. ∴ 1, 3, 5, 4, omitting 2.

Hilary, 297. Benedicite qui vos persequuntur, et orate pro calumniantibus vos ac persequentibus vos. ∴ 2, 4, 5, omitting the *first and third.*

Hilary, 303. Diligite inimicos vestros, et orate pro calumniantibus vos ac persequentibus vos. ∴ 1, 4, 5, omitting the *second and third.* Cf. 128.

Cyprian, 79 (cf. 146). Diligite inimicos vestros, et orate pro his qui vos persequuntur. ∴ 1, 5, omitting 2, 3, 4.

Tertullian. Diligite (enim) inimicos vestros, (inquit,) et orate pro maledicentibus vos—which apparently is meant for a quotation of 1, 2.

∴ 1, 2, omitting 3, 4, 5.

Tertullian. Diligite (enim) inimicos vestros, (inquit,) et maledicentibus benedicite, et orate pro persecutoribus vestris—which is a quotation of 1, 2, 5.

∴ 1, 2, 5, omitting 3, 4.

Tertullian. Diligere inimicos, et orare pro eis qui vos persequuntur.

∴ 1, 5, omitting 2, 3, 4.

Tertullian. Inimicos diligi, maledicentes benedici. ∴ 1, 2, omitting 3, 4, 5.

Ambrose. Diligite inimicos vestros benefacite its qui oderunt vos: orate pro calumniantibus et persequentibus vos.

∴ 1, 3, 4, 5, omitting 2.

Ambrose. Diligite inimicos vestros, orate pro calumniantibus et persequentibus vos.

∴ 1, 4, 5, omitting 2, 3.

Augustine. Diligite inimicos vestros benefacite his qui vos oderunt: et orate pro eis qui vos persequuntur.

∴ 1, 3, 5, omitting 2, 4.

'Benedicite qui vos persequuntur, et orate pro calumniantibus vos ac persequentibus vos.' Hilary, 297.

Cyril Al. twice (i. 270: 807) quotes the place thus,—

εὖ ποιεῖτε τοὺς ἐχθροὺς ὑμῶν, καὶ προσεύχεσθε ὑπὲρ τῶν ἐπηρεαζόντων ὑμᾶς.

Chrys. (iii. 355) says

αὐτὸς γὰρ εἶπεν, εὔχεσθε ὑπὲρ τῶν ἐχθρῶν [ὑμῶν],

and repeats the quotation at iii. 340 and xii. 453.

So Tertull. (Apol. c. 31), pro inimicis deum orare, et *persecutoribus* nostris bone precari.

∴ 1, 5.

If the lost Greek of Irenaeus (i. 521) were recovered, we should probably find

ἀγαπᾶτε τοὺς ἐχθροὺς ὑμῶν,

καὶ προσεύχεσθε ὑπὲρ τῶν μισούντων ὑμᾶς.

and of Polycarp (ad Philipp. c. 12),

προσεύχεσθε ὑπὲρ τῶν διωκόντων καὶ μισούντων ὑμᾶς.

[332] *Dialogus Adamantii* is not adducible within my limits, because it is in all probability the production of a later age.' My number was eight.

[333] Observe that 5 = ὑπὲρ . . . τῶν διωκόντων.

For—

Didache (§ 1), 2 (3), 3 (2), 4, 5.

Polycarp (xii), 3 (2), 5.

Justin Martyr, Apol. 15, 3 (2), 2 (3), 4 (4), 5? ὑπὲρ τῶν ἐχθρῶν (= διωκόντων?) but the passage more like St. Luke, the context more like St. Matt., ver. 45.

Athenagoras (Leg. pro Christian. 11), 1, 2 (3), 5, ver. 45.

Tertullian (De Patient. vi), 1, 2 (3), 5, pt. ver. 45. Add Apol. c. 31. 1, 5.

Theophilus Ant. (Ad Autolycum iii. 14), 1, 4 (4), ὑπέρand ver. 46.

Clemens Alex. (Strom. iv. 14), 1, 2 (3), 4 (4), pt. ver. 45; (Strom. vii. 14), favours St. Matt.

Origen (De Orat. i), 1, 4 (4), ὑπέρ and in the middle of two quotations from St. Matthew; (Cels. viii. 45), 1, 4 (4), ὑπέρ and all ver. 45.

Eusebius (Praep. Evan. xiii. 7), 2 (3), 4 (4), 5, all ver. 45; (Comment. in Is. 66), 1, 3 (2), 4 (4), 5, also ver. 45; (In Ps. cviii), 4, 5.

Apost. Const. (i. 2), 1, 3 (2), 4 (4), 5, ὑπέρ and ver. 45.

Greg. Naz. (Orat. iv. 124), 2 (3), 4 (4), 5, ὑπερεύχεσθαι.

Greg. Nyss. (In Bapt. Christi), 3 (2), 4 (4), 5, ὑπέρ, ver. 45.

Lucifer (Pro S. Athan. ii) omits 4 (4), but quotes ver. 44 . . . end of chapter.

Pacianus (Epist. ii), 2 (3), 5.

Hilary (Tract. in Ps. cxviii. 9. 9), 2 (3), 4 (4), 5; (ibid. 10. 16), 1, 4 (4), 5. (The reviewer omits 'ac persequentibus vos' in both cases.)

Ambrose (In Ps. xxxviii. 2), 1, 3, 4, 5; (In Ps. xxxviii. 10), 1, 4 (4), 5.

Aphraates (Dem. ii), 1, 2 (3), 4 (4), 5, ἐθνικοί.

Apocryphal Acts of the Apostles (p. 89), 2 (3), 3 (2), 4 (4), ver. 45.

Number = 25.

[334] See Traditional Text, p. 55.

[335] For one of the two most important omissions in the New Testament, viz. *the Pericope de Adultera,* see Appendix I. See also Appendix II.

[336] Westcott and Hort, Introduction, p. 134.

Chapter Eleven - Causes of Corruption Chiefly Intentional - V. Transposition, VI. Substitution, and VII. Addition

§ 1.

ONE of the most prolific sources of Corrupt Readings, is Transposition, or the arbitrary inversion of the order of the sacred words,—generally in the subordinate clauses of a sentence. The extent to which 'this prevails in Codexes of the type of BאCD passes belief. It is not merely the occasional writing of ταῦτα πάντα for πάντα ταῦτα,—or ὁ λαὸς οὗτος for οὗτος ὁ λαός, to which allusion is now made: for if that were all, the phenomenon would admit of loyal explanation and excuse. But what I speak of is a systematic putting to wrong of the inspired words throughout the entire Codex; an operation which was evidently regarded in certain quarters as a lawful exercise of critical ingenuity,—perhaps was looked upon as an elegant expedient to be adopted for improving the style of the original without materially interfering with the sense.

Let me before going further lay before the reader a few specimens of Transposition.

Take for example St. Mark i. 5,—καὶ ἐβαπτίζοντο πάντες,—is unreasonably turned into πάντες καὶ ἐβαπτίζοντο; whereby the meaning of the Evangelical record becomes changed, for πάντες is now made to agree with Ἱεροσολυμῖται, and the Evangelist is represented as making the very strong assertion that *all* the people of Jerusalem came to St. John and were baptized. This is the private property of BDLΔ.

And sometimes I find short clauses added which I prefer to ascribe to the misplaced critical assiduity of ancient Critics. Confessedly spurious, these accretions to the genuine text often bear traces of pious intelligence, and occasionally of considerable ability. I do not suppose that they 'crept in' from the margin: but that they were inserted by men who entirely failed to realize the wrongness of what they did,—the mischievous consequences which might possibly ensue from their well-meant endeavours to improve the work of the Holy Ghost.

[Take again St. Mark ii. 3, in which the order in πρὸς αὐτὸν, παραλυτικὸν φέροντες,—is changed by אBL into φέροντες πρὸς αὐτὸν παραλυτικόν. A few words are needed to explain to those who have not carefully examined the passage the effect of this apparently slight alteration. Our Lord was in a house at Capernaum with a thick crowd of people around Him: there was no room even at the door. Whilst He was there teaching, a company of people come to Him (ἔρχονται πρὸς αὐτὸν), four of the party carrying a paralytic on a bed. When they arrive at the house, a few of the company, enough to represent the whole, force their way in and reach Him: but on looking back they see that the rest are unable to bring the paralytic near to Him (προσέγγισαι αὐτῷ[337]). Upon which they all go out and uncover the roof, take up the sick man on his bed, and the rest of the familiar *story* unfolds itself. Some officious scribe wished to remove all antiquity arising from the separation of παραλυτικόν from αἰρόμενον which agrees with it, and transposed φέροντες to the verb it is attached to, thus clumsily excluding the exquisite hint, clear enough to those who can read between the lines, that in the ineffectual at-

98

tempt to bring in the paralytic only some of the company reached our Lord's Presence. Of course the scribe in question found followers in אBL.]

It will be seen therefore that some cases of transposition are of a kind which is without excuse and inadmissible. Such transposition consists in drawing back a word which occurs further on, but is thus introduced into a new context, and gives a new sense. It seems to be assumed that since the words are all there, so long as they be preserved, their exact collocation is of no moment. Transpositions of that kind, to speak plainly, are important only as affording conclusive proof that such copies as BאD preserve a text which has undergone a sort of critical treatment which is so obviously indefensible that the Codexes themselves, however interesting as monuments of a primitive age,—however valuable commercially and to be prized by learned and unlearned alike for their unique importance,—are yet to be prized chiefly as beacon-lights preserved by a watchful Providence to warn every voyaging bark against making shipwreck on a shore already strewn with wrecks[338].

Transposition may sometimes be as conveniently illustrated in English as in Greek. St. Luke relates (Acts ii. 45, 46) that the first believers sold their goods 'and parted them to all men, as every man had need. And they, continuing daily,' &c. For this, Cod. D reads, 'and parted them daily to all men as every man had need. And they continued in the temple.'

§ 2.

It is difficult to divine for what possible reason most of these transpositions were made. On countless occasions they do not in the least affect the sense. Often, they are incapable of being idiomatically represented, in English. Generally speaking, they are of no manner of importance, except as tokens of the licence which was claimed by disciples, as I suspect, of the Alexandrian school [or exercised unintentionally by careless or ignorant Western copyists]. But there arise occasions when we cannot afford to be so trifled with. An important change in the meaning of a sentence is sometimes effected by transposing its clauses; and on one occasion, as I venture to think, the prophetic intention of the Speaker is obscured in consequence. I allude to St. Luke xiii. 9, where under the figure of a barren fig-tree, our Lord hints at what is to befall the Jewish people, because in the fourth year of His Ministry it remained unfruitful. 'Lo, these three years,' (saith He to the dresser of His Vineyard), 'come I seeking fruit on this fig-tree, and find none; cut it down; why cumbereth it the ground?' 'Spare it for this year also,' (is the rejoinder), 'and if it bear fruit,—well: but if not, next year thou shalt cut it down.' But on the strength of אBLT^w, some recent Critics would have us read,—'And if it bear fruit next year,—well: but if not, thou shalt cut it down':—which clearly would add a year to the season of the probation of the Jewish race. The limit assigned in the genuine text is the fourth year: in the corrupt text of אBLT^w, two bad Cursives, and the two chief Egyptian versions, this period becomes extended to the fifth.

To reason about such transpositions of words, a wearisome proceeding at best, soon degenerates into the veriest trifling. Sometimes, the order of the words is really immaterial to the sense. Even when a different shade of meaning is the result of a different collocation, that will seem the better order to one man which seems not to be so to another. The best order of course is that which most accurately exhibits the Author's precise shade of meaning: but of this the Author is probably the only competent judge. On our side, an appeal to actual evidence is obviously the only resource: since in no other way can we reasonably expect to ascertain what was the order of the words in the original document. And surely such an appeal can be attended with only one result: viz. the unconditional rejection of the peculiar and often varying order advocated by the very few Codexes,—a cordial acceptance of the order exhibited by every document in the world besides.

I will content myself with inviting attention to one or two samples of my meaning. It has been made a question whether St. Luke (xxiv. 7) wrote,— λέγων, Ὅτι δεῖ τὸν υἱὸν τοῦ ἀνθρώπου παραδοθῆναι as all the MSS. in the world but four, all the Versions, and all the available Fathers'[339] evidence from A.D. 150 downwards attest: or whether he wrote,—λέγων τὸν υἱὸν τοῦ ἀνθρώπου ὅτι δεῖ παραδοθῆναι, as אBCL,—and those four documents only— would have us believe? [The point which first strikes a scholar is that there is in this reading a familiar classicism which is alien to the style of the Gospels, and which may be a symptom of an attempt on the part of some early critic who was seeking to bring them into agreement with ancient Greek models.] But surely also it is even obvious that the correspondence of those four Codexes in such a particular as this must needs be the result of their having derived the reading from one and the same original. On the contrary, the agreement of all the rest in a trifling matter of detail like the present can be accounted for in only one way, viz., by presuming that they also have all been derived through various lines of descent from a single document: but *that* document the autograph of the Evangelist. [For the great number and variety of them necessitates their having been derived through various lines of descent. Indeed, they must have the notes of number, variety, as well as continuity, and weight also.]

§ 3.

On countless occasions doubtless, it is very difficult—perhaps impossible—to determine, apart from external evidence, which collocation of two or more words is the true one, whether e. g. ἔχει ζωήν for instance or ζωὴν ἔχει[340],—ἠγέρθη εὐθὲως or εὐθέως ἠγέρθη[341],—χωλούς, τυφλούς—or τυφλούς, χωλούς[342],—shall be preferred. The burden of proof rests evidently with innovators on Traditional use.

Obvious at the same time is it to foresee that if a man sits down before the Gospel with the deliberate intention of improving the style of the Evangelists by transposing their words on an average of seven (B), eight (א), or twelve (D) times in every page, he is safe to convict himself of folly in repeated instances, long before he has reached the end of his task. Thus, when the scribe of ℵ, in place of ἐξουσίαν ἔδωκεν αὐτῷ καὶ κρίσιν ποιεῖν[343], presents us with καὶ κρίσιν ἔδωκεν αὐτῷ ἐξουσίαν ποιεῖν, we hesitate not to say that he has written nonsense[344]. And when BD instead of εἰσί τινες τῶν ὧδε ἑστηκότων exhibit εἰσί τινες ὧδε τῶν ἑστηκότων, we cannot but conclude that the credit of those two MSS. must be so far lowered in the eyes of every one who with true appreciation of the niceties of Greek scholarship observes what has been done.

[This characteristic of the old uncials is now commended to the attention of students, who will find in the folios of those documents plenty of instances for examination. Most of the cases of Transposition are petty enough, whilst some, as the specimens already presented to the reader indicate, constitute blots not favourable to the general reputation of the copies on which they are found. Indeed, they are so frequent that they have grown to be a very habit, and must have propagated themselves. For it is in this secondary character rather than in any first intention, so to speak, that Transpositions, together with Omissions and Substitutions and Additions, have become to some extent independent causes of corruption. Originally produced by other forces, they have acquired a power of extension in themselves.

It is hoped that the passages already quoted may be found sufficient to exhibit the character of the large class of instances in which the pure Text of the original Autographs has been corrupted by Transposition. That it has been so corrupted, is proved by the evidence which is generally overpowering in each case. There has clearly been much intentional perversion: carelessness also and ignorance of Greek combined with inveterate inaccuracy, characteristics especially of Western corruption as may be seen in Codex D and the Old Latin versions, must have had their due share in the evil work. The result has been found in constant slurs upon the sacred pages, lessening the beauty and often perverting the sense,—a source of sorrow to the keen scholar and reverent Christian, and reiterated indignity done in wantonness or heedlessness to the pure and easy flow of the Holy Books.]

---

337 προσέγγισαι is transitive here, like ἐγγίζω in Gen. xlviii. 10, 13: 2 Kings iv. 6: Isaiah xlvi. 13.
338 The following are the numbers of Transpositions supplied by B, ℵ, and D in the Gospels:—2,098: ℵ, 2,299: D, 3,471. See Revision Revised, pp. 12, 13.
339 Marcion (Epiph. i. 317): Eusebius (Mai, iv. 266): Epiphanius (i. 348): Cyril (Mai, ii. 438): John Thess. (Gall. xiii. 188).

340 St. John v. 26, in ℵ.
341 St. Mark ii. 12, in D.
342 St. Luke xiv. 13, in ℵB.
343 St. John v. 27.
344 'Nec aliter' (says Tischendorf) 'Tertull.' (Prax. 21),—'et judicium dedit illi facere in potestate.' But this (begging the learned critic's pardon) is quite a different thing.

Chapter Eleven (*continued*) - Causes of Corruption Chiefly Intentional - VI. Substitution

§ 4.

[ALL the Corruption in the Sacred Text may be classed under four heads, viz. Omission, Transposition, Substitution, and Addition. We are entirely aware that, in the arrangement adopted in this Volume for purposes of convenience, Scientific Method has been neglected. The inevitable result must be that passages are capable of being classed under more heads than one. But Logical exactness is of less practical value than a complete and suitable treatment of the corrupted passages that actually occur in the four Gospels.

It seems therefore needless to supply with a scrupulousness that might bore our readers a disquisition upon Substitution which has not forced itself into a place amongst Dean Burgon's papers, although it is found in a fragmentary plan of this part of the treatise. Substituted forms or words or phrases, such as OC (ὅς) for θ̄σ̄ (Θεός)[345] ἠπόρει for ἐποίει (St. Mark vi. 20), or εὐκ οἴδατε δοκιμάζειν for δοκιμάζετε (St. Luke xii. 56), have their own special causes of substitution, and are naturally and best considered under the cause which in each case gave them birth.

Yet the class of Substitutions is a large one, if Modifications, as they well may be, are added to it[346]. It will be readily concluded that some substitutions are serious, some of less importance, and many trivial. Of the more important class, the reading of ἀμαρτήματος for κρίσεως (St. Mark iii. 29) which the Revisers have adopted in compliance with אBLΔ and three Cursives, is a specimen. It is true that D reads ἀμαρτίας supported by the first corrector of C, and three of the Ferrar group (13, 69, 346) and that the change adopted is supported by the Old Latin versions except f, the Vulgate, Bohairic, Armenian, Gothic, Lewis, and Saxon. But the opposition which favours κρίσεως is made up of A, C under the first reading and the second correction, ΦΣ and eleven other Uncials, the great bulk of the Cursives, f, Peshitto, and Harkleian, and is superior in strength. The internal evidence is also in favour of the Traditional reading, both as regards the usage of ἔνοχός, and the natural meaning given by κρίσεως. Ἀμαρτήματος has clearly crept in from ver. 28. Other instances of Substitution may be found *in* the well-known St. Luke xxiii. 45 (τοῦ ἡλίου ἐκλιπόντος), St. Matt. xi. 27 (βούληται ἀποκαλύψαι), St. Matt. xxvii. 34 (οἶνον for ὄξος), St. Mark i. 2 (Ἠσαΐᾳ for τοῖς προφήταις), St. John i. 18 (ὁ Μονογένης Θεός being a substitution made by heretics for ὁ Μονογένης Υἱός), St. Mark vii. 31 (διὰ Σιδῶνος for καὶ Σιδῶνος). These instances may perhaps suffice: many more may suggest themselves to intelligent readers. Though most are trivial, their cumulative force is extremely formidable. Many of these changes arose from various causes which are described in many other places in this book.]

345   See the very learned, ingenious, and satisfactory disquisition in The Revision Revised, pp. 424-501.
346   The numbers are:— B, substitutions, 935; modifications, 1,132; total, 2,067. 2,379 " ;1,265 " ;1,114 " א. D, " 2,121; " 1,772; " 3,893.
Revision Revised, pp. 12, 13.

Chapter Eleven (*continued*) - Causes of Corruption Chiefly Intentional - VII. Addition

§ 5.

[THE smallest of the four Classes, which upon a pure survey of the outward form divide among themselves the surface of the entire field of Corruption, is that of Additions[347]. And the reason of their smallness of number is discoverable at once. Whilst it is but too easy for scribes or those who have a love of criticism to omit words and passages under all circumstances, or even to vary the order, or to use another word or form instead of the right one, to insert anything into the sacred Text which does not proclaim too glaringly its own unfitness—in a word, to invent happily—is plainly a matter of much greater difficulty. Therefore to increase the Class of Insertions or Additions or Interpolations, so that it should exceed the Class of Omissions, is to go counter to the natural action of human forces. There is no difficulty in leaving out large numbers of the Sacred Words: but there is much difficulty in placing in the midst of them human words, possessed of such a character and clothed in such an uniform, as not to betray to keen observation their earthly origin.

A few examples will set this truth in clearer light. It is remarkable that efforts at interpolation occur most copiously amongst the books of those who are least fitted to make them. We naturally look amongst the representatives of the Western school where Greek was less understood than in the East where Greek acumen was imperfectly represented by Latin activity, and where translation into Latin and retranslation into Greek was a prolific cause of corruption. Take then the following passage from the Codex D (St. Luke vi. 4):—

'On the same day He beheld a certain man working on the sabbath, and said to him, "Man, blessed art thou if thou knowest what thou doest; but if thou knowest not, thou art cursed and a transgressor of the law."'

And another from the Curetonian Syriac (St. Matt. xx. 28), which occurs under a worse form in D.

'But seek ye from little to become greater, and not from greater to become less. When ye are invited to supper in a house, sit not down in the best place, lest some one come who is more honourable than thou, and the lord of the supper say to thee, "Go down below," and thou be ashamed in the presence of them that have sat down. But if thou sit down in the lower place, and one who is inferior to thee come in, the lord also of the supper will say to thee, "Come near, and come up, and sit down," and thou shalt have greater honour in the presence of them that have sat down.'

Who does not see that there is in these two passages no real 'ring of genuineness'?

Take next some instances of lesser insertions.]

§ 6.

Conspicuous beyond all things in the Centurion of Capernaum (St. Matt. viii. 13) was his faith. It occasioned wonder even in the Son of Man. Do we not, in the significant statement, that when they who had been sent returned to the house, they found the servant whole that had been sick[348],' recognize by implication the assurance that the Centurion, because he needed no such confirmation of his belief, went *not* with them; but enjoyed the twofold blessedness of remaining with Christ, and of believing without seeing? I think so. Be this however as it may, אCEMUX besides about fifty cursives, append to St. Matt. viii. 13 the clearly apocryphal statement, 'And the Centurion returning to his house in that same hour found the servant whole.' It does not improve the matter to find that Eusebius[349], besides the Harkleian and the Ethiopic versions, recognize the same appendix. We are thankful, that no one yet has been found to advocate the adoption of this patent accretion to the inspired text. Its origin is not far to seek. I presume it was inserted in order to give a kind of finish to the story[350].

[Another and that a most remarkable Addition may be found in St. Matt. xxiv. 36, into which the words οὐδὲ ὁ Υἱός, 'neither the Son' have been transferred from St. Mark xiii. 32 in compliance with a wholly insufficient body of authorities[351]. Lachmann was the leader in this proceeding, and he has been followed by Tischendorf, Westcott and Hort, and the Revisers. The latter body add in their margin, 'Many authorities, some ancient, omit *neither the Son*.' How inadequate to the facts of the case this description is, will be seen when the authorities are enumerated. But first of those who have been regarded by the majority of the Revisers as the disposers of their decision, according to the information supplied by Tischendorf.

They are (*a*) of Uncials א (in the first reading and as re-corrected in the seventh century) BD; (*b*) five Cursives (for a present of 346 may be freely made to Tischendorf); (*c*) ten Old Latin copies also the Aureus (Words.), some of the Vulgate (four according to Wordsworth), the Palestinian, Ethiopic, Armenian; (*d*) Origen (Lat. iii. 874), Hilary (733a), Cyril Alex. (Mai Nova Pp. Bibliotheca, 481), Ambrose (i. 147⁸ᶠ). But Irenaeus (Lat. i. 386), Cyril (Zach. 800), Chrysostom (ad locum) seem to quote from St. Mark. So too, as Tischendorf admits, Amphilochius.

On the other hand we have, (*a*) the chief corrector of א (cᵃ) ΦΣ with thirteen other Uncials and the Greek MSS. of Adamantius and Pierius mentioned by Jerome[352]; (*b*) all the Cursives, as far as is known (except the aforenamed); (*c*) the Vulgate, with the Peshitto, Harkleian, Lewis, Bohairic, and the Sahidic; (d) Jerome (in the place just now quoted), St. Basil who contrasts the text of St. Matthew with that of St. Mark, Didymus, who is also express in declaring that the three words in dispute are not found in St. Matthew (Trip., 195), St. John Damascene (ii. 346), Apollonius Philosophus (Galland. ix. 247), Euthymius Zigabenus (in loc.), Paulinus (iii. 12), St. Ambrose (ii. 656ᵃ), and Anastasius Sinaita (Migne, lxxxix. 941).

Theophylact (i. 133), Hesychius Presb. (Migne, lxiii. 142) Eusebius (Galland. ix. 580), Facundus Herm. (Galland. xi. 782), Athanasius (ii. 660), quote the words as from the Gospel without reference, and may therefore refer to St. Mark. Phoebadius (Galland. v. 251), though quoted against the Addition by Tischendorf, is doubtful.

On which side the balance of evidence inclines, our readers will judge. But at least they cannot surely justify the assertion made by the majority of the Revisers, that the Addition is opposed only by 'many authorities, some ancient,' or at any rate that this is a fair and adequate description of the evidence opposed to their decision.

An instance occurs in St. Mark iii. 16 which illustrates the carelessness and tastelessness of the handful of authorities to which it pleases many critics to attribute ruling authority. In the fourteenth verse, it had been already stated that our Lord 'ordained twelve,' καὶ ἐποίησε δώδεκα; but because אBA and C (which was corrected in the ninth century with a MS. of the Ethiopic) reiterate these words two verses further on, Tischendorf with Westcott and Hort assume that it is necessary to repeat what has been so recently told. Meanwhile eighteen other uncials (including ΑΦΣ and the third hand of C); nearly all the Cursives; the Old Latin, Vulgate, Peshitto, Lewis, Harkleian, Gothic, Armenian, and the other MSS. of the Ethiopic omit them. It is plainly unnecessary to strengthen such an opposition by researches in the pages of the Fathers.

Explanation has been already given, how the introductions to Lections, and other Liturgical formulae, have been added by insertion to. the Text in various places. Thus ὁ Ἰησοῦς has often been inserted, and in some places remains wrongly (in the opinion of Dean Burgon) in the pages of the Received Text. The three most important additions to the Received Text occur, as Dean Burgon thought, in St. Matt. vi. 18, where ἐν τῷ φανερῷ has crept in from v. 6 against the testimony of a large majority both of Uncial and of Cursive MSS.: in St. Matt. xxv. 13, where the clause ἐν ᾗ ὁ υἱὸς τοῦ ἀνθρώοου ἔρχεται seemed to him to be condemned by a superior weight of authority: and in St. Matt. xxvii. 35, where the quotation (ἵνα πληρωθῇ . . . ἔβαλον κλῆρον) must be taken for similar reasons to have been originally a gloss.]

---

347 B has 536 words added in the Gospels: א, 839: D, 2,213. Revision Revised, pp. 12, 13. The interpolations of D are notorious.
348 St. Luke vii. 10.

349 Theoph. p. 212.
350 3 An opposite fate, strange to say, has attended a short clause in the same narrative, which however is even worse authenticated. Instead of οὐδὲ ἐν

τῷ Ἰσραὴλ τοσαύτην πίστιν εὗρον (St. Matt. viii. 10), we are invited henceforth to read παρ' οὐδενὶ τοσαύτην πίστιν ἐν τῷ Ἰσραὴλ εὗρον;—a tame and tasteless gloss, witnessed to by only B, and five cursives,—but having no other effect, if it should chance to be inserted, than to mar and obscure the Divine utterance.

For when our Saviour declares 'Not even in Israel have I found so great faith,' He is clearly contrasting this proficiency of an earnest Gentile against whatever of a like nature lie had experienced in His dealing with the Jewish people; and declaring the result. He is contrasting Jacob's descendants, the heirs of so many lofty privileges, with this Gentile soldier: their spiritual attainments with his; and assigning the palm to him. Substitute 'With no one in Israel have I found so great faith,' and the contrast disappears. Nothing else is predicated but a greater measure of faith in one man than in any other. The author of this feeble attempt to improve upon St. Matthew's Gospel is found to have also tried his hand on the parallel place in St. Luke, but with even inferior success: for there his misdirected efforts survive only in certain copies of the Old Latin. Ambrose notices his officiousness, remarking that it yields an intelligible sense; but that, 'juxta Graecos,' the place is to be read differently (i. 1376.).

It is notorious that a *few* copies of the Old Latin (Augustine *once* (iv. 322), though he quotes the place nearly twenty times in the usual way.) and the Egyptian versions exhibit the same depravation. Cyril habitually employed an Evangelium which was disfigured in the same way (iii. 833, also Opp. v. 544, ed. Pusey.). But are we out of such materials as these to set about reconstructing the text of Scripture?

351 This disquisition is made up in part from the Dean's materials.

352 'In quibusdam Latinis codicibus additum est, *neque Filius*: quum in Graecis, et maxime Adamantii et Pierii exemplaribus hoc non habeatur adscriptum. Sed quia in nonnullis legitur, disserendum videtur.' Hier. vii. 199 a. 'Gaudet Arius et Eunomius, quasi ignorantia magistri gloria discipulorum sit, et dicunt:—"Non potest aequalis esse qui novit et qui ignorat."' Ibid. 6.

In vi. 919, we may quote from St. Mark.

Chapter Twelve - Causes of Corruption Chiefly Intentional - VIII. Glosses

§ 1.

'GLOSSES,' properly so called, though they enjoy a conspicuous place in every enumeration like the present, are probably by no means so numerous as is commonly supposed. For certainly *every* unauthorized accretion to the text of Scripture is not a 'gloss': but only those explanatory words or clauses which have surreptitiously insinuated themselves into the text, and of which no more reasonable account can be rendered than that they were probably in the first instance proposed by some ancient Critic in the way of useful comment, or necessary explanation, or lawful expansion, or reasonable limitation of the actual utterance of the Spirit. Thus I do not call the clause νεκροὺς ἐγείρετε in St. Matt. x. 8 'a gloss.' It is a gratuitous and unwarrantable interpolation,—nothing else but a clumsy encumbrance of the text[353].

[Glosses, or *scholia*, or comments, or interpretations, are of various kinds, but are generally confined to Additions or Substitutions, since of course we do not omit in order to explain, and transposition of words already placed in lucid order, such as the sacred Text may be reasonably supposed to have observed, would confuse rather than illustrate the meaning. A clause, added in Hebrew fashion[354], which may perhaps appear to modern taste to be hardly wanted, must not therefore be taken to be a gloss.]

Sometimes a 'various reading' is nothing else but a gratuitous gloss;—the unauthorized substitution of a common for an uncommon word. This phenomenon is of frequent occurrence, but only in Codexes of a remarkable type like BℵCD. A few instances follow:—

1. The disciples on a certain occasion (St. Matt. xiii. 36), requested our LORD 'to explain' to them (ΦΡΑϹΟΝ ἡμῖν, 'they said') the parable of the tares. So every known copy, except two: so, all the Fathers who quote the place,— viz. Origen, five times[355],—Basil[356],—J. Damascene[357]. And so *all* the Versions[358]. But because B–ℵ, instead of φράσον, exhibit ΔΙΑϹΑΦΗϹΟΝ ('make clear to us'),—which is also *once* the reading of Origen[359], who was but too well acquainted with Codexes of the same depraved character as the archetype of B and ℵ,—Lachmann, Tregelles (not Tischendorf), Westcott and Hort, and the Revisers of 1881, assume that διασάφησον (a palpable gloss) stood in the inspired autograph of the Evangelist. They therefore thrust out φράσον and thrust in διασάφησον. I am wholly unable to discern any connexion between the premisses of these critics and their conclusions[360].

2. Take another instance. Πυγμῇ,—the obscure expression (Δ leaves it out) which St. Mark employs in vii. 3 to denote the strenuous frequency of the Pharisees' ceremonial washings,—is exchanged by Cod. ℵ, but by no other known copy of the Gospels, for πυκνά, which last word is of course nothing else but a sorry gloss. Yet Tischendorf degrades πυγμῇ and promotes πυκνά to honour,—happily standing alone in his infatuation. Strange, that the most industrious of modern accumulators of evidence should not have been aware that by such extravagances he marred his pretension to critical discernment! Origen and Epiphanius—the only Fathers who quote the place—both read πυγμῇ. It ought to be universally admitted that it is a mere waste of time that we should argue out a point like this[361].

§ 2.

A gloss little suspected, which—not without a pang of regret—I proceed to submit to hostile scrutiny, is the expression 'daily' (καθ' ἡμέραν) in St. Luke ix. 23. Found in the Peshitto and in Cureton's Syriac,—but only in some Copies of the Harkleian version[362]: found in most Copies of the Vulgate,—but largely disallowed by copies of the Old Latin[363]: found also in Ephraem Syrus[364],—but clearly not recognized by Origen[365]: found again in ℵAB and six other uncials,—but not found in CDE and ten others: the expression referred to cannot, at all events, plead for its own retention in the text higher antiquity than can be pleaded for its exclusion. Cyril, (if in such a matter the Syriac translation of his Commentary on St. Luke may be trusted,) is clearly an authority for reading καθ' ἡμέραν in St. Luke ix. 23[366]; but then he elsewhere twice quotes St. Luke ix. 23 in Greek without it[367]. Timotheus of Antioch, of the fifth century, omits the phrase[368]. Jerome again, although he suffered 'quotidie' to stand in the Vulgate, yet, when for his own purposes he quotes the place in St. Luke[369],—ignores the word. All this is calculated to inspire grave distrust. On the other hand, καθ' ἡμέραν enjoys the support of the two Egyptian Versions,—of the Gothic,—of the Armenian,—of the Ethiopic. And this, in the present state of our knowledge, must be allowed to be a weighty piece of evidence in its favour.

But the case assumes an entirely different aspect the instant it is discovered that out of the cursive copies only eight are found to contain καθ' ἡμέραν in St. Luke ix. 23[370]. How is it to be explained that nine manuscripts out of every ten in existence should have forgotten how to transmit such a remarkable message, had it ever been really so committed to writing by the Evangelist? The omission (says Tischendorf) is explained by the parallel places[371]. Utterly incredible, I reply; as no one ought to have known better than Tischendorf himself. We now scrutinize the problem more closely; and discover that the very *locus* of the phrase is a matter of uncertainty. Cyril once makes it part of St. Matt. x. 38[372]. Chrysostom twice connects it with St. Matt. xvi. 24[373]. Jerome, evidently regarding the phrase as a curiosity, informs us that 'juxta antiqua exemplaria' it was met with in St. Luke xiv. 27[374]. All this is in a high degree unsatisfactory. We suspect that we ourselves enjoy some slight familiarity with the 'antiqua exemplaria' referred to by the Critic; and we freely avow that we have learned to reckon them among the least reputable of our acquaintance. Are they not represented by those Evangelia, of which several copies are extant, that profess to have been 'transcribed from, and collated with, ancient copies at Jerusalem'? These uniformly exhibit καθ' ἡμέραν in St. Luke ix. 23[375]. But then, if the phrase be a gloss,—it is obvious to inquire,—how is its existence in so many quarters to be accounted for?

Its origin is not far to seek. Chrysostom, in a certain place, after quoting our Lord's saying about taking up the cross and following Him, remarks that the words 'do not mean that we are actually to bear the wood upon our shoulders, but to keep the prospect of death steadily before us, and like St. Paul to "die daily"[376].' The same Father, in the two other places already quoted from his writings, is observed similarly to connect the Saviour's mention of 'bearing the Cross' with the Apostle's announcement—'I die daily.' Add, that Ephraem Syrus[377], and Jerome quoted already,—persistently connect the same two places together; the last named Father even citing them in immediate succession;—and the inference is unavoidable. The phrase in St. Luke ix. 23 must needs be a very ancient as well as very interesting expository

gloss, imported into the Gospel from 1 Cor. xv. 31,—as Mill[378] and Matthaei[379] long since suggested.

Sincerely regretting the necessity of parting with an expression with which
one has been so long familiar, we cannot suffer the sentimental plea to weigh
with us when the Truth of the Gospel is at stake. Certain it is that but for
Erasmus, we should *never* have known the regret: for it was he that introduced καθ᾽ ἡμέραν into the Received Text. The MS. from which he printed is
without the expression: which is also not found in the Complutensian. It is
certainly a spurious accretion to the inspired Text.

[The attention of the reader is particularly invited to this last paragraph.
The learned Dean has been sneered at for a supposed sentimental and effem-
inate attachment to the Textus Receptus. He was always ready to reject
words and phrases, which have not adequate support; but he denied the va-
lidity of the evidence brought against many texts by the school of Westcott
and Hort, and therefore he refused to follow them in their surrender of the
passages.]

§ 3.

Indeed, a great many 'various readings,' so called, are nothing else but very
ancient interpretations,—fabricated readings therefore,—of which the value
may be estimated by the fact that almost every trace of them has long since
disappeared. Such is the substitution of φεύγει for ἀνεχώρησεν in St. John vi.
15;—which, by the way, Tischendorf thrusts into his text on the sole authority of ℵ, some Latin copies including the Vulgate, and Cureton's Syriac[380]:
though Tregelles ignores its very existence. That our Lord's 'withdrawal' to
the mountain on that occasion was of the nature of 'flight,' or retreat' is obvious. Hence Chrysostom and Cyril remark that He '*fled* to the mountain.' And
yet both Fathers (like Origen and Epiphanius before them) are found to have
read ἀνεχώρησεν.

Almost as reasonably in the beginning of the same verse might Tischendorf
(with ℵ) have substituted ἀναδεικνύναι for ἵνα ποιήσωσιν αὐτὸν, on the plea
that Cyril[381] says, ζητεῖν αὐτὸν ἀναδεῖξαι καὶ βασιλέα. We may on no account
suffer ourselves to be imposed upon by such shallow pretences for tampering with the text of Scripture: or the deposit will never be safe. A patent
gloss,—rather an interpretation,—acquires no claim to be regarded as the
genuine utterance of the Holy Spirit by being merely found in two or three
ancient documents. It is the little handful of documents which loses in reputation,—not the reading which gains in authority on such occasions.

In this way we are sometimes presented with what in effect are new incidents. These are not unfrequently discovered to be introduced in defiance of
the reason of the case; as where (St. John xiii. 24) Simon Peter is represented
(in the Vulgate) as *actually saying* to St. John, 'Who is it concerning whom He
speaks?' Other copies of the Latin exhibit, 'Ask Him who it is,' &c.: while ℵBC
(for on such occasions we are treated to any amount of apocryphal matter)
would persuade us that St. Peter only required that the information should
be furnished him by St. John—'Say who it is of whom He speaks.' Sometimes

a very little licence is sufficient to convert the *oratio obliqua* into the *recta*. Thus, by the change of a single letter (in אBX) Mary Magdalene is made to say to the disciples '*I have seen* the Lord' (St. John xx. 18). But then, as might have been anticipated, the new does not altogether agree with the old. Accordingly D and others paraphrase the remainder of the sentence thus,—'and she signified to them what He had said unto her.' How obvious is it to foresee that on such occasions the spirit of officiousness never know when to stop! In the Vulgate and Sahidic versions the sentence proceeds, 'and He told these things unto me.'

Take another example. The Hebraism μετὰ σάλπιγγος φωνῆς μεγάλης (St. Matt. xxiv. 31) presents an uncongenial ambiguity to Western readers, as our own incorrect A.V. sufficiently shows. Two methods of escape from the difficulty suggested themselves to the ancients:—(*a*) Since 'a trumpet of great sound' means nothing else but a loud trumpet,' and since this can be as well expressed by σάλπιγγος μεγάλης, the scribes at a very remote period are found to have omitted the word φωνῆς. The Peshitto and Lewis (interpreting rather than translating) so deal with the text. Accordingly, φωνῆς is not found in אLΔ and five cursives. Eusebius[382], Cyril Jerus.[383], Chrysostom[384], Theodoret[385], and even Cyprian[386] are also without the word. (*b*) A less violent expedient was to interpolate καὶ before φωνῆς. This is accordingly the reading of the best Italic copies, of the Vulgate, and of D. So Hilary[387] and Jerome[388], Severianus[389], Asterius[390], ps.-Caesarius[391], Damascene[392] and at least eleven cursive copies, so read the place.—There can be no doubt at all that the commonly received text is right. It is found in thirteen uncials with B at their head: in Cosmas[393], Hesychius[394], Theophylact[395]. But the decisive consideration is that the great body of the cursives have faithfully retained the uncongenial Hebraism, and accordingly imply the transmission of it all down the ages: a phenomenon which will not escape the unprejudiced reader. Neither will he overlook the fact that the three 'old uncials' (for A and C are not available here) advocate as many different readings: the two wrong readings being respectively countenanced by our two most ancient authorities, viz. the Peshitto version and the Italic. It only remains to point out that Tischendorf blinded by his partiality for א contends here for the mutilated text, and Westcott and Hort are disposed to do the same.

§ 4.

Recent Editors are agreed that we are henceforth to read in St. John xviii. 14 ἀπο4ανεῖν instead of ἀπολέσθαι:—'Now Caiaphas was he who counselled the *Jews* that it was expedient that one man should *die*' (instead of '*perish*') for the people.' There is certainly a considerable amount of ancient testimony in favour of this reading: for besides אBC, it is found in the Old Latin copies, the Egyptian, and Peshitto versions, besides the Lewis MS., the Chronicon, Cyril, Nonnus, Chrysostom. Yet may it be regarded as certain that St. John wrote ἀπολέσθαι in this place. The proper proof of the statement is the consentient voice of all the copies,—except about nineteen of loose character:—we know their vagaries but too well, and decline to let them impose upon us. In real fact, nothing else is ἀποθανεῖν but a critical assimilation of St. John xviii. 14 to xi. 50,—somewhat as 'die' in our A.V. has been retained by King James' translators, though they certainly had λέσθαι before them.

Many of these glosses are rank, patent, palpable. Such is the substitution (St. Mark vi. 11) of ὃς ἂν τόπος μὴ δέξηται ὑμᾶς by אBLΔ for ὅσοι ἂν μὴ δέξωνται ὑμᾶς,—which latter is the reading of the Old Latin and Peshitto, as well as of the whole body of uncials and cursives alike. Some Critic evidently considered that the words which follow, 'when you go out *thence*,' imply that *place*, not *persons*, should have gone before. Accordingly, he substituted '*whatsoever place*' for '*whosoever*[396]': another has bequeathed to us in four uncial MSS. a lasting record of his rashness and incompetency. Since however he left behind the words μηδὲ ἀκούσωσιν ὑμῶν, which immediately follow, who sees not that the fabricator has betrayed himself? I am astonished that so patent a fraud should have imposed upon Tischendorf, and Tregelles, and Lachmann, and Alford, and Westcott and Hort. But in fact it does not stand alone. From the same copies אBLΔ (with two others, CD) we find the woe denounced in the same verse on the unbelieving city erased (ἀμὴν λέγω ὑμῖν, ἀνεκτοτερον ἔσται Σοδόμοις ἤ Γομόρροις ἐν ἡμέρᾳ κρίσεως, ἤ τῇ πόλει ἐκείνῃ). Quite idle is it to pretend (with Tischendorf) that these words are an importation from the parallel place in St. Matthew. A memorable note of diversity has been set on the two places, which in *all* the copies is religiously maintained, viz. Σοδόμοις ἤ Γομόρροις, in St. Mark: γῇ Σοδόμων καὶ Γομόρρων, in St. Matt. It is simply incredible that this could have been done if the received text in this place had been of spurious origin.

§ 5.

The word ἀπέχει in St. Mark xiv. 41 has proved a stumbling-block. The most obvious explanation is probably the truest. After a brief pause[397], during which the Saviour has been content to survey in silence His sleeping disciples;—or perhaps, after telling them that they will have time and opportunity enough for sleep and rest when He shall have been taken from them;— He announces the arrival of 'the hour,' by exclaiming, Ἀπέχει,—'It is enough;' or, 'It is sufficient;' i.e. *The season for repose is over.*

But the Revisers' of the second century did not perceive that ἀπέχει is here used impersonally[398]. They understood the word to mean 'is fully come'; and supplied the supposed nominative, viz. τὸ τέλος[399]. Other critics who rightly understood ἀπέχει to signify 'sufficit,' still subjoined 'finis.' The Old Latin and the Syriac versions must have been executed from Greek copies which exhibited,— ἀπέχει τὸ τέλος. This is abundantly proved by the renderings *adest finis* (f),—*consummatus est finis* (a); from which the change to ἀπέχει τὸ τέλος KAI ἡ ὥρα (the reading of D) was obvious: *sufficit finis et hora* (d q); *adest enim consummatio; et* (ff² *venit*) *hora* (c); or, (as the Peshitto more fully gives it), *appropinquavit finis, et venit hora*[400]. Jerome put this matter straight by simply writing *sufficit*. But it is a suggestive circumstance, and an interesting proof how largely the reading ἀπέχει τὸ τέλος must once have prevailed, that it is frequently met with in cursive copies of the Gospels to this hour[401]. Happily it is an 'old reading' which finds no favour at the present day. It need not therefore occupy us any longer.

As another instance of ancient Glosses introduced to help out the sense, the reading of St. John ix. 22 is confessedly ἵνα ἐάν τις αὐτὸν ὁμολογήσῃ Χριστόν. So all the MSS. but one, and so the Old Latin. So indeed all the ancient versions except the Egyptian. Cod. D alone adds εἶναι: but εἶναι must once have been a familiar gloss: for Jerome retains it in the Vulgate: and indeed Cyril, whenever he quotes the place[402], exhibits τὸν Χριστὸν εἶναι. Not so however Chrysostom[403] and Gregory of Nyssa[404].

§ 6.

There is scarcely to be found, amid the incidents immediately preceding our Saviour's Passion, one more affecting or more exquisite than the anointing of His feet at Bethany by Mary the sister of Lazarus, which received its unexpected interpretation from the lips of Christ Himself. 'Let her alone. Against the day of My embalming hath she kept it.' (St. John xii. 7.) He assigns to her act a mysterious meaning of which the holy woman little dreamt. She had treasured up that precious unguent against the day,—(with the presentiment of true Love, she knew that it could not be very far distant),—when His dead limbs would require embalming. But lo, she beholds Him reclining at supper in her sister's house: and yielding to a Divine impulse she brings forth her reserved costly offering and bestows it on Him at once. Ah, she little knew,—she could not in fact have known,—that it was the only anointing those sacred feet were destined ever to enjoy! . . . . In the meantime through a desire, as I suspect, to bring this incident into an impossible harmony with what is recorded in St. Mark xvi. 1, with which obviously it has no manner of connexion, a scribe is found at some exceedingly remote period to have improved our Lord's expression into this:—'Let her alone in order that against the day of My embalming she may keep it.' Such an exhibition of the Sacred Text is its own sufficient condemnation. What that critic exactly meant, I fail to discover: but I am sure he has spoilt what he did not understand: and though it is quite true that ℵBD with five other Uncial MSS. and Nonnus, besides the Latin and Bohairic, Jerusalem, Armenian, and Ethiopic versions, besides four errant cursives so exhibit the place, this instead of commending the reading to our favour, only proves damaging to the witnesses by which it is upheld. We learn that no reliance is to be placed even in such a combination of authorities. This is one of the places which the Fathers pass by almost in silence. Chrysostom[405] however, and evidently Cyril Alex.[406], as well as Ammonius[407] convey though roughly a better sense by quoting the verse with ἐποίησε for τετήρηκεν. Antiochus[408] is express. [A and eleven other uncials, and the cursives (with the petty exception already noted), together with the Peshitto, Harkleian (which only notes the other reading in the margin), Lewis, Sahidic, and Gothic versions, form a body of authority against the palpable emasculation of the passage, which for number, variety, weight, and internal evidence is greatly superior to the opposing body. Also, with refer-

112

ence to continuity and antiquity it preponderates plainly, if not so decisively; and the context of D is full of blunders, besides that it omits the next verse, and B and ℵ are also inaccurate hereabouts[409]. So that the Traditional text enjoys in this passage the support of all the Notes of Truth.]

In accordance with what has been said above, for Ἄφες αὐτήν· εἰς τὴν ἡμέραν τοῦ ἐνταφιασμοῦ μου τετηρήκεν αὐτό (St. John xii. 7), the copies which it has recently become the fashion to adore, read ἄφες αὐτήν ἵνα . . . τηρήσῃ αὐτό. This startling innovation,—which destroys the sense of our Saviour's words, and furnishes a sorry substitute which no one is able to explain[410],—is accepted by recent Editors and some Critics: yet is it clearly nothing else but a stupid correction of the text,—introduced by some one who did not understand the intention of the Divine Speaker. Our Saviour is here discovering to us an exquisite circumstance,—revealing what until now had been a profound and tender secret: viz. that Mary, convinced by many a sad token that the Day of His departure could not be very far distant, had some time before provided herself with this costly ointment, and 'kept it' by her,—intending to reserve it against the dark day when it would be needed for the 'embalming' of the lifeless body of her Lord. And now it wants only a week to Easter. She beholds Him (with Lazarus at His side) reclining in her sister's house at supper, amid circumstances of mystery which fill her soul with awful anticipation. She divines, with love's true instinct, that this may prove her only opportunity. Accordingly, she 'anticipates to anoint' (προέλαβε μυρίσαι, St. Mark xiv. 8) His Body: and, yielding—to-an overwhelming impulse, bestows upon Him all her costly offering at once! . . . How does it happen that some professed critics have overlooked all this? Any one who has really studied the subject ought to know, from a mere survey of the evidence, on which side the truth in respect of the text of this passage must needs lie.

§ 7.

Our Lord, in His great Eucharistic address to the eternal Father, thus speaks:—I have glorified Thee on the earth. I have perfected the work which Thou gavest Me to do' (St. John xvii. 4). Two things are stated: first, that the result of His Ministry had been the exhibition upon earth of the Father's 'glory[411]': next, that the work which the Father had given the Son to do[412] was at last finished[413]. And that this is what St. John actually wrote is certain: not only because it is found in all the copies, except twelve of suspicious character (headed by ℵABCL); but because it is vouched for by the Peshitto[414] and the Latin, the Gothic and the Armenian versions[415]: besides a whole chorus of Fathers; viz. Hippolytus[416], Didymus[417], Eusebius[418], Athanasius[419], Basil[420], Chrysostom[421], Cyril[422], ps.-Polycarp[423], the interpolator of Ignatius[424], and the authors of the Apostolic Constitutions[425]: together with the following among the Latins:—Cyprian[426], Ambrose[427], Hilary[428], Zeno[429], Cassian[430], Novatian[431], certain Arians[432], Augustine[433].

But the asyndeton (so characteristic of the fourth Gospel) proving uncongenial to certain of old time, D inserted καὶ. A more popular device was to substitute the participle (τελειώσας) for ἐτελείωσα: whereby our Lord is made to say that He had glorified His Father's Name 'by perfecting' or 'completing'—'in that He had finished'—the work which the Father had given Him to do; which damages the sense by limiting it, and indeed introduces a new idea. A more patent gloss it would be hard to find. Yet has it been adopted as the genuine text by all the Editors and all the Critics. So general is the delusion in favour of any reading supported by the combined evidence of אABCL, that the Revisers here translate—'I glorified Thee on the earth, *having accomplished* (τελειώσας) the work which Thou hast given Me to do:' without so much as vouchsafing a hint to the English reader that they have altered the text.

When some came with the message 'Thy daughter is dead: why troublest thou the Master further?' the Evangelist relates that Jesus '*as soon as He heard* (εὐθέως ἀκούσας) what was being spoken, said to the ruler of the synagogue, Fear not: only believe.' (St. Mark v. 36.) For this, אBLΔ substitute 'disregarding (παρακούσας) what was being spoken': which is nothing else but a sorry gloss, disowned by every other copy, including ACD, and all the versions. Yet does παρακούσας find favour with Tischendorf, Tregelles, and others.

§ 8.

In this way it happened that in the earliest age the construction of St. Luke i. 66 became misapprehended. Some Western scribe evidently imagined that the popular saying concerning John Baptist,—τί ἄρα τὸ παιδίον τοῦτο ἔσται, extended further, and comprised the Evangelist's record,:—καὶ χεὶρ Κυρίου ἦν μετ' αὐτοῦ. To support this strange view, καί was altered into καὶ γὰρ, and ἐστὶ was substituted for ἦν. It is thus that the place stands in the Verona copy of the Old Latin (b). In other quarters the verb was omitted altogether: and that is how D, Evan. 59 with the Vercelli (a) and two other copies of the Old Latin exhibit the place. Augustine[434] is found to have read indifferently— 'manus enim Domini cum illo,' and 'cum illo est': but he insists that the combined clauses represent the popular utterance concerning the Baptist[435]. Unhappily, there survives a notable trace of the same misapprehension in א–BCL which, alone of MSS., read καὶ γὰρ ... ἦν[436]. The consequence might have been anticipated. All recent Editors adopt this reading, which however is clearly inadmissible. The received text, witnessed to by the Peshitto, Harkleian, and Armenian versions, is obviously correct. Accordingly, A and all the uncials not already named, together with the whole body of the cursives, so read the place. With fatal infelicity the Revisers exhibit 'For indeed the hand of the Lord was with him.' They clearly are to blame: for indeed the MS. evidence admits of no uncertainty. It is much to be regretted that not a single very ancient Greek Father (so far as I can discover) quotes the place.

§ 9.

It seems to have been anciently felt, in connexion with the first miraculous draught of fishes, that St. Luke's statement (v. 7) that the ships were so full that 'they were sinking' (ὥστε βυθίζεσθαι αὐτά) requires some qualification.

114

Accordingly C inserts ἤδη (were 'just' sinking); and D, παρα τι ('within a lit-tle'): while the Peshitto the Lewis and the Vulgate, as well as many copies of the Old Latin, exhibit 'ita ut *pene*.' These attempts to improve upon Scripture, and these paraphrases, indicate laudable zeal for the truthfulness of the Evangelist; but they betray an utterly mistaken view of the critic's office. The truth is, βυθίζεσθαι, as the Bohairic translators perceived and as most of us are aware, means 'were beginning to sink.' There is no need of further quali-fying the expression by the insertion with Eusebius[437] of any additional word.

I strongly suspect that the introduction of the name of 'Pyrrhus into Acts xx. 4 as the patronymic of 'Sopater of Beraea,' is to be accounted for in this way. A very early gloss it certainly is, for it appears in the Old Latin: yet, the Peshitto knows nothing of it, and the Harkleian rejects it from the text, though not from the margin. Origen and the Bohairic recognize it, but not Chrysostom nor the Ethiopic. I suspect that some foolish critic of the primi-tive age invented Πύρου (or Πύρρου) out of Βεροιαῖος (or Βερροιαῖος) which follows. The Latin form of this was 'Pyrus[438],' 'Pyrrhus,' or 'Pirrus[439].' In the Sahidic version he is called the 'son of Berus' (υἱὸς Βεροῦ),—which confirms me in my conjecture. But indeed, if it was with some *Beracan* that the gloss originated,—and what more likely?—it becomes an interesting circumstance that the inhabitants of that part of Macedonia are known to have confused the *p* and *b* sounds[440]. . . . This entire matter is unimportant in itself, but the letter of Scripture cannot be too carefully guarded: and let me invite the reader to consider,—If St. Luke actually wrote Σώπατρος Πύρρου Βεροιαῖος, why at the present day should five copies out of six record nothing of that second word?

[353] See The Traditional Text, pp. 51-52.
[354] St. Mark vi. 33. See The Traditional Text, p. 80.
[355] iii. 3 e: 4 b and c: 442 a: 481 b. Note, that the ῥῆσις in which the first three of these quotations occur seems to have been obtained by De la Rue from a Catena on St. Luke in the Mazarine Library (see his Monitum, iii. i). A large portion of it (viz. from p. 3, line 25, to p. 4, line 29) is ascribed to 'I. Geometra in Proverbia' in the Catena in Luc. of Corderius, p. 217.
[356] ii. 345.
[357] ii. 242.
[358] The Latin is *edissere* or *dissere*, *cnarra* or *narra*, both here and in xv. 15.

[359] iv. 254 a.
[360] In St. Matthew xiii. 36 the Peshitto Syriac has 'declare to us' and in St. Mat-thew xv. 15 the very same words, there being *no* various reading in either of these two passages.

The inference is, that the translators had the same Greek word in each place, especially considering that in the only other place where, besides St. Matt. xiii. 36, v. 1., διασαφεῖν occurs, viz. St. Matt. xviii. 31, they render διεσάφησαν by = they made known.

Since φράζειν only occurs in St. Matt. xiii. 36 and xv. 15, we cannot generalize about the Peshitto rendering of this verb. Conversely, is used as the render-ing of other Greek words besides φράζειν, e.g. of ἐπιλύειν, St. Mark iv.

34;
of διερμηνεύειν, St. Luke xxiv. 27;
of διανοίγειν, St. Luke xxiv. 32 and
Acts xvii. 3.

On the whole I have *no doubt* (though it is not susceptible of *proof*) that the Peshitto had, in both the places quoted above, φράσον. N.B. The Cureton and Lewis have, in St. Matt. xiii. 36, } = Peshitto. in ” xv. 15, ” in ” xviii. 31, for the διεσάφησαν, ,

The Cureton (Lewis defective) has a word often used in Syriac for 'shew,' 'declare.' [Rev. G. H. Gwilliam.]

361 In St. Mark vii. 3, the translators of the Peshitto render whatever Greek they had before them by, which means 'eagerly,' 'sedulously'; cf. use of the word for σπουδαίως, St. Luke vii. 4; ἐπιμελῶς, St. Luke xv. 8.

The Root means to 'cease'; thence 'to have leisure for a thing': it has nothing to do with 'Fist.' [Rev. G. H. Gwilliam.]

362 Harkl. Marg. *in loc.*, and Adler, p. 115.

363 Viz. a b c e ff² l q.

364 Ὀφείκει ψυχή, ἐν τῷ λόγῳ τοῦ Κυρίου κατακολουθοῦσα, τὸν σταυρὸν αὐτοῦ καθ' ἡμέραν αἴρειν, ὡς γέγραπται· τοῦτ' ἔστιν, ἑτοίμως ἔχουσα ὑπομένειν διὰ Χριστὸν πᾶσαν θλῖψιν καὶ πειρασμόν, κ.τ.λ. (ii. 326 e). In the same spirit, further on, he exhorts to constancy and patience,—τὸν ἐπὶ τοῦ Κυρίου θάνατον ἐν ἐπιθυμίᾳ πάντοτε πρὸ ὀφθαλμῶν ἔχοντες, καὶ (καθὼς εἴρηται ὑπὸ τοῦ Κυρίου) καθ' ἡμέραν τὸν σταυρὸν αἴροντες, ὅ ἐστι θάνατος (ii. 332 e). It is fair to assume that Ephraem's reference is to St. Luke ix. 23, seeing that he wrote not in Greek but in Syria; and that in the Peshitto the clause is found only in that place.

365 Ἄκουε Λουκᾶ λέγοντος,—i. 281 f. Also, int. iii. 543.

366 Pp. 221 (text), 222, 227.

367 ii. 751 e, 774 e (in Es.)—the proof that these quotations are from St. Luke; that Cyril exhibits ἀρνησάσθω instead of ἀπαρν. (see Tischendorf's note on St. Luke ix. 23). The quotation in i. 40 (Glaph.) *may* be from St. Matt. xvi. 24.

368 Migne, vol. lxxxvi. pp. 256 and 257.

369 After quoting St. Mark viii. 34,— 'aut juxta Lucam, *dicebat ad cunctos: Si quis vult post me venire, abneget semetipsum; et tollat crucem suam, et sequetur me.*'—i. 852 c.

This is found in his solution of *XI Quaestiones,* 'ad Algasiam,'—free translations probably from the Greek of some earlier Father. Six lines lower down (after quoting words found nowhere in the Gospels), Jerome proceeds:—'*Quotidie* credens in Christum *tollit crucem suam, et negat seipsum.*'

370 This spurious clause adorned the lost archetype of Evann. 13, 69, 346 (Ferrar's four); and survives in certain other Evangelia which enjoy a similar repute,—as 1, 33, 72 (with a marginal note of distrust), 131.

371 They are St. Matt. xvi. 24: St. Mark viii. 34.

372 i. 597 c (Adorat.)—elsewhere (viz. i. 21 d: 528 c: 580 b: iv. 1058 a; v². 83 c) Cyril quotes the place correctly. Note, that the quotation found in Mai, iii. 226, which Pusey edits (v. 418), in Ep. ad Hebr., is nothing else but an excerpt from the treatise de Adorat. 528 c.

373 In his Commentary on St. Matt. xvi. 24:—Διὰ παντὸς τοῦ βίου τοῦτο δεῖ ποιεῖν. Διηνεκῶς γάρ, φησι, περίφερε τὸν θάνατον τοῦτον, καὶ καθ' ἡμέραν ἕτοιμος ἔσο πρὸς σφαγήν (vii. 557 b). Again, commenting on ch. xix. 21,—Δεῖ προηγουμένως ἀκολουθεῖν τῷ Χριστῷ· τουτέστι, πάντα τὰ παρ' αὐτοῦ κελευόμενα ποιεῖν, πρὸς σφαγὰς εἶνα ἕτοιμον, καὶ θάνατον καθημερινόν (p. 629 e):—words which Chrysostom

immediately follows up by quoting ch. xvi. 24 (630 a).

374   i. 949 b,—'*Quotidie* (inquit Apostolus) *morior propter vestram salutem. Et Dominus, juxta antiqua exemplaria, Nisi quis tulerit crucem suam quotidie, et sequutus fuerit me, non potest meus esse discipulus.*' — Commenting on St. Matt. x. 38 (vol. vii. p. 65 b), Jerome remarks,—'in alio Evangelio scribitur,—*Qui non accipit crucem suam quotidie*': but the corresponding place to St. Matt. x. 38, in the sectional system of Eusebius (Greek and Syriac), is St. Luke xiv. 27.

375   Viz. Evan. 473 (2ᵖᵒ).

376   ii. 66 c, d.

377   See above, p. 175, note 2.

378   Proleg. p. cxlvi.

379   N. T. (1803), i. 368.

380   Lewis here agrees with Peshitto.

381   iv. 745.

382   In Ps. 501.

383   229 and 236.

384   vii. 736: xi. 478.

385   ii. 1209.

386   269.

387   577.

388   i. 881.

389   *Ap.* vi. 460.

390   *Ap.* Greg. Nyss. ii. 258.

391   Galland. vi. 53.

392   ii. 346.

393   ii. 261, 324.

394   *Ap.* Greg. Nyss. iii. 429.

395   i. 132.

396   The attentive student of the Gospels will recognize with interest how gracefully the third Evangelist St. Luke (ix. 5) has overcome this difficulty.

397   Augustine, with his accustomed acuteness, points out that St. Mark's narrative shews that after the words of 'Sleep on now and take your rest,' our Lord must have been silent for a brief space in order to allow His disciples a slight prolongation of the refreshment which his words had already permitted them to enjoy. Presently, He is heard to say,—'It is enough'—(that is, 'Ye have now slept and rested enough'); and adds, 'The hour is come. Behold, the Son of Man is betrayed into the hands of sinners.' 'Sed quia commemorata non est ipsa interpositio silentii Domini, propterea coartat intellectum, ut in illis verbis alia pronuntiatio requiratur.'—iii². 106 a, b. The passage in question runs thus;—Καθείδετε τὸ λοιπὸν καὶ ἀναπαύεσθε. ἀπέχει· ἦλθεν ἡ ὥρα· ἰδού. κ.τ.λ..

398   Those who saw this, explain the word amiss. Note the Scholion (Anon. Vat.) in Possinus, p. 321:—ἀπέχει, τουτέστι, πεπλήρωται, τέλος ἔχει τὸ κατ' ἐμέ., Last Twelve Verses, p. 226, note.

399   I retract unreservedly what I offered on this subject in a former work (Last Twelve Verses, &c., pp. 225, 226). I was misled by one who seldom indeed misleads,—the learned editor of the Codex Bezae (*in loco*).

400   So Peshitto. Lewis, *venit hora, appropinquat finis.* Harkleian, *adest consummatio, venit hora.*

401   απεχει. Vg. *sufficit.* + το τελος, 13, 69, 124, 2ᴾᵉ, cˢᵉʳ, 47, 54, 56, 61, 184, 346, 348, 439. d, q, *sufficit finis et hora.* f, *adest finis, venit hora.* c, ff², *adest enim consummatio,* et (ff² venit) *hora.* a, *consummatus est finis, advenit hora.* It is certain that one formidable source of danger to the sacred text has been its occasional obscurity. This has resulted,—(1) sometimes in the omission of words: Δευτερόπρωτον. (2) Sometimes in substitution, as πυγμῇ. (3) Sometimes in the insertion of unauthorized matter: thus, τὸ τέλος, as above.

402   iii. 105: iv. 913. So also iv. 614.

403   vi. 283.

404   i. 307.

405   viii. 392.

406 iv. 696.

407 Cramer's Cat. *in loc.*

408 1063.

409 E.g. ver. 1. All the three officiously insert (ὁ Ἰησοῦς, in order to prevent people from imagining that Lazarus raised Lazarus from the dead; ver. 4, D gives the gloss, ἀπὸ Καρυώτου for Ἰσκαρίωτης; ver. 13, spells thus,— ὡσσανά; besides constant inaccuracies, in which it is followed by none. א omits nineteen words in the first thirty-two verses of the chapter, besides adding eight and making other alterations. B is far from being accurate.

410 'Let her alone, that she may keep it against the day of My burying' (Alford). But how *could* she keep it after she had poured it all out?—'Suffer her to have kept it against the day of My preparation unto burial' (McClellan). But ἵνα τηρήσῃ could hardly mean that: and the day of His ἐνταφιασμός had not yet arrived.

411 Consider ii. 11 and xi. 40: St. Luke xiii. 17: Heb. i. 3.

412 Consider v. 36 and iv. 34.

413 Consider St. John xix. 30. Cf. St. Luke xxii. 37.

414 Lewis, 'and the work I have perfected': Harkleian, "because the work, &c., "because' being obelized.

415 The Bohairic and Ethiopic are hostile.

416 i. 245 (= Constt. App. viii. i; *ap.* Galland. iii. 199).

417 P. 419.

418 M^cell p. 157.

419 i. 534.

420 ii. 196, 238: iii. 39.

421 v. 256: viii. 475 *bis.*

422 iii. 542: iv. 954: v1. 599, 601, 614: v2. 152.—In the following places Cyril shews himself acquainted with the other reading,—iv. 879: v1. 167, 366: vi. 124.

423 Polyc. frg. v (ed. Jacobson).

424 Ps.-Ignat. 328.

425 *Ap.* Gall. iii. 215.

426 P. 285.

427 ii. 545.

428 Pp. 510, 816, 1008. But *opere consummato*, pp. 812, 815.—Jerome also once (iv. 563) has *opere completo.*

429 *Ap.* Gall. v. 135.

430 P. 367.

431 *Ap.* Gall. iii. 308.

432 *Ap.* Aug. viii. 622.

433 iii2. 761: viii. 640.

434 v. 1166.

435 Ibid. 1165 g, 1165 a.

436 Though the Bohairic, Gothic, Vulgate, and Ethiopic versions are disfigured in the same way, and the Lewis reads 'is.'

437 Theoph. 216 note: ὡς κινδυνεύειν αὐτὰ βυθισθῆναι.

438 Cod. Amiat.

439 g,—at Stockholm.

440 Stephanus De Urbibus in voc. Βέροια.

Chapter Thirteen - Causes of Corruption Chiefly Intentional - IX. Corruption by Heretics

§ 1.

THE Corruptions of the Sacred Text which we have been hitherto considering, however diverse the causes from which they may have resulted, have yet all agreed in this: viz. that they have all been of a lawful nature. My meaning is, that apparently, at no stage of the business has there been *mala fides* in any quarter. We are prepared to make the utmost allowance for careless, even for licentious transcription; and we can invent excuses for the mistaken zeal, the officiousness if men prefer to call it so, which has occasionally not scrupled to adopt conjectural emendations of the Text. To be brief, so long as an honest reason is discoverable for a corrupt reading, we gladly adopt the plea. It has been shewn with sufficient clearness, I trust, in the course of the foregoing chapters, that the number of distinct causes to which various readings may reasonably be attributed is even extraordinary.

But there remains after all an alarmingly large assortment of textual perturbations which absolutely refuse to fall under any of the heads of classification already enumerated. They are not to be accounted for on any ordinary principle. And this residuum of cases it is, which occasions our present embarrassment. They are in truth so exceedingly numerous; they are often so very considerable; they are, as a rule, so very licentious; they transgress to such an extent all regulations; they usurp so persistently the office of truth and faithfulness, that we really know not what to think about them. Sometimes we are presented with gross interpolations,—apocryphal stories: more often with systematic lacerations of the text, or transformations as from an angel of light.

We are constrained to inquire, How all this can possibly have come about? Have there even been persons who made it their business of set purpose to corrupt the [sacred deposit of Holy Scripture entrusted to the Church for the perpetual illumination of all ages till the Lord should come?]

At this stage of the inquiry, we are reminded that it is even notorious that in the earliest age of all, the New Testament Scriptures were subjected to such influences. In the age which immediately succeeded the Apostolic there were heretical teachers not a few, who finding their tenets refuted by the plain Word of God bent themselves against the written Word with all their power. From seeking to evacuate its teaching, it was but a single step to seeking to falsify its testimony. Profane literature has never been exposed to such hostility. I make the remark in order also to remind the reader of one more point of [dissimilarity between the two classes of writings. The inestimable value of the New Testament entailed greater dangers, as well as secured superior safeguards. Strange, that a later age should try to discard the latter].

It is found therefore that Satan could not even wait for the grave to close over St. John. 'Many' there were already who taught that Christ had not come in the flesh. Gnosticism was in the world already. St. Paul denounces it by name[441] and significantly condemns the wild fancies of its professors, their dangerous speculations as well as their absurd figments. Thus he predicts and condemns[442] their pestilential teaching in respect of meats and drinks and concerning matrimony. In his Epistle to Timothy[443] he relates that Hymeneus and Philetus taught that the Resurrection was past already. What wonder if a flood of impious teaching[444] broke loose on the Church when the last of the Apostles had been gathered in, and another generation of men had arisen, and the age of Miracles was found to be departing if it had not already departed[445], and the loftiest boast which any could make was that they had known those who had [seen and heard the Apostles of the Lord].

The 'grievous wolves' whose assaults St. Paul predicted as imminent, and against which he warned the heads of the Ephesian Church[446], did not long 'spare the flock.' Already, while St. John was yet alive, had the Nicolaitans developed their teaching at Ephesus[447] and in the neighbouring Church of Pergamos[448]. Our risen Lord in glory announced to His servant John that in the latter city Satan had established his dwelling-place[449]. Nay, while those awful words were being spoken to the Seer of Patmos, the men were already born who first dared to lay their impious hands on the Gospel of Christ.

No sooner do we find ourselves out of Apostolic lines and among monuments of the primitive age than we are made aware that the sacred text must have been exposed at that very early period to disturbing influences which, on no ordinary principles, can be explained. Justin Martyr, Irenaeus, Origen, Clement of Alexandria,—among the Fathers: some Old Latin MSS.[450], the Bohairic and Sahidic, and coming later on, the Curetonian and Lewis,—among the Versions: of the copies Codd. B and ℵ: and above all, coming later down still, Cod. D:—these venerable monuments of a primitive age occasionally present us with deformities which it is worse than useless to extenuate,—quite impossible to overlook. Unauthorized appendixes, —tasteless and stupid amplifications,—plain perversions of the meaning of the Evangelists,—wholly gratuitous assimilations of one Gospel to another,—the unprovoked omission of passages of profound interest and not unfrequently of high doctrinal import:—How are such phenomena as these to be accounted for? Again, in one quarter, we light upon a systematic mutilation of the text so extraordinary that it is as if some one had amused himself by running his pen through every clause which was not absolutely necessary to the intelligibleness of what remained. In another quarter we encounter the thrusting in of fabulous stories and apocryphal sayings which disfigure as well as encumber the text.—How will any one explain all this?

Let me however at the risk of repeating what has been already said dispose at once of an uneasy suspicion which is pretty sure to suggest itself to a person of intelligence after reading what goes before. If the most primitive witnesses to our hand are indeed discovered to bear false witness to the text of Scripture,—whither are we to betake ourselves for the Truth? And what security can we hope ever to enjoy that any given exhibition of the text of Scripture is the true one? Are we then to be told that in this subject-matter the maxim 'id verius quod prius' does not hold? that the stream instead of getting purer as we approach the fountain head, on the contrary grows more and more corrupt?

Nothing of the sort, I answer. The direct reverse is the case. Our appeal is always made to antiquity; and it is nothing else but a truism to assert that the oldest reading is also the best. A very few words will make this matter clear;

because a very few words will suffice to explain a circumstance already adverted to which it is necessary to keep always before the eyes of the reader.

The characteristic note, the one distinguishing feature, of all the monstrous and palpable perversions of the text of Scripture just now under consideration is this:—that they are never vouched for by the oldest documents generally, but only by a few of them,—two, three, or more of the oldest documents being observed as a rule to yield conflicting testimony, (which in this subject-matter is in fact contradictory). In this way the oldest witnesses nearly always refute one another, and indeed dispose of one another's evidence almost as often as that evidence is untrustworthy. And now I may resume and proceed.

I say then that it is an adequate, as well as a singularly satisfactory explanation of the greater part of those gross depravations of Scripture which admit of no legitimate excuse, to attribute them, however remotely, to those licentious free-handlers of the text who are declared by their contemporaries to have falsified, mutilated, interpolated, and in whatever other way to have corrupted the Gospel; whose blasphemous productions of necessity must once have obtained a very wide circulation: and indeed will never want some to recommend and uphold them. What with those who like Basilides and his followers invented a Gospel of their own:—what with those who with the Ebionites and the Valentinians interpolated and otherwise perverted one of the four Gospels until it suited their own purposes:—what with those who like Marcion shamefully maimed and mutilated the inspired text:—there must have been a large mass of corruption festering in the Church throughout the immediate post-Apostolic age. But even this is not all. There were those who like Tatian constructed Diatessarons, or attempts to weave the fourfold narrative into one,—'Lives of Christ,' so to speak;—and productions of this class were multiplied to an extraordinary extent, and as we certainly know, not only found their way into the remotest corners of the Church, but established themselves there. And will any one affect surprise if occasionally a curious scholar of those days was imposed upon by the confident assurance that by no means were those many sources of light to be indiscriminately rejected, but that there must be some truth in what they advanced? In a singularly uncritical age, the seductive simplicity of one reading,—the interesting fullness of another,—the plausibility of a third,—was quite sure to recommend its acceptance amongst those many eclectic recensions which were constructed by long since forgotten Critics, from which the most depraved and worthless of our existing texts and versions have been derived. Emphatically condemned by Ecclesiastical authority, and hopelessly outvoted by the universal voice of Christendom, buried under fifteen centuries, the corruptions I speak of survive at the present day chiefly in that little handful of copies which, calamitous to relate, the school of Lachmann and Tischendorf and Tregelles look upon as oracular: and in conformity with which many scholars are for refashioning the Evangelical text under the mistaken title of 'Old Readings.' And now to proceed with my argument.

§ 2.

Numerous as were the heresies of the first two or three centuries of the Christian era, they almost all agreed in this;—that they involved a denial of the eternal Godhead of the Son of Man: denied that He is essentially very and eternal God. This fundamental heresy found itself hopelessly confuted by the whole tenor of the Gospel, which nevertheless it assailed with restless ingenuity: and many are the traces alike of its impotence and of its malice which have survived to our own times. It is a memorable circumstance that it is precisely those very texts which relate either to the eternal generation of the Son,—to His Incarnation,—or to the circumstances of His Nativity, —which have suffered most severely, and retain to this hour traces of having been in various ways tampered with. I do not say that Heretics were the only offenders here. I am inclined to suspect that the orthodox were as much to blame as the impugners of the Truth. But it was at least with a pious motive that the latter tampered with the Deposit. They did but imitate the example set them by the assailing party. It is indeed the calamitous consequence of extravagances in one direction that they are observed ever to beget excesses in the opposite quarter. Accordingly the piety of the primitive age did not think it wrong to fortify the Truth by the insertion, suppression, or substitution of a few words in any place from which danger was apprehended. In this way, I am persuaded, many an unwarrantable 'reading' is to be explained. I do not mean that 'marginal glosses have frequently found their way into the text':— that points to a wholly improbable account of the matter. I mean, that expressions which seemed to countenance heretical notions, or at least which had been made a bad use of by evil men, were deliberately falsified. But I must not further anticipate the substance of the next chapter.

The men who first systematically depraved the text of Scripture, were as we now must know the heresiarchs Basilides (fl. 134), Valentinus (fl. 140), and Marcion (fl. 150): three names which Origen is observed almost invariably to enumerate together. Basilides[451] and Valentinus[452] are even said to have written Gospels of their own. Such a statement is not to be severely pressed: but the general fact is established by the notices, and those are exceedingly abundant, which the writers against Heresies have cited and left on record. All that is intended by such statements is that these old heretics retained, altered, transposed, just so much as they pleased of the fourfold Gospel: and further, that they imported whatever additional matter they saw fit:—not that they rejected the inspired text entirely, and substituted something of their own invention in its place[453]. And though, in the case of Valentinus, it has been contended, apparently with reason, that he probably did not individually go to the same length as Basilides,—who, as well in respect of St. Paul's Epistles as of the four Gospels, was evidently a grievous offender[454],—yet, since it is clear that his principal followers, who were also his contemporaries, put forth a composition which they were pleased to style the 'Gospel of Truth[455],' it is idle to dispute as to the limit of the rashness and impiety of the individual author of the heresy. Let it be further stated, as no slight confirmation of the view already hazarded as to the probable contents of the (so-called) Gospels of Basilides and of Valentinus, that one particular Gospel is related to have been preferred before the rest and specially adopted by certain schools of ancient Heretics. Thus, a strangely mutilated and depraved text of St. Matthew's Gospel is related to have found especial favour with the Ebionites[456], with whom the Corinthians are associated by Epiphanius: though Irenaeus seems to say that it was St. Mark's Gospel which was adopted by the heretical followers of Cerinthus. Marcion's deliberate choice of St. Luke's Gospel is sufficiently well known. The Valentinians appropriated to themselves St. John[457]. Heracleon, the most distinguished disciple of this school, is deliberately censured by Origen for having corrupted the text of the fourth Evangelist in many places[458]. A considerable portion of his Commentary on St. John has been preserved to us: and a very strange production it is found to have been.

Concerning Marcion, who is a far more conspicuous personage, it will be necessary to speak more particularly. He has left a mark on the text of Scripture of which traces are distinctly recognizable at the present day[459]. A great deal more is known about him than about any other individual of his school. Justin Martyr and Irenaeus wrote against him: besides Origen and Clement of Alexandria, Tertullian in the West[460], and Epiphanius in the East, elaborately refuted his teaching, and give us large information as to his method of handling Scripture.

Another writer of this remote time who, as I am prone to think, must have exercised sensible influence on the text of Scripture was Ammonius of Alexandria.

But Tatian beyond every other early writer of antiquity [appears to me to have caused alterations in the Sacred Text.]

It is obviously no answer to anything that has gone before to insist that the Evangelium of Marcion (for instance), so far as it is recognizable by the notices of it given by Epiphanius, can very rarely indeed be shewn to have resembled any extant MS. of the Gospels. Let it be even freely granted that many of the charges brought against it by Epiphanius with so much warmth, collapse when closely examined and severely sifted. It is to be remembered that Marcion's Gospel was known to be an heretical production: one of the many creations of the Gnostic age,—it must have been universally execrated and abhorred by faithful men. Besides this lacerated text of St. Luke's Gospel, there was an Ebionite recension of St. Matthew: a Cerinthian exhibition of St. Mark: a Valentinian perversion of St. John. And we are but insisting that the effect of so many corruptions of the Truth, industriously propagated within far less than 100 years of the date of the inspired verities themselves, must needs have made itself sensibly felt. Add the notorious fact, that in the second and third centuries after the Christian era the text of the Gospels is found to have been grossly corrupted even in orthodox quarters,—and that traces of these gross corruptions are discoverable in certain circles to the present hour,—and it seems impossible not to connect the two phenomena together.

The wonder rather is that, at the end of so many centuries, we are able distinctly to recognize any evidence whatever.

The proneness of these early Heretics severally to adopt one of the four Gospels for their own, explains why there is no consistency observable in the corruptions they introduced into the text. It also explains the bringing into one Gospel of things which of right clearly belong to another—as in St. Mark iii. 14 οὓς καὶ ἀποστόλους ὠνόμασεν.

I do not propose (as will presently appear) in this way to explain any considerable number of the actual corruptions of the text: but in no other way is it possible to account for such systematic mutilations as are found in Cod. B,—such monstrous additions as are found in Cod. D,—such gross perturbations as are continually met with in one or more, but never in all, of the earliest Codexes extant, as well as in the oldest Versions and Fathers.

The plan of Tatian's Diatessaron will account for a great deal. He indulges in frigid glosses, as when about the wine at the feast of Cana in Galilee he reads that the servants knew 'because they had drawn the water'; or in tasteless and stupid amplifications, as in the going back of the Centurion to his house. I suspect that the τί με ἐρωτᾷς περὶ τοῦ ἀγαθοῦ, 'Why do you ask me about that which is good?' is to be referred to some of these tamperers with the Divine Word.

§ 3.

These professors of 'Gnosticism' held no consistent theory. The two leading problems on which they exercised their perverse ingenuity are found to have been (1) the origin of Matter, and (2) the origin of Evil.

(1) They taught that the world's artificer ('the Word') was Himself a creature of the 'Father[461].' Encountered on the threshold of the Gospel by the plain declaration that, 'In the beginning was the Word: and the Word was with God: and the Word was God': and presently, 'All things were made by Him';—they were much exercised. The expedients to which they had recourse were certainly extraordinary. That 'Beginning' (said Valentinus) was the first thing which 'the Father' created: which He called 'Only begotten Son,' and also 'God' and in whom he implanted the germ of all things. Seminally, that is, whatsoever subsequently came into being was in Him. 'The Word' (he said) was a product of this first-created thing. And 'All things were made by Him,' because in 'the Word' was the entire essence of all the subsequent worlds (Aeons), to which he assigned forms[462]. From which it is plain that, according to Valentinus, 'the Word' was distinct from 'the Son'; who was *not* the world's Creator. Both alike, however, he acknowledged to be 'God[463]': but only, as we have seen already, using the term in an inferior sense.

Heracleon, commenting on St. John i. 3, insists that 'all things' can but signify this perishable world and the things that are therein: not essences of a loftier nature. Accordingly, after the words 'and without Him was not anything made,' he ventures to interpolate this clause,—of the things that are in the world and in the creation[464].' True, that the Evangelist had declared with unmistakable emphasis, 'and without Him was not anything' (literally, 'was not even one thing ') 'made that was made.' But instead of 'not even one thing,' the Valentinian Gnostics appear to have written 'nothing[465]'; and the concluding clause 'that was made,' because he found it simply unmanageable, Valentinus boldly severed from its context, making it the beginning of a fresh sentence. With the Gnostics, ver. 4 is found to have begun thus,— 'What was made in Him was life.'

Of the change of οὐδὲ ἕν into οὐδέν[466] traces survive in many of the Fathers[467]: but ℵ and D are the only Uncial MSS. which are known to retain that corrupt reading.—The uncouth sentence which follows (ὃ γέγονεν ἐν αὐτῷ ζωὴ ἦν), singular to relate, was generally tolerated, became established in many quarters, and meets us still at every step. It was evidently put forward so perseveringly by the Gnostics, with whom it was a kind of article of the faith, that the orthodox at last became too familiar with it. Epiphanius, though he condemns it, once employs it[468]. Occurring first in a fragment of Valentinus[469]: next, in the Commentary of Heracleon[470]: after that, in the pages of Theodotus the Gnostic (A.D. 192)[471]: then, in an exposure by Hippolytus of the tenets of the Naäseni[472], (a subsection of the same school);— the baseness of its origin at least is undeniable. But inasmuch as the words may be made to bear a loyal interpretation, the heretical construction of St. John i. 3 was endured by the Church for full 200 years. Clemens Alex. is observed thrice to adopt it[473]: Origen[474] and Eusebius[475] fall into it repeatedly. It is found in Codd. ℵCD: apparently in Cod. A, where it fills one line exactly. Cyril comments largely on it[476]. But as fresh heresies arose which the depraved text seemed to favour, the Church bestirred herself and remonstrated. It suited the Arians and the Macedonians[477], who insisted that the Holy Ghost is a creature. The former were refuted by Epiphanius, who points out that the sense is not complete until you have read the words ὃ γέγονεν. A fresh sentence (he says) begins at ἐν αὐτῷ ζωὴ ἦν[478]. Chrysostom deals with the latter. 'Let us beware of putting the full stop' (he says) 'at the words οὐδὲ ἕν,—as do the heretics. In order to make out that the Spirit is a creature, they read ὃ γέγονεν ἐν αὐτῷ ζωὴ ἦν: by which means the Evangelist's meaning becomes unintelligible[479].'

But in the meantime, Valentinus, whose example was followed by Theodotus and by at least two of the Gnostic sects against whom Hippolytus wrote, had gone further, The better to conceal St. John's purpose, the heresiarch falsified the inspired text. In the place of, 'What was made in Him, was life,' he substituted 'What was made in Him, is life.' Origen had seen copies so depraved, and judged the reading not altogether improbable. Clement, on a single occasion, even adopted it. It was the approved reading of the Old Latin versions,—a memorable indication, by the way, of a quarter from which the Old Latin derived their texts,—which explains why it is found in Cyprian, Hilary, and Augustine; and why Ambrose has so elaborately vindicated its sufficiency. It also appears in the Sahidic and in Cureton's Syriac; but not in the Peshitto, nor in the Vulgate. [Nor in the Bohairic.] In the meantime, the only

Greek Codexes which retain this singular trace of the Gnostic period at the present day, are Codexes ℵ and D.

§ 4.

[We may now take some more instances to shew the effects of the operations of Heretics.]

The good Shepherd in a certain place (St. John x. 14, 15) says concerning Himself—'I know My sheep and am known of Mine, even as the Father knoweth Me and I know the Father': by which words He hints at a mysterious knowledge as subsisting between Himself and those that are His. And yet it is worth observing that whereas He describes the knowledge which subsists between the Father and the Son in language which implies that it is strictly identical on either side, He is careful to distinguish between the knowledge which subsists between the creature and the Creator by slightly varying the expression,—thus leaving it to be inferred that it is not, neither indeed can be, on either side the same. God knoweth us with a perfect knowledge. Our so-called 'knowledge' of God is a thing different not only in degree, but in kind[480]. Hence the peculiar form which the sentence assumes[481]:—γινώσκω τὰ ἐμά, καὶ γινώσκομαι ὑπὸ τῶν ἐμῶν And this delicate diversity of phrase has been faithfully retained all down the ages, being witnessed to at this hour by every MS. in existence except four now well known to us: viz. ℵBDL. The Syriac also retains it,—as does Macarius[482], Gregory Naz.[483], Chrysostom[484], Cyril[485], Theodoret[486], Maximus[487]. It is a point which really admits of no rational doubt: for does any one suppose that if St. John had written 'Mine own know Me,' 996 MSS. out of 1000 at the end of 1,800 years would exhibit, 'I am known of Mine'?

But in fact it is discovered that these words of our Lord experienced depravation at the hands of the Manichaean heretics. Besides inverting the clauses, (and so making it appear that such knowledge begins on the side of Man,) Manes (A.D. 261) obliterated the peculiarity above indicated. Quoting from his own fabricated Gospel, he acquaints us with the form in which these words were exhibited in that mischievous production: viz. γινώσκει με τὰ ἐμά, καὶ γινώσκω τὰ ἐμά. This we learn from Epiphanius and from Basil[488]. Cyril, in a paper where he makes clear reference to the same heretical Gospel, insists that the order of knowledge must needs be the reverse of what the heretics pretended[489].—But then, it is found that certain of the orthodox contented themselves with merely reversing the clauses, and so restoring the true order of the spiritual process discussed —regardless of the exquisite refinement of expression to which attention was called at the outset. Copies must once have abounded which represented our Lord as saying, 'I know My own and My own know Me, even as the Father knoweth Me and I know the Father'; for it is the order of the Old Latin, Bohairic, Sahidic, Ethiopic, Lewis, Georgian, Slavonic, and Gothic, though not of the Peshitto, Harkleian, and Armenian; and Eusebius[490], Nonnus, and even Basil[491] so read the place. But no token of this clearly corrupt reading survives in any known copy of the Gospels,—except ℵBDL. Will it be believed that nevertheless all the recent

126

Editors of Scripture since Lachman insist on obliterating this refinement of language, and going back to the reading which the Church has long since deliberately rejected,—to the manifest injury of the deposit? 'Many words about a trifle,'—some will be found to say. Yes, to deny God's truth is a very facile proceeding. Its rehabilitation always requires many words. I request only that the affinity between אBDL and the Latin copies which universally exhibit this disfigurement[492], may be carefully noted. [Strange to say, the true reading receives no notice from Westcott and Hort, or the Revisers[493].]

§ 5. DOCTRINAL.

The question of Matrimony was one of those on which the early heretics freely dogmatized. Saturninus[494] (A.D. 120) and his followers taught that marriage was a production of Hell.

We are not surprised after this to find that those places in the Gospel which bear on the relation between man and wife exhibit traces of perturbation. I am not asserting that the heretics themselves depraved the text. I do but state two plain facts: viz. (1) That whereas in the second century certain heretical tenets on the subject of Marriage prevailed largely, and those who advocated as well as those who opposed such teaching relied chiefly on the Gospel for their proofs: (2) It is accordingly found that not only does the phenomenon of 'various readings' prevail in those places of the Gospel which bear most nearly on the disputed points, but the 'readings' are exactly of that suspicious kind which would naturally result from a tampering with the text by men who had to maintain, or else to combat, opinions of a certain class. I proceed to establish what I have been saying by some actual examples[495].

St. Matt. xix. 29.	St. Mark x. 29.	St. Luke xviii. 29.
η γυναικα,	η γυναικα,	η γυναικα,
—BD abc Orig.	—אBDΔ, abc, &c.	all allow it.

ὅταν δὲ λέγῃ· ὅτι "πᾶς ὅστις ἀφῆκε γυναῖκα," οὐ τοῦτό φησιν, ὥστε ἁπλῶς διασπᾶσθαι τοὺς γάμους, κ.τ.λ. Chrys. vii. 636 E.

Παραδειγματίσαι (in St. Matt. i. 19) is another of the expressions which have been disturbed by the same controversy. I suspect that Origen is the author (see the heading of the Scholion in Cramer's Catenae) of a certain uncritical note which Eusebius reproduces in his 'quaestiones ad Stephanum[496]' on the difference between δειγματίσαι and παραδειγματίσαι; and that with him originated the substitution of the uncompounded for the compounded verb in this place. Be that as it may, Eusebius certainly read παραδειγματίσαι (Dem. 320), with all the uncials but two (BZ): all the cursives but one (1). Will it be believed that Lachmann, Tregelles, Tischendorf, Alford, Westcott and Hort, on such slender evidence as that are prepared to reconstruct the text of St. Matthew's Gospel?

It sounds so like trifling with a reader's patience to invite his attention to an elaborate discussion of most of the changes introduced into the text by Tischendorf and his colleagues, that I knowingly pass over many hundreds of instances where I am nevertheless perfectly well aware of my own strength,—my opponent's weakness. Such discussions in fact become un-bearable when the points in dispute are confessedly trivial. No one however will deny that when three consecutive words of our LORD are challenged they are worth contending for. We are invited then to believe (St. Luke xxii. 67-8) that He did not utter the bracketed words in the following sentence,—'If I tell you, ye will not believe; and if I ask you, ye will not answer (Me, nor let Me go).' Now, I invite the reader to inquire for the grounds of this asser-tion. Fifteen of the uncials (including AD), and every known cursive, besides all the Latin and all the Syriac copies recognize the bracketed words. They are only missing in אBLT and their ally the Bohairic. Are we nevertheless to be assured that the words are to be regarded as spurious? Let the reader then be informed that Marcion left out seven words more (viz. all from, 'And if I ask you' to the end), and will he doubt either that the words are genuine or that their disappearance from four copies of bad character, as proved by their constant evidence, and from one version is sufficiently explained?

441 ψευδωνύμου γνώσεως 1 Tim. vi. 20.

442 1 Tim. iv. 1-3.

443 ii. 17.

444 γενεαλογίαι 1 Tim. i. 4: Titus iii. 9. Dangerous speculation (ἃ μὴ ἑώρακεν ἐμβατεύων Col. ii. 18). 'Old wives' fa-bles' (2 Tim : iv. 7. Tit. i. 24).

445 See the fragment of Irenaeus in Euseb. H. E. i .

446 Acts xx. 29.

447 Rev. ii. 6.

448 Rev. ii. 15.

449 Rev. ii. 13.

450 Chiefly the Low Latin amongst them. Tradit. Text. chap. vii. p. 137.

451 'Ausus fuit et Basilides scribere Evangelium, et suo illud nomine titulare.'— Orig. Opp. iii. 933 c: Iren. 23: Clem. Al. 409, 426, 506, 509, 540, 545: Tertull. c. 46: Epiph. 24: Theodor. i. 4.

452 'Evangelium habet etiam suum, praeter haec nostra' (De Praescript., ad calcem).

453 Origen (commenting on St. Luke x. 25-28) says,—ταῦτα δὲ εἴρηται πρὸς τοὺς ἀπὸ Οὐαλεντίνου, καὶ Βασιλίδου, καὶ τοὺς ἀπὸ Μαρκίωνος. ἔχουσι γὰρ καὶ αὐτοὶ τὰς λέξεις ἐν τῷ καθ᾽ ἑαυτοὺς εὐαγγελίῳ. Opp. iii. 981 A.

454 'Licet non sint digni fide, qui fidem primam irritam fecerunt, Marcionem loquor et Basilidem et omnes Haereticos qui vetus laniant Testamentum: tamen eos aliqua ex parte ferremus, si saltem in novo continerent manus suas; et non auderent Christi (ut ipsi iactitant) boni Dei Filii, vel Evangelistas violare, vel Apostolos. Nunc vero, quum et Evangelia eius dissipaverint; et Apostolorum epistolas, non Apostolorum Christi fecerunt esse, sed proprias; miror quomodo sibi Christianorum nomen audeant vindicare. Ut enim de caeteris Epistolis taceam, (de quibus quidquid contrarium suo dogmati viderant, evaserunt, nonnullas integras repudiandas crediderunt); ad Timotheum videlicet utramque, ad Hebraeos, et ad Titum, quam nunc conamur exponere.' Hieron. Praef. ad Titum.

455 'Hi vero, qui sunt a Valentino, exsistentes extra omnem timorem, suas conscriptiones praeferentes, plura habere gloriantur, quam sint ipsa Evangelia. Siquidem in tantum processerunt audaciae, uti quod ab his

non olim conscriptum est, Veritatis Evangelium titulent.' Iren. iii. xi. 9.

⁴⁵⁶ See, by all means, Epiphanius, Haer. xxx. c. xiii; also c. iii.

⁴⁵⁷ 'Tanta est circa Evangelia haec firmitas, ut et ipsi haeretici testimonium reddant eis, et ex ipsis egrediens unusquisque eorum conetur suam confirmare doctrinam. Ebionaei etenim eo Evangelio quod est secundum Matthaeum, solo utentes, ex illo ipso convincuntur, non recte praesumentes de Domino. Marcion autem id quod est secundum Lucam circumcidens, ex his quae adhuc servantur penes eum, blasphemus in solum existentem Deum ostenditur. Qui autem Iesum separant a Christo, et impassibilem perseverasse Christum, passum vero Iesum dicunt, id quod secundum Marcum est praeferentes Evangelium; cum amore veritatis legentes illud, corrigi possunt. Hi autem qui a Valentino sunt, eo quod est secundum Joannem plenissime utentes,' &c. Iren. iii. xi. 7.

⁴⁵⁸ Ἡρακλέων, ὁ τῆς Οὐαλεντίνου σχολῆς δοκιμώτατος. Clem. Al. p. 595. Of Heracleon it is expressly related by Origen that he depraved the text of the Gospel. Origen says (iv. 66) that Heracleon (regardless of the warning in Prov. xxx. 6) added to the text of St. John i. 3 (viz. after the words ἐγένετο οὐδὲ ἕν) the words τῶν ἐν τῷ κόσμῳ, καὶ τῷ κτίσει, Heracleon clearly read ὃ γέγονεν ἐν αὐτῷ ζωὴ ἦν; See Orig. iv. 64. In St. John ii. 19, for ἐν τρισί, he wrote ἐν τρίτῃ. He also read (St. John iv. 18) (for πέντε), ἐξ ἄγδρας ἔσχες.

⁴⁵⁹ Celsus having objected that believers had again and again falsified the text of the Gospel, refashioning it, in order to meet the objections of assailants, Origen replies: Μεταχαράξαντας δὲ τὸ εὐαγγέλιον ἄλλους οὐκ οἶδα, ἢ τοὺς ἀπὸ Μαρκίωνος, καὶ τοὺς ἀπὸ

Οὐαλεντίνου, οἶμαι δὲ καὶ τοὺς ἀπὸ Λουκάνου. τοῦτο δὲ λεγόμενον οὐ τοῦ λόγου ἐστὶν ἔγκλημα, ἀλλὰ τῶν τολμησάντων ῥαδιουργῆσαι τα εὐαγγέλια. Opp. i. 411 B.

⁴⁶⁰ De Praesc. Haer. c. 51.

⁴⁶¹ Οὗτος δὲ δημιουργὸς καὶ ποιητὴς τοῦδε τοῦ παντὸς κόσμου καὶ τῶν ἔθν αὐτῷ... ἔσται μὲν καταδεέστερος τοῦ τελείου Θεοῦ... ἅτε δὴ καὶ γεννητὸς ὤν, καὶ οὐκ ἀγέννητος. Ptolemaeus, ap. Epiph. p. 217. Heracleon saw in the nobleman of Capernaum an image of the Demiurge who, βασιλικὸς ὠνομάσθη οἰονεὶ μικρός τις βασιλεύς, ὑπὸ καθολικοῦ βασιλέως τεταγμένος ἐπὶ μικρὰς βασιλείας p. 373.

⁴⁶² Ὁ Ἰωάννης... βουλόμενος εἰπεῖν τὴν τῶν ὅλων γένεσιν, καθ᾽ ἣν τὰ πάντα προέβαλεν ὁ Πατήρ, ἀρχήν τινα ὑποτίθεται, τὸ πρῶτον γεννηθὲν ὑπὸ τοῦ Θεοῦ, ὃν δὴ καὶ υἱὸν Μονογενῆ καὶ Θεὸν κέκληκεν, ἐν ᾧ τὰ πάντα ὁ Πατὴρ προέβαλε σπερματικᾶς. Ὑπὸ δὲ τούτου φησὶ τὸν Λόγον προβεβλῆσθαι, καὶ ἐν αὐτῷ τὴν ὅλην τῶν Αἰώνων οὐσίαν, ἣν αὐτὸς ὕστερον ἐμόρφωσεν ὁ Λόγος... Πάντα δι᾽ αὐτοῦ ἐγένετο, καὶ χωρὶς αὐτοῦ ἐγένετο οὐδὲ ἕν· πᾶσι γὰρ τοῖς μετ᾽ αὐτὸν Αἰῶσι μορφῆς καὶ γενέσεως αἴτ.ος ὁ Λόγος ἐγένετο.

⁴⁶³ Ἐν τῷ Πατρὶ καὶ ἐκ τοῦ Πατρὸς ἡ ἀρχή, καὶ ἐκ τῆς ἀρχῆς ὁ Λόγος. Καλῶς οὖν εἶπεν· ἐν ἀρχῇ ἦν ὁ Λόγος· ἦν γὰρ ἐν τῷ Υἱῷ. Καὶ ὁ Λόγος ἦν πρὸς τόν Θεόν· καὶ γὰρ ἡ Ἀρχή· καὶ Θεὸς ἦν ὁ Λόγοςπ ἀκολούθως. Τὸ γὰρ ἐκ Θεοῦ γεννηθὲν Θεός ἐστιν.—Ibid. p. 102. Compare the Excerpt. Theod. ap. Clem. Al. c. vi. p. 963.

⁴⁶⁴ Ap. Orig. 938. 9.

⁴⁶⁵ So Theodotus (p. 980), and so Ptolemaeus (ap. Epiph. i. 217), and so Heracleon (ap. Orig. p. 954). Also Meletius the Semi-Arian (ap. Epiph. 1. 882).

⁴⁶⁶ See The Traditional Text, p. 113.

467 Clem. Al. always has οὐδὲ ἕν (viz. pp. 134, 156, 273, 769, 787, 803, 812, 815, 820): but when he quotes the Gnostics (p. 838) he has οὐδέν. Cyril, while writing his treatise De Trinitate, read οὐδέν in his copy. Eusebius, for example, has οὐδὲ ἕν, fifteen times; οὐδέν only twice, viz. Praep. 322: Esai. 529.

468 Opp. 74.

469 *Ap.* Iren. 102.

470 Ibid. 940.

471 *Ap.* Clem. Al. 968, 973.

472 Philosoph. 107. But not when he is refuting the tenets of the Peratae: οὐδὲ ἕν, ὃ γέγονεν. ἐν αὐτῷ ζωή ἐστιν. ἐν αὐτῷ δέ, φησίν, ἡ Εὔα γέγονεν, ἡ Εὔα ζωή. Ibid. p. 134.

473 Opp. 114, 218, 1009.

474 Cels. vi. 5: Princip. II. ix. 4: IV. i. 30: In Joh. i. 22, 34: 6, 10, 12, 13 bis: In Rom. iii. 10, 15: Haer. v. 151.

475 Psalm. 146, 235, 245: Marcell. 237. Not so in Ecl. 100: Praep. 322, 540.

476 Ἀναγκαίως φησίν, "ὃ γέγονεν, ἐν αὐτῷ ζωὴ ἦν." οὐ μόνον φησί, "δι' αὐτοῦ τὰ πάντα ἐγένετο," ἀλλὰ καὶ εἴ τι γέγονεν ἦν ἐν αὐτῷ ἡ ζωή. τοῦτ' ἔστιν, ὁ μονογενὴς τοῦ Θεοῦ λόγος, ἡ πάντων ἀρχή, καὶ σύστασις ὁρατῶν τε καὶ ἀοράτων ... αὐτὸς γὰρ ὑπάρχων ἡ κατὰ φύσιν ζωή, τὸ εἶναι καὶ ζῆν καὶ κινεῖσθαι πολυτρόπως τοῖς οὖσι χαρίσεται. Opp. iv. 49 e.

He understood the Evangelist to declare concerning the Λόγος, that, πάντα δι' αὐτοῦ ἐγένετο, καὶ ἦν ἐν τοῖς γενομένοις ὡς ζωή. Ibid. 60 c.

477 Οὗτοι δὲ βούλονται αὐτὸ εἶναι κτίσμα κτίσματος. φασὶ γάρ, ὅτι πάντα δι' αὐτοῦ γέγονε, καὶ χωρὶς αὐτοῦ ἐγένετο οὐδὲ ἕν. ἄρα, φασί, καὶ τὸ Πνεῦμα ἐκ τῶν ποιημάτων ὑπάρχει, ἐπειδὴ πάντα δι' αὐτοῦ γέγονε. Opp. 741. Which is the teaching of Eusebius, Marcell. 333-4. The Macedonians were an offshoot of the Arians.

478 i. 778 D, 779 B. See also ii. 80.

479 Opp. viii. 40.

480 Consider 1 John ii. 3, 4: and read Basil ii. 188 b, c. See p. 207, note 4. Consider also Gal. iv. 9. So Cyril Al. [iv. 655 a], καὶ προέγνω μᾶλλον ἢ ἐγνώσθη παρ' ἡμῶν.

481 Chrysostom alone seems to have noticed this:—ἵνα μὴ τῆς γνώσεως ἴσον τὸν μέτρον νομίσῃς, ἄκουσον πῶς διορθοῦται αὐτὸ τῇ ἐπαγωγῇ· γινώσκω τὰ ἐμά, φησι, καὶ γινώσκομαι ὑπὸ τῶν ἐμῶν. ἀλλ' οὐκ ἴση ἡ γνῶσις, κ.τ.λ. viii. 352 d.

482 P. 38. (Gall. vii. 26.)

483 i. 298, 613.

484 viii. 351, 352 d and e.

485 iv. 652 c, 653 a, 654 d.

486 i. 748: iv. 274, 550.

487 In Dionys. Ar. 192.

488 Φησὶ δὲ ὁ αὐτὸς Μάνης ... τὰ ἐμὰ πρόβατα γινώσκει μέ, καὶ γινώσκω ᾳἀ ἐ μὰ πρόβατα. (Epiphan. 697.)— Again,—ἥρπασεν ὁ αἱρετικὸς πρὸς τὴν ἰδίαν κατασκευὴν τῆς βλασφημίας. ἰδού, φησιν, εἴρηται· ὅτι γινώσκουσί (lower down, γινώσκει) με τὰ ἐμά, καὶ γινώσκω τὰ ἐμά. (Basil ii. 188 a, b.)

489 Ἐν τάξει τῇ οἰκείᾳ καὶ πρεπωδεστάτῃ τῶν πραγμάτων ἕκαστα τιθείς. οὐ γὰρ ἔφη, γινώσκει με τὰ ἐμά, καὶ γινώσκω τὰ ἐμά, ἀλλ' ἑαυτὸν ἐγνωκότα πρότερον εἰσφέρει τὰ ἴδια πρόβατα, εἶθ' οὕτως γνωσθήσεσθαί φησι παρ' αὐτῶν ... οὐχ ἡμεῖς αὐτὸν ἐπεγνώκαμεν πρῶτοι, ἐπέγνω δὲ ἡμᾶς πρῶτον αὐτός ... οὐχ ἡμεῖς ἠρξάμεθα τοῦ πράγματος, ἀλλ' ὁ ἐκ Θεοῦ Θεὸς μονογενής—iv. 654 d, 655 a. (Note, that this passage appears in a mutilated form, viz. words are omitted, in the Catena of Corderius, p. 267,—where it is wrongly assigned to Chrysostom: an instructive instance.)

490 In Ps. 489: in Es. 509: Theoph. 185, 258, 260.

491   ii. 188 a:—which is the more remarkable, because Basil proceeds exquisitely to shew (1886) that man's
'knowledge' of God consists in his keeping of God's Commandments. (1 John ii.
3, 4.) See p. 206, note 1.

492   So Jerome, iv. 484: vii. 455.
Strange, that neither Ambrose nor Augustine should quote the place.

493   See Revision Revised, p. 220.

494   Or Saturnilus—τὸ δὲ γαμεῖν καὶ
γεννᾷν ἀπὸ τοῦ Σατανᾶ φησὶν εἶναι. p.
245, 1. 38. So Marcion, 253.

495   [The MS. breaks off here, with references to St. Mark x. 7, Eph. v. 31-2
(on which the Dean had accumulated a
large array of references), St. Mark x.
29-30, with a few references, but no
more. I have not had yet time or
strength to work out the subject.]

496   Mai, iv. 221.

Appendices

Appendix I - Pericope De Adultera

I HAVE purposely reserved for the last the most difficult problem of all: viz. those twelve famous verses of St. John's Gospel (chap. vii. 53 to viii. 11) which contain the history of 'the woman taken in adultery,'—the *pericope de adultera*, as it is called. Altogether indispensable is it that the reader should approach this portion of the Gospel with the greatest amount of experience and the largest preparation. Convenient would it be, no doubt, if he could further divest himself of prejudice; but that is perhaps impossible. Let him at least endeavour to weigh the evidence which shall now be laid before him in impartial scales. He must do so perforce, if he would judge rightly: for the matter to be discussed is confessedly very peculiar: in some respects, even unique. Let me convince him at once of the truth of what has been so far spoken.

It is a singular circumstance that at the end of eighteen centuries two instances, and but two, should exist of a considerable portion of Scripture left to the mercy, so to speak, of 'Textual Criticism.' Twelve consecutive Verses in the second Gospel—as many consecutive Verses in the fourth—are in this predicament. It is singular, I say, that the Providence which has watched so marvellously over the fortunes of the, Deposit,— the Divine Wisdom which has made such ample provision for its security all down the ages, should have so ordered the matter, that these two co-extensive problems have survived to our times to be tests of human sagacity,—trials of human faithfulness and skill. They present some striking features of correspondence, but far more of contrast,—as will presently appear. And yet the most important circumstance of all cannot be too soon mentioned: viz. that both alike have experienced the same calamitous treatment at the hands of some critics. By common consent the most recent editors deny that either set of Verses can have formed part of the Gospel as it proceeded from the hands of its inspired author. How mistaken is this opinion of theirs in respect of the 'Last twelve verses of the Gospel according to St. Mark,' has been already demonstrated in a separate treatise. I must be content in this place to deal in a far less ceremonious manner with the hostile verdict of many critics concerning St. John vii. 53–viii. 11. That I shall be able to satisfy those persons who profess themselves unconvinced by what was offered concerning St. Mark's last twelve verses, I am not so simple as to expect. But I trust that I shall have with me all candid readers who are capable of weighing evidence impartially, and understanding the nature of logical proof, when it is fully drawn out before them,—which indeed is the very qualification that I require of them.

And first, the case of the *pericope de adultera* requires to be placed before the reader in its true bearings. For those who have hitherto discussed it are observed to have ignored certain preliminary considerations which, once clearly apprehended, are all but decisive of the point vat issue. There is a fundamental obstacle, I mean, in the way of any attempt to dislodge this portion of the sacred narrative from the context in which it stands, which they seem to have overlooked. I proceed to explain.

Sufficient prominence has never yet been given to the fact that in the present discussion the burden of proof rests entirely with those who challenge the genuineness of the Pericope under review. In other words, the question before us is not by any means,—Shall these Twelve Verses be admitted—or, Must they be refused admission—into the Sacred Text? That point has been settled long, long ago. St. John's Twelve verses are in possession. Let those eject them who can. They are known to have occupied their present position for full seventeen hundred years. There never was a time—as far as is known—when they were not *where*,—and to all intents and purposes *what*—they now are. Is it not evident, that no merely ordinary method of proof,—no merely common argument,—will avail to dislodge Twelve such Verses as these?

'Twelve such Verses,' I say. For it is the extent of the subject-matter which makes the case so formidable. We have here to do with no dubious clause, concerning which ancient testimony is divided; no seeming gloss, which is suspected to have overstepped its proper limits, and to have crept in as from the margin; no importation from another Gospel; no verse of Scripture which has lost its way; no weak amplification of the Evangelical meaning; no tasteless appendix, which encumbers the narrative and almost condemns itself. Nothing of the sort. If it were some inconsiderable portion of Scripture which it was proposed to get rid of by shewing that it is disallowed by a vast amount of ancient evidence, the proceeding would be intelligible. But I take leave to point out that a highly complex and very important incident—as related in twelve consecutive verses of the Gospel—cannot be so dealt with. Squatters on the waste are liable at any moment to be served with a notice of ejectment: but the owner of a mansion surrounded by broad acres which his ancestors are known to have owned before the Heptarchy, may on no account be dispossessed by any such summary process. This—to speak without a figure—is a connected and very striking portion of the sacred narrative:—the description of a considerable incident, complete in itself, full of serious teaching, and of a kind which no one would have ever dared to invent. Those who would assail it successfully must come forward with weapons of a very different kind from those usually employed in textual warfare.

It shall be presently shewn that these Twelve Verses hold their actual place by a more extraordinary right of tenure than any other twelve verses which can be named in the Gospel: but it would be premature to enter upon the proof of that circumstance now. I prefer to invite the reader's attention, next to the actual texture of the *pericope de adultera*, by which name (as already explained) the last verse of St. John vii. together with verses 1-11 of ch. viii. are familiarly designated. Although external testimony supplies the sole proof of genuineness, it is nevertheless reasonable to inquire what the verses in question may have to say for themselves. Do they carry on their front the tokens of that baseness of origin which their impugners so Confidently seek to fasten upon them? Or do they, on the contrary, unmistakably bear the impress of Truth?

The first thing which strikes me in them is that the actual narrative concerning 'the woman taken in adultery' is entirely contained in the last nine of these verses: being preceded by two short paragraphs of an entirely different character and complexion. Let these be first produced and studied:

'and every man went to his own house: but Jesus went to the Mount of Olives.' 'And again, very early in the morning, He presented Himself in the Temple; and all the people came unto Him: and He sat down and taught them.'

Now as every one must see, the former of these two paragraphs is unmistakably not the beginning but the end of a narrative. It purports to be the conclusion of something which went before, not to introduce something which conies after. Without any sort of doubt, it is St. John's account of what occurred at the close of the debate between certain members of the Sanhedrin which terminates his history of the last day of the Feast of Tabernacles. The verse in question marks the conclusion of the Feast,—implies in short that all is already finished. Remove it, and the antecedent narrative ends abruptly. Retain it, and all proceeds methodically; while an affecting contrast is established, which is recognized to be strictly in the manner of Scripture[578]. Each one had gone to his home: but the homeless One had repaired to the Mount of Olives. In other words, the paragraph under discussion is found to be an integral part of the immediately antecedent narrative: proves to be a fragment of what is universally admitted to be genuine Scripture. By consequence, itself must needs be genuine also[579].

It is vain for any one to remind us that these two verses are in the same predicament as those which follow: are as ill supported by MS. evidence as the other ten: and must therefore share the same fate as the rest. The statement is incorrect, to begin with; as shall presently be shewn. But, what is even better deserving of attention, since confessedly these twelve verses are either to stand or else to fall together, it must be candidly admitted that whatever begets a suspicion that certain of them, at all events, must needs be genuine, throws real doubt on the justice of the sentence of condemnation which has been passed in a lump upon all the rest.

I proceed to call attention to another inconvenient circumstance which some Critics in their eagerness have overlooked.

The reader will bear in mind that—contending, as I do, that the entire Pericope under discussion is genuine Scripture which has been forcibly wrenched away from its lawful context,—I began by examining the upper extremity, with a view to ascertaining whether it bore any traces of being a fractured edge. The result is just what might have been anticipated. The first two of the verses which it is the fashion to brand with ignomy were found to carry on their front clear evidence that they are genuine Scripture. How then about the other extremity?

Note, that in the oracular Codexes B and א immediate transition is made from the words out of Galilee ariseth no prophet,' in ch. vii. 52, to the words Again therefore Jesus spake unto them, saying,' in ch. viii. 12. And we are invited by all the adverse Critics alike to believe that so the place stood in the inspired autograph of the Evangelist.

But the thing is incredible. Look back at what is contained between ch. vii. 37 and 52, and note—(a) That two hostile parties crowded the Temple courts (ver. 40-42): (b) That some were for laying violent hands on our LORD (ver. 44): (c) That the Sanhedrin, being assembled in debate, were reproaching their servants for not having brought Him prisoner, and disputing one against another[580] (ver. 45-52). How can the Evangelist have proceeded, — 'Again therefore Jesus spake unto them, saying, I am the light of the world'? What is it supposed then that St. John meant when he wrote such words?

But on the contrary, survey the context in any ordinary copy of the New Testament, and his meaning is perfectly clear. The last great day of the Feast of Tabernacles is ended. It is the morrow and 'very early in the morning.' The Holy One has 'again presented Himself in the Temple' where on the previous night He so narrowly escaped violence at the hands of His enemies, and He teaches the people. While thus engaged,—the time, the place, His own occupation suggesting thoughts of peace and holiness and love,—a rabble rout, headed by the Scribes and Pharisees, enter on the foulest of errands; and we all remember with how little success. Such an interruption need not have occupied much time. The Woman's accusers having departed, our Saviour resumes His discourse which had been broken off. 'Again therefore' it is said in ver. 12, with clear and frequent reference to what had preceded in ver. 2— 'Jesus spake unto them, saying, I am the light of the world.' And had not that saying of His reference as well to the thick cloud of moral darkness which His words, a few moments before, had succeeded in dispelling, as to the orb of glory which already flooded the Temple Court with the effulgence of its rising,—His own visible emblem and image in the Heavens? . . . I protest that with the incident of 'the woman taken in adultery,'—so introduced, so dismissed,—all is lucid and coherent: without those connecting links, the story is scarcely intelligible. These twelve disputed verses, so far from 'fatally interrupting the course of St. John's Gospel, if retained in the text[581],' prove to be even necessary for the logical coherency of the entire context in which they stand.

But even that is not all. On close and careful inspection, the mysterious texture of the narrative, no less than its 'edifying and eminently Christian' character, vindicates for the *Pericope de adultera* a right to its place in the Gospel. Let me endeavour to explain what seems to be its spiritual significancy: in other words, to interpret the transaction.

The Scribes and Pharisees bring a woman to our Saviour on a charge of adultery. The sin prevailed to such an extent among the Jews that the Divine enactments concerning one so accused had long since fallen into practical oblivion. On the present occasion our Lord is observed to revive His own ancient ordinance after a hitherto unheard of fashion. The trial by the bitter water, or water of conviction[582], was a species of ordeal, intended for the vindication of innocence, the conviction of guilt. But according to the traditional belief the test proved inefficacious, unless the husband was himself innocent of the crime whereof he accused his wife.

Let the provisions of the law, contained in Num. v. 16 to 24, be now considered. The accused Woman having been brought near, and set before the Lord, the priest took 'holy water in an earthen vessel,' and put of the dust of the, floor of the tabernacle into the water.' Then, with the bitter water that causeth the curse in his hand, he charged the woman by an oath. Next, he wrote the curses in a book and blotted them out with the bitter water; causing the woman to drink the bitter water that causeth the curse. Whereupon if she were guilty, she fell under a terrible penalty,—her body testifying visibly to her sin. If she was innocent, nothing followed.

And now, who sees not that the Holy One dealt with His hypocritical assailants, as if they had been the accused parties? Into the presence of incarnate Jehovah verily they had been brought: and perhaps when He stooped down and wrote upon the ground, it was a bitter sentence against the adulterer and adulteress which He wrote. We have but to assume some connexion between the curse which He thus traced in the dust of the floor of the tabernacle' and the words which He uttered with His lips, and He may with truth be declared to have 'taken of the dust and put in on the water,' and 'caused them to drink of the bitter water which causeth the curse.' For when, by His Holy Spirit, our great High Priest in His human flesh addressed these adulterers,— what did He but present them with living water[583] 'in an earthen vessel[584]'? Did He not further charge them with an oath of cursing, saying, 'If ye have not gone aside to uncleanness, be ye free from this bitter water: but if ye be defiled '—On being presented with which alternative, did they not, self-convicted, go out one by one? And what else was this but their own acquittal of the sinful woman, for whose condemnation they shewed themselves so impatient? 'Surely it was the water of conviction' (τὸ ὕδωρ τοῦ ἐλεγμοῦ) as it is six times called, which *they* had been compelled to drink; whereupon, convicted (ἐλεγχόμενοι) by their own conscience,' as St. John relates, they had pronounced the other's acquittal. Finally, note that by Himself declining to 'condemn' the accused woman, our Lord also did in effect blot out those curses which He had already written against her in the dust,—when He made the floor of the sanctuary His 'book.'

Whatever may be thought of the foregoing exposition—and I am not concerned to defend it in every detail,—on turning to the opposite contention, we are struck with the slender amount of actual proof with which the assailants of this passage seem to be furnished. Their evidence is mostly negative—a proceeding which is constantly observed to attend a bad cause: and they are prone to make up for the feebleness of their facts by the strength of their assertions. But my experience, as one who has given a considerable amount of attention to such subjects, tells me that the narrative before us carries on its front the impress of Divine origin. I venture to think that it vindicates for itself a high, unearthly meaning. It seems to me that it cannot be the work of a fabricator. The more I study it, the more I am impressed with its Divinity. And in what goes before I have been trying to make the reader a partaker of my own conviction.

To come now to particulars, we may readily see from its very texture that it must needs have been woven in a heavenly loom. Only too obvious is the remark that the very subject-matter of the chief transaction recorded in these twelve verses, would be sufficient in and by itself to preclude the suspicion that these twelve verses are a spurious addition to the genuine Gospel. And then we note how entirely in St. John's manner is the little explanatory clause in ver. 6,—'This they said, tempting Him, that they might have to accuse Him[585].' We are struck besides by the prominence given in verses 6 and 8 to the act of writing,—allusions to which, are met with in every work of the last Evangelist[586]. It does not of course escape us how utterly beyond the reach of a Western interpolator would have been the insertion of the article so faithfully retained to this hour before λίθον in ver. 7. On completing our survey, as to the assertions that the *pericope de adultera* 'has no right to a place in the text of the four Gospels,'— is 'clearly a Western interpolation, though not Western of the earliest type[587],' (whatever *that* may mean), and so forth,—we can but suspect that the authors very imperfectly realize the difficulty of the problem with which they have to deal. Dr. Hort finally assures us that 'no accompanying marks would prevent' this portion of Scripture 'from fatally interrupting the course of St. John's Gospel if retained in the text': and when they relegate it accordingly to a blank page at the end of the Gospels within 'double brackets,' in order 'to shew its inferior authority';— we can but read and wonder at the want of perception, not to speak of the coolness, which they display. *Quousque tandem?*

But it is time to turn from such considerations as the foregoing, and to inquire for the direct testimony, which is assumed by recent Editors and Critics to be fatal to these twelve verses. Tischendorf pronounces it 'absolutely certain that this narrative was not written by St. John[588].' One, vastly his superior in judgement (Dr. Scrivener) declares that 'on all intelligent principles of mere Criticism, the passage must needs be abandoned[589].' Tregelles is 'fully satisfied that this narrative is not a genuine part of St. John's Gospel[590].' Alford shuts it up in brackets, and like Tregelles puts it into his footnotes. Westcott and Hort, harsher than any of their predecessors, will not, as we have seen, allow it to appear even at the foot of the page. To reproduce all that has been written in disparagement of this precious portion of God's written Word would be a joyless and an unprofitable task. According to Green, 'the genuineness of the passage cannot be maintained[591].' Hammond is of opinion that it would be more satisfactory to separate it from its present context, and place it by itself as an appendix to the Gospel[592].' A yet more recent critic 'sums up,' that 'the external evidence must be held fatal to the genuineness of the passage[593].' The opinions of Bishops Wordsworth, Ellicott, and Lightfoot, shall be respectfully commented upon by-and-by. In the meantime, I venture to join issue with every one of these learned persons. I contend that on all intelligent principles of sound Criticism the passage before us must be maintained to be genuine Scripture; and that without a particle of doubt. I cannot even admit that it has been transmitted to us under circumstances widely different from those connected with any other passage of Scripture whatever[594].' I contend that it has been transmitted in precisely the same way as all the rest of Scripture, and therefore exhibits the same notes of genuineness as any other twelve verses of the same Gospel which can be named: but—like countless other places—it is found for whatever reason to have given offence in certain quarters: and in consequence has experienced very ill usage at the hands of the ancients and of the moderns also:—but especially of the latter. In other words, these twelve verses exhibit the required notes of genuineness *less conspicuously* than any other twelve consecutive verses in the same Gospel. But that is all. The one only question to be decided is the following:—On a review of the whole of the evidence,—is it more reasonable to stigmatize these twelve verses as a spurious accretion to the Gospel? Or to admit that they must needs be accounted to be genuine? . . . I shall shew that they are at this hour supported by a weight of testimony which is absolutely overwhelming. I read with satisfaction that my own convictions were shared by Mill, Matthaei, Adler, Scholz, Vercellone. I have also the learned Ceriani on my side. I should have been just as confident had I stood alone:—such is the imperative strength of the evidence.

To begin then. Tischendorf—(who may be taken as a fair sample of the assailants of this passage)—commences by stating roundly that the Pericope is omitted by אABCLTXΔ, and about seventy cursives. I will say at once, that no sincere inquirer after truth could so state the evidence. It is in fact not a true statement. A and C are hereabout defective. No longer possible therefore is it to know with certainty what they either did, or did not, contain. But this is not merely all. I proceed to offer a few words concerning Cod. A.

Woide, the learned and accurate[595] editor of the Codex Alexandrinus, remarked (in 1785)—'Historia adulterae *videtur* in hoc codice defuisse.' But this modest inference of his, subsequent Critics have represented as an ascertained fact, Tischendorf announces it as 'certissimum.' Let me be allowed to investigate the problem for myself. Woide's calculation,—(which has

138

passed unchallenged for nearly a hundred years, and on the strength of which it is now-a-days assumed that Cod. A must have exactly resembled Codd. אB in *omitting* the *pericope de adultera*,)—was far too roughly made to be of any critical use[596].

Two leaves of Cod. A have been here lost: viz. from the word καταβαίνων in vi. 50 to the word λέγεις in viii. 52: a *lacuna* (as I find by counting the letters in a copy of the ordinary text) of as nearly as possible 8,805 letters,—allowing for contractions, and of course not reckoning St. John vii. 53 to viii. 11. Now, in order to estimate fairly how many letters the two lost leaves actually contained, I have inquired for the sums of the letters on the leaf immediately preceding, and also on the leaf immediately succeeding the hiatus; and I find them to be respectively 4,337 and 4,303: together, 8,640 letters. But this, it will be seen, is insufficient by 165 letters, or eight lines, for the assumed contents of these two missing leaves. Are we then to suppose that one leaf exhibited somewhere a blank space equivalent to eight lines? Impossible, I answer. There existed, on the contrary, a considerable redundancy of matter in at least the second of those two lost leaves. This is proved by the circumstance that the first column on the next ensuing leaf exhibits the unique phenomenon of being encumbered, at its summit, by two very long lines (containing together fifty-eight letters), for which evidently no room could be found on the page which immediately preceded. But why should there have been any redundancy of matter at all? Something extraordinary must have produced it. What if the *Pericope de adultera*, without being actually inserted in full, was recognized by Cod. A? What if the scribe had proceeded as far as the fourth word of St. John viii. 3, and then had suddenly checked himself? We cannot tell what appearance St. John vii. 53–viii. 11 presented in Codex A, simply because the entire leaf which should have contained it is lost. Enough however has been said already to prove that it is incorrect and unfair to throw אAB into one and the same category,—with a 'certissimum,'—as Tischendorf does.

As for L and Δ, they exhibit a vacant space after St. John vii. 52,—which testifies to the consciousness of the copyists that they were leaving out something. These are therefore witnesses *for*,—not witnesses *against*,—the passage under discussion.—X being a Commentary on the Gospel as it was read in Church, of course leaves the passage out.—The only uncial MSS. therefore which *simply* leave out the pericope, are the three following—אBT: and the degree of attention to which such an amount of evidence is entitled, has been already proved to be wondrous small. We cannot forget moreover that the two former of these copies enjoy the unenviable distinction of standing alone on a memorable occasion:—they *alone* exhibit St. Mark's Gospel mutilated in respect of its twelve concluding verses.

But I shall be reminded that about seventy MSS. of later date are without the *pericope de adultera*: that the first Greek Father who quotes the pericope is Euthymius in the twelfth century: that Tertullian, Origen, Chrysostom, Cyril, Nonnus, Cosmas, Theophylact, knew nothing of it: and that it is not con-

139

tained in the Syriac, the Gothic, or the Egyptian versions. Concerning every one of which statements I remark over again that no sincere lover of Truth, supposing him to understand the matter about which he is disputing, could so exhibit the evidence for this particular problem. First, because so to state it is to misrepresent the entire case. Next, because some of the articles of indictment are only half true:—in fact are *untrue*. But chiefly, because in the foregoing enumeration certain considerations are actually suppressed which, had they been fairly stated, would have been found to reverse the issue. Let me now be permitted to conduct this inquiry in my own way.

The first thing to be done is to enable the reader clearly to understand what the problem before him actually is. Twelve verses then, which, as a matter of fact, are found dovetailed into a certain context of St. John's Gospel, the Critics insist must now be dislodged. But do the Critics in question prove that they must? For unless they do, there is no help for it but the *pericope de adultera* must be left where it is. I proceed to shew first, that it is im possible, on any rational principle to dislodge these twelve verses from their actual context.—Next, I shall point out that the facts adduced in evidence and relied on by the assailants of the passage, do not by any means prove the point they are intended to prove; but admit of a sufficient and satisfactory explanation.—Thirdly, it shall be shewn that the said explanation carries with it, and implies, a weight of testimony in support of the twelve verses in dispute, which is absolutely overwhelming.—Lastly, the positive evidence in favour of these twelve verses shall be proved to outweigh largely the negative evidence, which is relied upon by those who contend for their removal. To some people I may seem to express myself with too much confidence. Let it then be said once for all, that my confidence is inspired by the strength of the arguments which are now to be unfolded. When the Author of Holy Scripture supplies such proofs of His intentions, I cannot do otherwise than rest implicit confidence in them.

Now I begin by establishing as my firtt proposition that,

(1) *These twelve verses occupied precisely the same position which they now occupy from the earliest period to which evidence concerning the Gospels reaches.*

And this, because it is a mere matter of fact, is sufficiently established by reference to the ancient Latin version of St. John's Gospel. We are thus carried back to the second century of our era: beyond which, testimony does not reach. The pericope is observed to stand *in situ* in Codd. b c e ff² g h j. Jerome (A.D. 385), after a careful survey of older Greek copies, did not hesitate to retain it in the Vulgate. It is freely referred to and commented on by himself[597] in Palestine: while Ambrose at Milan (374) quotes it at least nine times[598]; as well as Augustine in North Africa (396) about twice as often[599]. It is quoted besides by Pacian[600], in the north of Spain (370),—by Faustus[601] the African (400),—by Rufinus[602] at Aquileia (400),—by Chrysologus[603] at Ravenna (433),—by Sedulius[604] a Scot (434). The unknown authors of two famous treatises[605] written at the same period, largely quote this portion of the narrative. It is referred to by Victorius or Victorinus (457),—by Vigilius of Tapsus[606] (484) in North Africa,—by Gelasius[607], bp. of Rome (492),—by Cassiodorus[608] in Southern Italy,—by Gregory the Great[609], and by other Fathers of the Western Church.

To this it is idle to object that the authors cited all wrote in Latin. For the purpose in hand their evidence is every bit as conclusive as if they had written in Greek,—from which language no one doubts that they derived their knowledge, through a translation. But in fact we are not left to Latin authorities. [Out of thirty-eight copies of the Bohairic version the *pericope de adultera* is read in fifteen, but in three forms which will be printed in the Oxford edition. In the remaining twenty-three, it is left out.] How is it intelligible that this passage is thus found in nearly half the copies—except on the hypothesis that they formed an integral part of the Memphitic version? They might have been easily omitted: but how could they have been inserted?

Once more. The Ethiopic version (fifth century),—the Palestinian Syriac (which is referred to the fifth century),—the Georgian (probably fifth or sixth century),—to say nothing of the Slavonic, Arabic and Persian versions, which are of later date,—all contain the portion of narrative in dispute. The Armenian version also (fourth–fifth century) originally contained it; though it survives at present in only a few copies. Add that it is found in Cod. D, and it will be seen that in all parts of ancient Christendom this portion of Scripture was familiarly known in early times.

But even this is not all. Jerome, who was familiar with Greek MSS. (and who handled none of later date than B and ℵ), expressly relates (380) that the *pericope de adultera* 'is found in many copies both Greek and Latin[610].' He calls attention to the fact that what is rendered 'sine peccato' is ἀναμάρτητος in the Greek: and lets fall an exegetical remark which shews that he was familiar with copies which exhibited (in ver. 8) εγραψεν ενος εκαστου αυτων τας αμαρτιας,—a reading which survives to this day in one uncial (U) and at least eighteen cursive copies of the fourth Gospel[611]. Whence is it—let me ask in passing—that go many Critics fail to see that *positive* testimony like the foregoing far outweighs the adverse *negative* testimony of ℵBT,—aye, and of AC to boot if they were producible on this point? How comes it to pass that the two Codexes, ℵ and B, have obtained such a mastery—rather exercise such a tyranny—over the imagination of many Critics as quite to overpower their practical judgement? We have at all events established our first proposition: viz. that from the earliest period to which testimony reaches, the incident of 'the woman taken in adultery' occupied its present place in St. John's Gospel. The Critics eagerly remind us that in four cursive copies (13, 69, 124, 346), the verses in question are found tacked on to the end of St. Luke xxi. But have they then forgotten that 'these four Codexes are derived from a common archetype,' and therefore represent one and the same ancient and, I may add, corrupt copy? The same Critics are reminded that in the same four Codexes [commonly called the Ferrar Group] 'the agony and bloody sweat' (St. Luke xxii. 43, 44) is found thrust into St. Matthew's Gospel between ch.

xxvi. 39 and 40. Such licentiousness on the part of a solitary exemplar of the Gospels no more affects the proper place of these or of those verses than the superfluous digits of a certain man of Gath avail to disturb the induction that to either hand of a human being appertain but five fingers, and to either foot but five toes.

It must be admitted then that as far back as testimony reaches the passage under discussion stood where it now stands in St. John's Gospel. And this is my first position. But indeed, to be candid, hardly any one has seriously called that fact in question. No, nor do any (except Dr. Hort[612]) doubt that the passage is also of the remotest antiquity. Adverse Critics do but insist that however ancient, it must needs be of spurious origin: or else that it is an afterthought of the Evangelist:—concerning both which imaginations we shall have a few words to offer by-and-by.

It clearly follows,—indeed it may be said with truth that it only remains,—to inquire what may have led to its so frequent exclusion from the sacred Text? For really the difficulty has already resolved itself into that.

And on this head, it is idle to affect perplexity. In the earliest age of all,—the age which was familiar with the universal decay of heathen virtue, but which had not yet witnessed the power of the Gospel to fashion society afresh, and to build up domestic life on a new and more enduring basis;—at a time when the greatest laxity of morals prevailed, and the enemies of the Gospel were known to be on the look out for grounds of cavil against Christianity and its Author;—what wonder if some were found to remove the *pericope de adultera* from their copies, lest it should be pleaded in extenuation of breaches of the seventh commandment? The very subject-matter, I say, of St. John viii. 3–11 would sufficiently account for the occasional omission of those nine verses. Moral considerations abundantly explain what is found to have here and there happened. But in fact this is not a mere conjecture of my own. It is the reason assigned by Augustine for the erasure of these twelve verses from many copies of the Gospel[613]. Ambrose, a quarter of a century earlier, had clearly intimated that danger was popularly apprehended from this quarter[614]: while Nicon, five centuries later, states plainly that the mischievous tendency of the narrative was the cause why it had been expunged from the Armenian version[615]. Accordingly, just a few Greek copies are still to be found mutilated in respect of those nine verses only. But in fact the indications are not a few that all the twelve verses under discussion did not by any means labour under the same degree of disrepute. The first three (as I shewed at the outset) clearly belong to a different category from the last nine,—a circumstance which has been too much overlooked.

The Church in the meantime for an obvious reason had made choice of St. John vii. 37–viii. 12—the greater part of which is clearly descriptive of what happened at the Feast of Tabernacles—for her Pentecostal lesson: and judged it expedient, besides omitting as inappropriate to the occasion the incident of the woman taken in adultery, to ignore also the three preceding verses;—making the severance begin, in fact, as far back as the end of ch. vii.

52. The reason for this is plain. In this way the allusion to a certain departure at night, and return early next morning (St. John vii. 53: viii. 1), was avoided, which entirely marred the effect of the lection as the history of a day of great and special solemnity,—'the great day of the Feast.' And thus it happens that the gospel for the day of Pentecost was made to proceed directly from 'Search and look: for out of Galilee ariseth no prophet,' in ch. vii. 52,—to 'Then spake Jesus unto them, saying, I am the light of the world,' in ch. viii. 12; with which it ends. In other words, an omission which owed its beginning to a moral scruple was eventually extended for a liturgical consideration; and resulted in severing twelve verses of St. John's Gospel—ch. vii. 53 to viii. 11—from their lawful context.

We may now proceed to the consideration of my second proposition, which is

(2) *That by the very construction of her Lectionary, the Church in her corporate capacity and official character has solemnly recognized the narrative in question as an integral part of St. John's Gospel, and as standing in its traditional place, from an exceedingly remote time.*

Take into your hands at random the first MS. copy of St. John's Gospel which presents itself, and turn to the place in question. Nay, I will instance *all* the four Evangelia which I call mine,—all the seventeen which belong to Lord Zouch,—all the thirty-nine which Baroness Burdett-Coutts imported from Epirus in 1870-2. Now all these copies—(and nearly each of them represents a different line of ancestry)—are found to contain the verses in question. How did the verses ever get there?

But the most extraordinary circumstance of the case is behind. Some out of the Evangelia referred to are observed to have been prepared for ecclesiastical use: in other words, are so rubricated throughout as to shew where. every separate lection had its 'beginning' (ἀρχή), and where its 'end' (τέλος). And some of these lections are made up of disjointed portions of the Gospel. Thus, the lection for Whitsunday is found to have extended from St. John vii. 37 to St. John viii. 12; beginning at the words τῇ ἐσχάτῃ ἡμέρᾳ τῇ μεγάλῃ, and ending—τὸ φῶς τῆς ζωῆς: but *over-leaping* the twelve verses now under discussion: viz. vii. 53 to viii. 11. Accordingly, the word 'over-leap' (ὑπέρβα) is written in *all* the copies after vii. 52,—whereby the reader, having read on to the end of that verse, was directed to skip all that followed down to the words καὶ μηκέτι ἁμάρτανε in ch. viii. 11: after which he found himself instructed to "recommence' (ἄρξαι). Again I ask (and this time does not the riddle admit of only one solution?),— When and how does the reader suppose that the narrative of 'the woman taken in adultery' first found its way into the *middle of the lesson for Pentecost*? I pause for an answer: I shall perforce be told that it never 'found its way' into the lection at all: but having once crept into St. John's Gospel, however that may have been effected, and established itself there, it left those ancient men who devised the Church's Lectionary without choice. They could but direct its omission, and employ for that purpose the established liturgical formula in all similar cases.

143

But first,—How is it that those who would reject the narrative are not struck by the essential foolishness of supposing that twelve fabricated verses, purporting to be an integral part of the fourth Gospel, can have so firmly established themselves in every part of Christendom from the second century downwards, that they have long since become simply ineradicable? Did the Church then, *pro hac vice*, abdicate her function of 'being a witness and a keeper of Holy Writ'? Was she all of a sudden forsaken by the inspiring Spirit, who, as she was promised, should 'guide her into all Truth'? And has she been all down the ages guided into the grievous error of imputing to the disciple whom Jesus loved a narrative of which he knew nothing? For, as I remarked at the outset, this is not merely an assimilated expression, or an unauthorized nominative, or a weakly-supported clause, or any such trifling thing. Although be it remarked in passing, I am not aware of a single such trifling excrescence which we are not able at once to detect and to remove. In other words, this is not at all a question, like the rest, about the genuine text of a passage. Our inquiry is of an essentially different kind, viz. Are these twelve consecutive verses Scripture at all, or not? Divine or human? Which? They claim by their very structure and contents to be an integral part of the Gospel. And such a serious accession to the Deposit, I insist, can neither have 'crept into' the Text, nor have 'crept out' of it. The thing is unexampled, —is unapproached,—is impossible.

Above all,—(the reader is entreated to give the subject his sustained attention),—Is it not perceived that the admission involved in the hypothesis before us is fatal to any rational pretence that the passage is of spurious origin? We have got back in thought at least to the third or fourth century of our era. We are among the Fathers and Doctors of the Eastern Church in conference assembled: and they are determining what shall be the Gospel for the great Festival of Pentecost. 'It shall begin' (say they) 'at the thirty-seventh verse of St. John vii, and conclude with the twelfth verse of St. John viii. But so much of it as relates to the breaking up of the Sanhedrin,—to the withdrawal of our Lord to the Mount of Olives,—and to His return next morning to the Temple,—had better not be read. It disturbs the unity of the narrative. So also had the incident of the woman taken in adultery better not be read. It is inappropriate to the Pentecostal Festival.' The Authors of the great Oriental Liturgy therefore admit that they find the disputed verses in their copies: and thus they vouch for their genuineness. For none will doubt that, had they regarded them as a spurious accretion to the inspired page, they would have said so plainly. Nor can it be denied that if in their corporate capacity they had disallowed these twelve verses, such an authoritative condemnation would most certainly have resulted in the perpetual exclusion from the Sacred Text of the part of these verses which was actually adopted as a Lection. What stronger testimony on the contrary can be imagined to the genuineness of any given portion of the everlasting Gospel than that it should have been canonized or recognized as part of Inspired Scripture by the collective wisdom of the Church in the third or fourth century?

And no one may regard it as a suspicious circumstance that the present Pentecostal lection has been thus maimed and mutilated in respect of twelve of its verses. There is nothing at all extraordinary in the treatment which St. John vii. 37-viii. 12 has here experienced. The phenomenon is even of perpetual recurrence in the Lectionary of the East,—as will be found explained below[616].

Permit me to suppose that, between the Treasury and Whitehall, the remote descendant of some Saxon thane occupied a small tenement and garden which stood in the very middle of the ample highway. Suppose further, the property thereabouts being Government property, that the road on either side of this estate had been measured a hundred times, and jealously watched, ever since Westminster became Westminster. Well, an act of Parliament might no doubt compel the supposed proprietor of this singular estate to surrender his patrimony; but I submit that no government lawyer would ever think of setting up the plea that the owner of that peculiar strip of land was an impostor. The man might have no title-deeds to produce, to be sure; but counsel for the defendant would plead that neither did he require any. 'This man's title' (counsel would say) 'is—occupation for a thousand years. His evidences are—the allowance of the State throughout that long interval. Every procession to St. Stephen's—every procession to the Abbey— has swept by defendant's property—on this side of it and on that,—since the days of Edward the Confessor. And if my client refuses to quit the soil, I defy you—except by violence—to get rid of him.'

In this way then it is that the testimony borne to these verses by the Lectionary of the East proves to be of the most opportune and convincing character. The careful provision made for passing by the twelve verses in dispute:—the minute directions which fence those twelve verses off on this side and on that, directions issued we may be sure by the highest Ecclesiastical authority, because recognized in every part of the ancient Church,—not only establish them effectually in their rightful place, but (what is at least of equal importance) fully explain the adverse phenomena which are ostentatiously paraded by adverse critics; and which, until the clue has been supplied, are calculated to mislead the judgement.

For now, for the first time, it becomes abundantly plain why Chrysostom and Cyril, in publicly commenting on St. John's Gospel, pass straight from ch. vii. 52 to ch. viii. 12. Of course they do. Why should they,—how could they,— comment on what was not publicly read before the congregation? The same thing is related (in a well-known 'scholium') to have been done by Apolinarius and Theodore of Mopsuestia. Origen also, for aught I care,—though the adverse critics have no right to claim him, seeing that his commentary on all that part of St. John's Gospel is lost;but Origen's name, as I was saying, for aught I care, may be added to those who did the same thing. A triumphant refutation of the proposed inference from the silence of these many Fathers is furnished by the single fact that Theophylact must also be added to their number. Theophylact, I say, ignores the *pericope de adultera*—passes it by, I

145

mean,—exactly as do Chrysostom and Cyril. But will any one pretend that Theophylact,—writing in A.D. 1077,—did not know of St. John vii. 53–viii. 11? Why, in nineteen out of every twenty copies within his reach, the whole of those twelve verses must have been to be found.

The proposed inference from the silence of certain of the Fathers is therefore invalid. The argument *e silentio*—always an insecure argument,—proves inapplicable in this particular case. When the antecedent facts have been once explained, all the subsequent phenomena become intelligible. But a more effectual and satisfactory reply to the difficulty occasioned by the general silence of the Fathers, remains to be offered.

There underlies the appeal to Patristic authority an opinion,—not expressed indeed, yet consciously entertained by us all,—which in fact gives the appeal all its weight and cogency, and which must now by all means be brought to the front. The fact that the Fathers of the Church were not only her Doctors and Teachers, but also the living voices by which alone her mind could be proclaimed to the world, and by which her decrees used to be authoritatively promulgated;—this fact, I say, it is which makes their words, whenever they deliver themselves, so very important: their approval, if they approve, so weighty; their condemnation, if they condemn, so fatal. But then, in the present instance, they do not condemn. They neither approve nor condemn. They simply say nothing. They are silent: and in what precedes, I have explained the reason why. We wish it had been otherwise. We would give a great deal to persuade those ancient oracles to speak on the subject of these twelve verses: but they are all but inexorably silent. Nay, I am overstating the case against myself. Two of the greatest Fathers (Augustine and Ambrose) actually do utter a few words; and they are to the effect that the verses are undoubtedly genuine:—'Be it known to all men' (they say) 'that this passage *is* genuine: but the nature of its subject-matter has at once procured its ejection from MSS., and resulted in the silence of Commentators.' The most learned of the Fathers in addition practically endorses the passage; for Jerome not only leaves it standing in the Vulgate where he found it in the Old Latin version, but relates that it was supported by Greek as well as Latin authorities.

To proceed however with what I was about to say.

It is the authoritative sentence of the Church then on this difficult subject that we desiderate. We resorted to the Fathers for that: intending to regard any quotations of theirs, however brief, as their practical endorsement of all the twelve verses: to infer from their general recognition of the passage, that the Church in her collective capacity accepted it likewise. As I have shewn, the Fathers decline, almost to a man, to return any answer. But,—Are we then without the Church's authoritative guidance on this subject? For this, I repeat, is the only thing of which we are in search. It was only in order to get at this that we adopted the laborious expedient of watching for the casual utterances of any of the giants of old time. Are we, I say, left without the Church's opinion?

Not so, I answer. The reverse is the truth. The great Eastern Church speaks out on this subject in a voice of thunder. In all her Patriarchates, as far back as the written records of her practice reach,—and they reach back to the time of those very Fathers whose silence we felt to be embarrassing,—the Eastern Church has selected nine out of these twelve verses to be the special lesson for October 8. A more significant circumstance it would be impossible to adduce in evidence. Any pretence to fasten a charge of spuriousness on a portion of Scripture so singled out by the Church for honour, were nothing else but monstrous. It would be in fact to raise quite a distinct issue: viz. to inquire what amount of respect is due to the Church's authority in determining the authenticity of Scripture? I appeal not to an opinion, but to *a fact*: and that fact is, that though the Fathers of the Church for a very sufficient reason are very nearly silent on the subject of these twelve verses, the Church herself has spoken with a voice of authority so loud that none can affect not to hear it: so plain, that it cannot possibly be misunderstood.

And let me not be told that I am hereby setting up the Lectionary as the true standard of appeal for the Text of the New Testament: still less let me be suspected of charging on the collective body of the faithful whatever irregularities are discoverable in the Codexes which were employed for the public reading of Scripture. Such a suspicion could only be entertained by one who has hitherto failed to apprehend the precise point just now under consideration. We are not examining the text of St. John vii. 53–viii. 11. We are only discussing whether those twelve verses *en bloc* are to be regarded as an integral part of the fourth Gospel, or as a spurious accretion to it. And that is a point on which the Church in her corporate character must needs be competent to pronounce; and in respect of which her verdict must needs be decisive. She delivered her verdict in favour of these twelve verses, remember, at a time when her copies of the Gospels were of papyrus as well as 'old uncials' on vellum.—Nay, before 'old uncials' on vellum were at least in any general use. True, that the transcribers of Lectionaries have proved themselves just as liable to error as the men who transcribed Evangelia. But then, it is incredible that those men forged the Gospel for St. Pelagia's day: impossible, if it were a forgery, that the Church should have adopted it. And it is the significancy of the Church having adopted the *pericope de adultera* as the lection for October 8, which has never yet been sufficiently attended to: and which I defy the Critics to account for on any hypothesis but one: viz. that the pericope was recognized by the ancient Eastern Church as an integral part of the Gospel.

Now when to this has been added what is implied in the rubrical direction that a ceremonious respect should be shewn to the Festival of Pentecost by dropping the twelve verses, I submit that I have fully established my second position, viz. That by the very construction of her Lectionary the Church in her corporate capacity and official character has solemnly recognized the narrative in question, as an integral part of St. John's Gospel, and as standing in its traditional place, from an exceedingly remote time.

For,—(I entreat the candid reader's sustained attention),—the circumstances of the present problem altogether refuse to accommodate themselves to any hypothesis of a spurious original for these verses; as I proceed to shew.

Repair in thought to any collection of MSS. you please; suppose to the British Museum. Request to be shewn their seventy-three copies of St. John's Gospel, and turn to the close of his seventh chapter. At that particular place you will find, in sixty-one of these copies, these twelve verses: and in thirty-five of them you will discover, after the words Προφήτης ἐκ τῆς Γαλιλαίας οὐκ ἐγ. a rubrical note to the effect that 'on Whitsunday, these twelve verses are to be dropped; and the reader is to go on at ch. viii. 12.' What can be the meaning of this respectful treatment of the Pericope in question? How can it ever have come to pass that it has been thus ceremoniously handled all down the ages? Surely on no possible view of the matter but one can the phenomenon just now described be accounted for. Else, will any one gravely pretend to tell me that at some indefinitely remote period, (1) These verses were fabricated: (2) Were thrust into the place they at present occupy in the sacred text: (3) Were unsuspectingly believed to be genuine by the Church; and in consequence of which they were at once passed over by her direction on Whitsunday as incongruous, and appointed by the Church to be read on October 8, as appropriate to the occasion?

(3) But further. How is it proposed to explain why *one* of St. John's afterthoughts should have fared so badly at the Church's hands;—another, so well? I find it suggested that perhaps the subject-matter may sufficiently account for all that has happened to the *pericope de adultera*: And so it may, no doubt. But then, once admit *this*, and the hypothesis under consideration becomes simply nugatory: fails even to *touch* the difficulty which it professes to remove. For if men were capable of thinking scorn of these twelve verses when they found them in the 'second and improved edition of St. John's Gospel,' why may they not have been just as irreverent in respect of the same verses, when they appeared in the *first* edition? How is it one whit more probable that every Greek Father for a thousand years should have systematically overlooked the twelve verses in dispute when they appeared in the second edition of St. John's Gospel, than that the same Fathers should have done the same thing when they appeared in the first[617]?

(4) But the hypothesis is gratuitous and nugatory: for it has been invented in order to account for the phenomenon that whereas twelve verses of St. John's Gospel are found in the large majority of the later Copies,—the same verses are observed to be absent from all but one of the five oldest Codexes. But how, (I wish to be informed,) is that hypothesis supposed to square with these phenomena? It cannot be meant that the 'second edition' of St. John did not come abroad until after Codd. אABCT were written? For we know that the old Italic version (a document of the second century) contains all the three portions of narrative which are claimed for the second edition. But if this is not meant, it is plain that some further hypothesis must be invented in

order to explain why certain Greek MSS. of the fourth and fifth centuries are without the verses in dispute. And this fresh hypothesis will render that under consideration (as I said) nugatory and shew that it was gratuitous.

What chiefly offends me however in this extraordinary suggestion is its *irreverence.* It assumes that the Gospel according to St. John was composed like any ordinary modern book: capable therefore of being improved in the second edition, by recension, addition, omission, retractation, or what not. For we may not presume to limit the changes effected in a second edition. And yet the true Author of the Gospel is confessedly God the Holy Ghost: and I know of no reason for supposing that His works are imperfect when they proceed forth from His Hands.

The cogency of what precedes has in fact weighed so powerfully with thoughtful and learned Divines that they have felt themselves constrained, as their last resource, to cast about for some hypothesis which shall at once account for the absence of these verses from so many copies of St. John's Gospel, and yet retain them for their rightful owner and author,—St. John. Singular to relate, the assumption which has best approved itself to their judgement has been, that there must have existed two editions of St. John's Gospel,—the earlier edition without, the later edition with, the incident under discussion. It is I presume, in order to conciliate favour to this singular hypothesis, that it has been further proposed to regard St. John v. 3, 4 and the whole of St. John xxi, (besides St. John vii. 53-viii. 11), as after-thoughts of the Evangelist.

1. But this is unreasonable: for nothing else but *the absence* of St. John vii. 53-viii. 11, from so many copies of the Gospel has constrained the Critics to regard those verses with suspicion. Whereas, on the contrary, there is not known to exist a copy in the world which omits so much as a single verse of chap. xxi. Why then are we to assume that the whole of that chapter was away from the original draft of the Gospel? Where is the evidence for so extravagant an assumption?

2. So, concerning St. John v. 3, 4: to which there really attaches no manner of doubt, as I have elsewhere shewn[618]. Thirty-two precious words in that place are indeed omitted by אBC: twenty-seven by D. But by this time the reader knows what degree of importance is to be attached to such an amount of evidence. On the other hand, they are found in *all other copies*: are vouched for by the Syriac[619] and the Latin versions: in the Apostolic Constitutions, by Chrysostom, Cyril, Didymus, and Ammonius, among the Greeks,—by Tertullian, Ambrose, Jerome, Augustine among the Latins. Why a passage so attested is to be assumed to be an after-thought of the Evangelist has never yet been explained: no, nor ever will be.

(5) Assuming, however, just for a moment the hypothesis correct for argument's sake, viz. that in the second edition of St. John's Gospel the history of the woman taken in adultery appeared for the first time. Invite the authors of that hypothesis to consider what follows. The discovery that five out of six of the oldest uncials extant (to reckon here the fragment T) are without the

verses in question; which yet are contained in ninety-nine out of every hundred of the despised cursives:—what other inference can be drawn from such premisses, but that the cursives fortified by other evidence are by far the more trustworthy witnesses of what St. John in his old age actually entrusted to the Church's keeping?

[The MS. here leaves off, except that a few pencilled words are added in an incomplete form. I have been afraid to finish so clever and characteristic an essay.]

578   Compare 1 Sam. xxiv. 22:—'And Saul went home: *but David and his men gat them up into the hold.*' 1 Kings xviii. 42:—'So Ahab went up to eat and to drink: *and Elijah went up to the top of Carmel, and he cast himself down upon the earth, and put his face between his knees.*' Esther iii. 15:—'And the king and Haman sat down to drink; *but the city of Shushan was perplexed.*' Such are the idioms of the Bible.

579   Ammonius (Cord. Cat. p. 216), with evident reference to it, remarks that our Lord's words in verses 37 and 38 were intended as a *viaticum* which all might take home with them, at the close of this, 'the last, the great day of the feast.'

580   So Eusebius Ὅτε κατὰ τὸ αὐτὸ συναχθέντες οἱ τῶν Ἰουδαίων ἔθνους ἄρχοντες ἐπὶ τῆς Ἰερουσαλήμ, συνέδριον ἐποιήσαντο καὶ σκέψιν ὅπως αὐτὸν ἀπολέσωσιν· ἐν ᾧ οἱ μὲν θάνατον αὐτοῦ κατεψηφίσαντο· ἕτεροι δὲ ἀντέλεγον, ὡς ὁ Νικόδημος, κ.τ.λ. (in Psalmos, p. 230 a).

581   Westcott and Hort's prefatory matter (1870) to their revised Text of the New Testament, p. xxvii.

582   So in the LXX. See Num. v. 11-31.

583   Ver. 17. So the LXX.

584   2 Cor. iv. 7: v. 1.

585   Compare ch. vi. 6, 71: vii. 39: xi. 13, 51: xii. 6, 33: xiii. 11, 28: xxi. 19.

586   Consider ch. xix. 19, 20, 21, 22: xx. 30, 31: xxi. 24, 25.—1 John i. 4: ii. 1, 7, 8, 12, 13, 14, 21, 26: v. 13.—2 John 5, 12.—3 John 9, 13.—Rev. *passim,* espe-

cially i. 11, 19: ii. 1, &c.: x. 4: xiv. 13: xvii. 8: xix. 9: xx. 12, 15: xxi. 5, 27: xxii. 18, 29.

587   Westcott and Hort, ibid. pp. xxvii, xxvi.

588   Novum Testamentum, 1869, p. 829.

589   Plain Introduction, 1894, ii. 364.

590   Printed Texts, 1854, p. 241.

591   Developed Criticism, p. 82.

592   Outlines, &c., p. 103.

593   Nicholson's Gospel according to the Hebrews, p. 141.

594   Scrivener, ut supra, ii. 368.

595   I insert this epithet on sufficient authority. Mr. Edw. A. Guy, an intelligent young American,—himself a very accurate observer and a competent judge,—collated a considerable part of Cod. A in 1875, and assured me that he scarcely ever found any discrepancy between the Codex and Woide's reprint. One instance of *italicism* was in fact all that had been overlooked in the course of many pages.

596   It is inaccurate also. His five lines contain eight mistakes. Praefat. p. xxx, § 86.

597   ii. 630, addressing Rufinns, A.D. 403. Also ii. 748-9.

598   i. 291, 692, 707, 1367: ii. 668, 894, 1082: iii. 892-3, 896-7.

599   i. 30: ii. 527, 529-30: iii¹. 774: iii². 158, 183, 531-2 (where he quotes the place largely and comments upon it): iv. 149, 466 (largely quoted), 1120: v. 80, 1230 (largely quoted in both places): vi. 407, 413 viii. 377, 574.

[600] Pacian (A.D. 372) refers the Novatians to the narrative as something which all men knew. 'Nolite in Evangelio legere quod pepercerit Dominus etiam adulterae confitenti, quam nemo damnarat?' Pacianus, Op. Epist. iii. Contr. Novat. (A.D. 372). *Ap.* Galland. vii. 267.

[601] *Ap.* Augustin. viii. 463.

[602] In his translation of Eusebius. Nicholson, p. 53.

[603] Chrysologus, A.D. 433, Abp. of Ravenna. Venet. 1742. Ile mystically explains the entire incident. Serm. cxv. § 5.

[604] Sedulius (A.D. 435) makes it the subject of a poem, and devotes a whole chapter to it. *Ap.* Galland. ix. 553 and 590.

[605] 'Promiss.' De Promissionibus dimid. temp. (saec. iv). Quotes viii. 4, 5, 9. P. 2, c. 22, col. 147 b. Ignot. Auct., De Vocatione omnium Gentium (circa, A.D. 440), *ap.* Opp. Prosper. Aquit. (1782), i. p. 460-1:—'Adulteram ex legis constitutione lapidandam . . . liberavit . . . cum executores praecepti de conscientiis territi, trementem ream sub illius iudicio reliquissent. . . . Et inclinatus, id est ad humana dimissus . . . "digito scribebat in terram," ut legem mandatorum per gratiae decreta vacuaret,' &c.

[606] Wrongly ascribed to Idacius.

[607] Gelasius P. A.D. 492. Conc. iv. 1235. Quotes viii. 3, 7, 10, 11.

[608] Cassiodorus, A.D. 514. Venet. 1729. Quotes viii. 11. See ii. p. 96, 3, 5-180.

[609] Dialogues, xiv. 15.

[610] ii. 748:—In evangelio secundum Ioannem in multis et Graecis et Latinis codicibus invenitur de adultera muliere, quae accusata est apud Dominum.

[611] ἑνὸς ἑκάστου αὐτῶν τὰς ἁμαρτίας. Ev. 95, 40, 48, 64, 73, 100, 122, 127, 142, 234, 264, 267, 274, 433, 115, 121, 604, 736.

[612] Appendix, p. 88.

[613] vi. 407:—Sed hoc videlicet infidelium sensus exhorret, ita ut nonnulli modicae fidei vel potius inimici verae fidei, (credo metuentes peccandi impunitatem dari mulieribus suis), illud quod de adulterae indulgentia Dominus fecit, auferrent de codicibus suis: quasi permissionem peccandi tribuerit qui dixit, 'Iam deinceps noli peccare;' aut ideo non debuerit mulier a medico Deo illius peccati remissione sanari, ne offenderentur insani. De coniug. adult. ii. cap. 7. i. 707:—Fortasse non mediocrem scrupulum movere potuit imperitis Evangelii lectio, quae decursa est, in quo advertistis adulteram Christo oblatam, eamque sine damnatione dimissam. Nam profecto si quis ea auribus accipiat otiosis, incentivum erroris incurrit, cum leget quod Deus censuerit adulterium non esse damnandum.

[614] Epist. 58. Quid scribebat? nisi illud Propheticum (Jer. xxii. 29-30), *Terra, terra, scribe hos vivos abdicatos.*

[615] Constt. App. (Gen. iii. 49). Nicon (Gen. iii. 250). I am not certain about these two references.

[616] Two precious verses (viz. the forty-third and forty-fourth) used to be omitted from the lection for Tuesday before Quinquagesima,—viz. St. Luke xxii. 39-xxiii. 1.

The lection for the preceding Sabbath (viz. St. Luke xxi. 8-36) consisted of only the following verses,—ver. 8, 9, 25-27, 33-36. All the rest (viz. verses 10-24 and 28-32) was omitted.

On the ensuing Thursday, St. Luke xxiii was handled in a similar style: viz. ver. 1-31. 33, 44-56 alone were read,— all the other verses being left out.

On the first Sabbath after Pentecost

(All Saints'), the lesson consisted of St. Matt. x. 32, 33, 37-38: xix. 27-30.

On the fifteenth Sabbath after Pentecost, the lesson was St. Matt. xxiv. 1-9, 13 (leaving out verses 11, 12).

On the sixteenth Sabbath after Pentecost, the lesson was St. Matt. xxiv. 34-37, 42-44 (leaving out verses 38-41).

On the sixth Sabbath of St. Luke,—the lesson was ch. viii. 26-35 followed by verses 38 and 39.

[617] 'This celebrated paragraph . . . was probably not contained in the first edition of St. John's Gospel but added at the time when his last chapter was annexed to what had once been the close of his narrative,—xx. 30, 31.' Scrivener's Introduction to Cod. D, p. 50.
[618] In an unpublished paper.
[619] It is omitted in some MSS. of the Peshitto.

Appendix II - Conflation and the So-Called Neutral Text

SOME of the most courteous of our critics, in reviewing the companion volume to this, have expressed regret that we have not grappled more closely than we have done with Dr. Hort's theory. I have already expressed our reasons. Our object has been to describe and establish what we conceive to be the true principles of Sacred Textual Science. We are concerned only in a secondary degree with opposing principles. Where they have come in our way, we have endeavoured to remove them. But it has not entered within our design to pursue them into their fastnesses and domiciles. Nevertheless, in compliance with a request which is both proper and candid, I will do what I can to examine with all the equity that I can command an essential part of Dr. Hort's system, which appears to exercise great influence with his followers.

§ 1. CONFLATION.

Dr. Hort's theory of 'Conflation' may be discovered on pp. 93-107. The want of an index to his Introduction, notwithstanding his ample 'Contents,' makes it difficult to collect illustrations of his meaning from the rest of his treatise. Nevertheless, the effect of Conflation appears to be well described in his words on p. 133:—'Now however the three great lines were brought together, and made to contribute to a text different from all.' In other words, by means of a combination of the Western, Alexandrian, and 'Neutral' Texts— 'the great lines of transmission . . . to all appearance exclusively divergent,'— the 'Syrian' text was constructed in a form different from any one and all of the other three. Not that all these three were made to contribute on every occasion. We find (p. 93) Conflation, or Conflate Readings, introduced as proving the posteriority of Syrian to Western . . . and other . . . readings.' And in the analysis of eight passages, which is added, only in one case (St. Mark viii. 26) are more than two elements represented, and in that the third class consists of 'different conflations' of the first and second[620].

Perhaps I may present Dr. Hort's theory under the form of a diagram:—

Western Readings.   **Other Readings.**

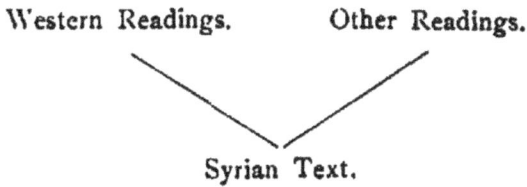

Syrian Text.

Our theory is the converse in main features to this. We utterly repudiate the term Syrian' as being a most inadequate and untrue title for the Text adopted and maintained by the Catholic Church with all her intelligence and learning, during nearly fifteen centuries according to Dr. Hort's admission: and we claim from the evidence that the Traditional Text of the Gospels, under the true name, is that which came fresh from the pens of the Evangelists; and that all variations from it, however they have been entitled, are nothing else than corrupt forms of the original readings. Our diagram in rough presentation will therefore assume this character:—

Traditional Text.

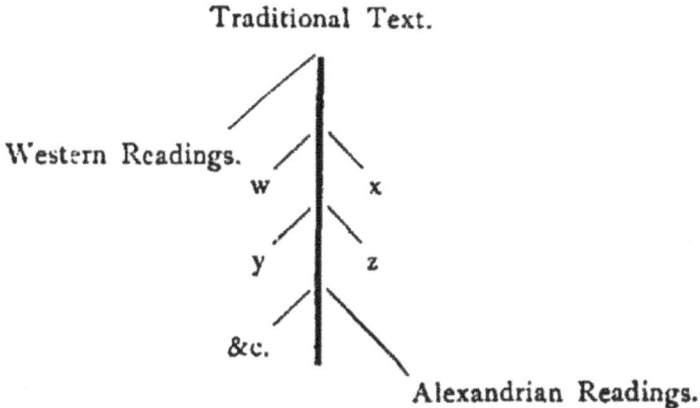

Western Readings.

w   x

y   z

&c.

Alexandrian Readings.

It should be added, that w, x, y, z, &c., denote forms of corruption. We do not recognize the 'Neutral' at all, believing it to be a Caesarean combination or recension, made from previous texts or readings of a corrupt character.

The question is, which is the true theory, Dr. Hort's or ours?

The general points that strike us with reference to Dr. Flores theory are:—

(1) That it is very vague and indeterminate in nature. Given three things, of which X includes what is in Y and Z, upon the face of the theory either X may have arisen by synthesis from Y and Z, or X and Z may owe their origin by analysis to X.

(2) Upon examination it is found that Dr. Hort's arguments for the posteriority of D are mainly of an internal character, and are loose and imaginative, depending largely upon personal or literary predilections.

(3) That it is exceedingly improbable that the Church of the fourth and fifth centuries, which in a most able period had been occupied with discussions

153

on verbal accuracy, should have made the gross mistake of adopting (what was then) a modern concoction from the original text of the Gospels, which had been written less than three or four centuries before; and that their error should have been acknowledged as truth, and perpetuated by the ages that succeeded them down to the present time.

But we must draw nearer to Dr. Hort's argument.

He founds it upon a detailed examination of eight passages, viz. St. Mark vi. 33; viii. 26; ix. 38; ix. 49; St. Luke ix. 10; xi. 54; xii. 18; xxiv. 53.

1. Remark that eight is a round and divisible number. Did the author decide upon it with a view of presenting two specimens from each Gospel? To be sure, he gives four from the first two, and four from the two last, only that he confines the batches severally to St. Mark and St. Luke. Did the strong style of St. Matthew, with distinct meaning in every word, yield no suitable example for treatment? Could no passage be found in St. John's Gospel, where not without parallel, but to a remarkable degree, extreme simplicity of language, even expressed in alternative clauses, clothes soaring thought and philosophical acuteness? True, that he quotes St. John v. 37 as an instance of Conflation by the Codex Bezae which is anything but an embodiment of the Traditional or 'Syrian' Text, and xiii. 24 which is similarly irrelevant. Neither of these instances therefore fill up the gap, and are accordingly not included in the selected eight. What can we infer from this presentment, but that Conflation' is probably not of frequent occurrence as has been imagined, but may indeed be—to admit for a moment its existence—nothing more than an occasional incident? For surely, if specimens in St. Matthew and St. John had abounded to his hand, and accordingly Conflation' had been largely employed throughout the Gospels, Dr. Hort would not have exercised so restricted, and yet so round a choice.

2. But we must advance a step further. Dean Burgon as we have seen has calculated the differences between B and the Received Text at 7,578, and those which divide ℵ and the Received Text as reaching 8,972. He divided these totals respectively under 2,877 and 3,455 omissions, 536 and 839 additions, 2,098 and 2,299 transpositions, and 2,067 and 2,379 substitutions and modifications combined. Of these classes, it is evident that Conflation has nothing to do with Additions or Transpositions. Nor indeed with Substitutions, although one of Dr. Hort's instances appears to prove that it has. Conflation is the combination of two (or more) different expressions into one. If therefore both expressions occur in one of the elements, the Conflation has been made beforehand, and a substitution then occurs instead of a conflation. So in St. Luke xii. 18, B, &c., read τὸν σῖτον καὶ τὰ ἀγαθά μου, which Dr. Hort[621] considers to be made by Conflation into τά γενήματά μου καὶ τὰ ἀγαθά μου, because τά γενήματά μου is found in Western documents. The logic is strange, but as Dr. Hort has claimed it, we must perhaps allow him to have intended to include with this strange incongruity some though not many Substitutions in his class of instances, only that we should like to know definitely what substitutions were to be. comprised in this class. For I

154

shrewdly suspect that there were actually none. Omissions are now left to us, of which the greater specimens can hardly have been produced by Conflation. How, for instance, could you get the last Twelve Verses of St. Mark's Gospel, or the Pericope de Adultera, or St. Luke xxii. 43-44, or any of the rest of the forty-five whole verses in the Gospels upon which a slur is cast by the Neologian school? Consequently, the area of Conflation is greatly reduced. And I venture to think, that supposing for a moment the theory to be sound, it could not account for any large number of variations, but would at the best only be a sign or symptom found every now and then of the derivation attributed to the Received Text.

3. But we must go on towards the heart of the question. And first to examine Dr. Hort's eight instances. Unfortunately, the early patristic evidence on these verses is scanty. We have little evidence of a direct character to light up the dark sea of conjecture.

(1) St. Mark (vi. 33) relates that on a certain occasion the multitude, when they beheld our Saviour and his disciples on their way in a ship crossing to the other side of the lake, ran together (συνέδραμον) from all their cities to the point which He was making for (ἐκεῖ), and arrived there before the Lord and His followers (προῆλθον αὐτούς), and on His approach came in a body to Him (συνῆλθον πρὸς αὐτν). And on disembarking (καὶ ἐξελθών, i.e. ἐκ τοῦ πλοίου, ver. 32), &c. It should be observed, that it was only the Apostles who knew that His ultimate object was a 'desert place' (ver. 31, 30): the indiscriminate multitude could only discern the bay or cape towards which the boat was going: and up to what I have described as the disembarkation (ver. 34), nothing has been said of His movements, except that He was in the boat upon the lake. The account is pictorial. We see the little craft toiling on the lake, the people on the shores running all in one direction, and on their reaching the heights above the place of landing watching His approach, and then descending together to Him to the point where He is going to land. There is nothing weak or superfluous in the description. Though condensed (what would a modern history have made of it?), it is all natural and in due place.

Now for Dr. Hort. He observes that one clause (καὶ προῆλθον αὐτούς) is attested by Bℵ and their followers; another (καὶ συνῆλθον αὐτοῦ, or ἦλθον αὐτοῦ, which is very different from the 'Syrian' συνῆλθον πρὸς αὐτόν) by some Western documents; and he argues that the entire form in the Received Text, καὶ προῆλθον αὐτούς, καὶ συνῆλθον πρὸς αὐτόν, was formed by Conflation from the other two. I cannot help observing that it is a suspicious mark, that even in the case of the most favoured of his chosen examples he is obliged to take such a liberty with one of his elements of Conflation as virtually to doctor it in order to bring it strictly to the prescribed pattern. When we come to his arguments he candidly admits, that 'it is evident that either δ (the Received Text) is conflate from α (Bℵ) and β (Western), or α and β are independent simplifications of δ'; and that 'there is nothing in the sense of δ that would tempt to alteration,' and that 'accidental' omission of one or other clause would 'be easy.' But he argues with an ingenuity that denotes a bad cause that the difference between αὐτοῦ and πρὸς αὐτόν is really in his favour, chiefly because αὐτοῦ would very likely *if* it had previously existed been changed into πρὸς αὐτόν—which no one can doubt; and that 'συνῆλθον πρὸς αὐτόν is certainly otiose after συνέδραμον ἐκεῖ,' which shews that he did not understand the whole meaning of the passage. His argument upon what he terms 'Intrinsic Probability' leads to a similar inference. For simply ἐξελθών cannot mean that He "came out" of His retirement in some sequestered nook to meet them,' such a nook being not mentioned by St. Mark, whereas πλοῖον is; nor can ἐκεῖ denote the desert region.' Indeed the position of that region or nook was known before it was reached solely to our Lord and His Apostles: the multitude was guided only by what they saw, or at least by vague surmise.

Accordingly, Dr. Hort's conclusion must be reversed. 'The balance of Internal Evidence of Readings, alike from Transcriptional and from Intrinsic Probability, is decidedly' *not* 'in favour of δ from α and β,' *but* 'of α and β from δ.' The reading of the Traditional Text is the superior both as regards the meaning, and as to the probability of its pre-existence. The derivation of the two others from that is explained by that besetting fault of transcribers which is termed Omission. Above all, the Traditional reading is proved by a largely over-balancing weight of evidence.

(2) 'To examine other passages equally in detail would occupy too much space.' So says Dr. Hort: but we must examine points that require attention.

St. Mark viii. 26. After curing the blind man outside Bethsaida, our Lord in that remarkable period of His career directed him, according to the Traditional reading, (α) neither to enter into that place, μηδὲ εἰς τὴν κώμην εἰσέλθῃς, nor (α) to tell what had happened to any inhabitant of Bethsaida (μηδὲ εἴπῃς τινὶ ἐν τῇ κώμῃ). Either some one who did not understand the Greek, or some matter-of-fact and officious scholar, or both, thought or maintained that τινὶ ἐν τῇ κώμῃ must mean some one who was at the moment actually in the place. So the second clause got to be omitted from the text of Bℵ, who are followed only by one cursive and a half (the first reading of 1 being afterwards corrected), and the Bohairic version, and the Lewis MS. The Traditional reading is attested by ACNΣ and thirteen other Uncials, all Cursives except eight, of which six with Φ read a consolidation of both clauses, by several versions, and by Theophylact (i. 210) who is the only Father that quotes the place. This evidence ought amply to ensure the genuineness of this reading.

But what says Dr. Hort? 'Here a is simple and vigorous, and it is unique in the New Testament: the peculiar Μηδὲ has the terse force of many sayings as given by St. Mark, but the softening into Μή by ℵ* shews that it might trouble scribes.' It is surely not necessary to controvert this. It may be said however that a is bald as well as simple, and that the very difficulty in β makes it probable that that clause was not invented. To take τινὶ ἐν τῇ κώμῃ Hebraistically for τινὶ τῶν ἐν τῇ κώμῃ like the τις ἐν ὑμῖν ig.av of St. James v. 19[622], need not trouble scholars, I think. Otherwise they can follow Meyer, according to Winer's Grammar (II. 511), and translate the second μηδέ *nor even*. At all events, this is a poor pillar to support a great theory.

(3) St. Mark ix. 38. 'Master, we saw one casting out devils in Thy name, (β) who doth not follow us, and we forbad him (α) because he followeth not us.'

Here the authority for α is אBCLΔ, four Cursives, f, Bohairic, Peshitto, Ethiopic, and the Lewis MS. For β there are D, two Cursives, all the Old Latin but f and the Vulgate. For the Traditional Text, i.e. the whole passage, ΑΦΣΝ + eleven Uncials, all the Cursives but six, the Harkleian (yet obelizes α) and Gothic versions, Basil (ii. 252), Victor of Antioch (Cramer, Cat. i. 365), Theophylact (i. 219): and Augustine quotes separately both omissions (α ix. 533, and β III. ii. 153). No other Fathers, so far as I can find, quote the passage.

Dr. Hort appears to advance no special arguments on his side, relying apparently upon the obvious repetition. In the first part of the verse, St. John describes the case of the man: in the second he reports for our Lord's judgement the grounds of the prohibition which the Apostles gave him. Is it so certain that the original text of the passage contained only the description, and omitted the reason of the prohibition as it was given to the non-follower of our Lord? To me it seems that the simplicity of St. Mark's style is best preserved by the inclusion of both. The Apostles did not curtly forbid the man: they treated him with reasonableness, and in the same spirit St. John reported to his Master all that occurred. Besides this, the evidence on the Traditional side is too strong to admit of it not being the genuine reading.

(4) St. Mark ix. 49. 'For (α) every one shall be salted with fire, (β) and every sacrifice shall be salted with salt.' The authorities are—

α. אBLΔ, fifteen Cursives, some MSS. of the Bohairic, some of the Armenian, and the Lewis.

β. D, six copies of the Old Latin, three MSS. of the Vulgate. Chromatius of Aquileia (Galland. viii. 338).

Trad. Text. ΑCΦΣΝ and twelve more Uncials, all Cursives except fifteen, two Old Latin, Vulgate, Peshitto, Harkleian, some MSS. of Ethiopic and Armenian, Gothic, Victor of Antioch (Cramer's Cat. i. 368), Theophylact (i. 221).

This evidence must surely be conclusive of the genuineness of the Traditional reading. But now for Dr. Hort.

'A reminiscence of Lev. vii. 13 . . . has created β out of α.' But why should not the reminiscence have been our Lord's? The passage appears like a quotation, or an adaptation, of some authoritative saying. He positively advances no other argument than the one just quoted, beyond stating two points in which the alteration might be easily effected.

(5) St. Luke ix. 10. 'He took (His Apostles) and withdrew privately

α. Into a city called Bethsaida (εἰς πόλιν καλουμένην Β.).

β. Into a desert place (εἰς τόπον ἔρημον), or Into a desert place called Bethsaida, or of Bethsaida.'

Trad. Text. Into a desert place belonging to a city called Bethsaida.'

The evidence for these readings respectively is—

α. BLXΞ, with one correction of א (Cᵃ), one Cursive, the Bohairic and Sahidic. D reads κώμην.

β. The first and later readings (Cᵇ) of four Cursives?, Curetonian, some variant Old Latin (β²), Peshitto also variant (β³).

Trad. Text. A (with ἔρημον τόπον) C + twelve Uncials, all Cursives except three or five, Harkleian, Lewis (omits ἔρημον), Ethiopic, Armenian, Gothic, with Theophylact (i. 332).

Remark the curious character of α and β. In Dr. Hort's Neutral Text, which he maintains to have been the original text of the Gospels, our Lord is represented here as having withdrawn in private (κατ᾽ ἰδίαν, which the Revisers shirking the difficulty translate inaccurately 'apart') *into the city called Bethsaida*. How could there have been privacy of life *in* a city in those days? In fact, κατ᾽ ἰδίαν necessitates the adoption of τόπον ἔρημον, as to which the Peshitto (β³) is in substantial agreement with the Traditional Text. Bethsaida is represented as the capital of a district, which included, at sufficient distance from the city, a desert or retired spot. The group arranged under β is so weakly supported, and is evidently such a group of fragments, that it can come into no sort of competition with the Traditional reading. Dr. Hort confines himself to shewing *how* the process he advocates might have arisen, not *that* it did actually arise. Indeed, this position can only be held by assuming the conclusion to be established that it *did* so arise.

(6) St. Luke xi. 54. 'The Scribes and Pharisees began to urge Him vehemently and to provoke Him to speak of many things (ἐνεδρεύοντες θηρεῦσαι),

α. Laying wait for Him to catch something out of His mouth.

β. Seeking to get some opportunity (ἀφορμήν τινα) for finding out how to accuse Him (ἵνα εὕρωσιν κατηγορῆσαι); or, for accusing Him (ἵνα κατηγορήσωσιν αὐτοῦ).

Trad. Text. Laying wait for Him, *and* seeking to catch something (ζητοῦντες θηρεῦσαί τι) out of His mouth, that they might accuse Him.'

The evidence is—

α. אBL, Bohairic, Ethiopic, Cyril Alex. (Mai, Nov. Pp. Bibliotheca, ii. 87, iii. 249, not accurately).

β. D, Old Latin except f, Curetonian.

Trad. Text. AC + twelve Uncials, all Cursives (except five which omit ζητοῦντες), Peshitto, Lewis (with omission), Vulgate, Harkleian, Theophylact (i. 363).

As to genuineness, the evidence is decisive. The reading α is Alexandrian, adopted by B-א, and is bad Greek into the bargain, ἐνεδρεύοντες θηρεῦσαι being very rough, and being probably due to incompetent acquaintance with the Greek language. If α was the original, it is hard to see how β could have come from it. That the figurative language of α was replaced in β by a simply descriptive paraphrase, as Dr. Hort suggests, seems scarcely probable. On the other hand, the derivation of either α or β from the Traditional Text is much easier. A scribe would without difficulty pass over one of the participles lying contiguously with no connecting conjunction, and having a kind of Homoe-oteleuton. And as to β, the distinguishing ἀφορμήν τινα would be a very natural gloss, requiring for completeness of the phrase the accompanying λαβεῖν. This is surely a more probable solution of the question of the mutual relationship of the readings than the laboured account of Dr. Hort, which is too long to be produced here.

(7) St. Luke xii. 18. 'I will pull down my barns, and build greater, and there will I bestow all

α. My corn and my goods.

β. My crops (τὰ γενήματά μου). My fruits (τοὺς καρπούς μου).

Trad. Text. My crops (τὰ γενήματά μου) and my goods.'

This is a faulty instance, because it is simply a substitution, as Dr. Hort admitted, in α of the more comprehensive word γενήματά for σῖτον, and a simple omission of καὶ τὰ ἀγαθὰ μου in β. And the admission of it into the selected eight shews the difficulty that Dr. Hort must have experienced in choosing his examples. The evidence is—

α. BTLX and a correction of ℵ(aᶜ), eight Cursives, Peshitto, Bohairic, Sahidic, Armenian, Ethiopic.

β. ℵ*D, three Cursives, b ff i q, Curetonian and Lewis, St. Ambrose (i. 573).

Trad. Text. AQ + thirteen Uncials. All Cursives except twelve, *f*, Vulgate, Harkleian, Cyril Alex. (Mai, ii. 294-5) *bis*, Theophylact (i. 370), Peter Chrysologus (Migne 52, 490-1) *bis*.

No more need be said: substitutions and omissions are too common to require justification.

(8) St. Luke xxiv. 53. 'They were continually in the temple

α. Blessing God (εὐλογοῦντες).

β. Praising God (αἰνοῦντες).

Trad. Text. Praising and blessing God.'

The evidence is—

α. ℵBC*L, Bohairic, Palestinian, Lewis.

β. D, seven Old Latin.

Trad. Text. AC² + twelve Uncials, all Cursives, c f q, Vulgate, Peshitto, Harkleian, Armenian, Ethiopic, Theophylact (i. 497).

Dr. Hort adds no remarks. He seems to have thought, that because he had got an instance which outwardly met all the requirements laid down, therefore it would prove the conclusion it was intended to prove. Now it is evidently an instance of the omission of either of two words from the complete account by different witnesses. The Evangelist employed both words in order to emphasize the gratitude of the Apostles. The words are not tautological. Αἶνος is the set praise of God, drawn out in more or less length, properly as offered in addresses to Him[623]. Εὐλογία includes all speaking well of ,Him, especially when uttered before other men. Thus the two expressions describe in combination the life of gratitude exhibited unceasingly by the expectant and the infant Church. Continually in the temple they praised Him in devotion, and told the people of His glorious works.

4. Such are the eight weak pillars upon which Dr. Hort built his theory which was to account for the existence of his Neutral Text, and the relation of it towards other Texts or classes of readings. If his eight picked examples can be thus demolished, then surely the theory of Conflation must be utterly unsound. Or if in the opinion of some of my readers my contention goes too far, then at any rate they must admit that it is far from being firm; if it does not actually reel and totter. The opposite theory of omission appears to be much more easy and natural.

But the curious phenomenon that Dr. Hort has rested his case upon so small an induction as is supplied by only eight examples—if they are not in fact only seven—has not yet received due explanation. Why, he ought to have referred to twenty-five or thirty at least. If Conflation is so common, he might have produced a large number of references without working out more than was enough for illustration as patterns. This question must be investigated further. And I do not know how to carry out such an investigation better, than to examine some instances which come naturally to hand from the earlier parts of each Gospel.

It must be borne in mind, that for Conflation two differently-attested phrases or words must be produced which are found in combination in some passage of the Traditional Text. If there is only one which is omitted, it is clear that there can be no Conflation because there must be at least two elements to conflate: accordingly our instances must be cases, not of single omission, but of double or alternative omission. If again there is no Western reading, it is not a Conflation in Dr. Hort's sense. And finally, if the remaining reading is not a 'Neutral' one, it is not to Dr. Hort's liking. I do not say that my instances will conform with these conditions. Indeed, after making a list of all the omissions in the Gospels, except those which are of too petty a character such as leaving out a pronoun, and having searched the list with all the care that I can command, I do not think that such instances can be found. Nevertheless, I shall take eight, starting from the beginning of St. Matthew, and choosing the most salient examples, being such also that, if Dr. Hort's theory be sound, they ought to conform to his requirements. Similarly, there will come then four from either of St. Mark and St. Luke, and eight from St. John. This course of proceeding will extend operations from the eight which form Dr. Hort's total to thirty-two.

A. In St. Matthew we have (1) i. 25, αὐτῆς τὸν πρωτότοκον and τὸν Υἱόν; (2) v. 22, εἰκῆ and τῷ ἀδελφῷ αὐτοῦ; (3) ix. 13, εἰς μετάνοιαν; (4) x. 3, Λεββαῖος and Θαδδαῖος; (5) xii. 22, τυφλὸν καὶ and κωφόν; (6) xv. 5, τὸν πατέρα αὐτοῦ and (ἢ) τὴν μητέρα αὐτοῦ; (7) xviii. 35, ἀπὸ τῶν καρδιῶν ὑμῶν and τὰ παραπτώματα αὐτῶν ; and (8) xxvi. 3, οἱ πρεσβύτεροι (καὶ) οἱ Γραμματεῖς. I have had some difficulty in making up the number. Of those selected as well as I could, seven are cases of single omission or of one pure omission apiece, though their structure presents a possibility of two members for Conflation; whilst the Western clement comes in sparsely or appears in favour of both the omission and the retention; and, thirdly, in some cases, as in (2) and (3), the support is not only Western, but universal. Consequently, all but (4) are excluded. Of (4) Dr. Hort remarks, (Notes on Select Readings, p. 11) that it is 'a case of Conflation of the true and the chief Western Texts,' and accordingly it does not come within the charmed circle.

B. From St. Mark we get, (1) i. 1, Υἱοῦ τοῦ Θεοῦ, and Ἰησοῦ Χριστοῦ; (2) i. 2, ἔμπροσθέν σου and πρὸ προσώπου σου (cp. ix. 38); (3) iii. 15, θεραπεύειν τὰς νόσοις (καὶ) and ἐκβάλλειν τὰ δαιμόνια; (4) xiii. 33, ἀγρυπνεῖτε and (καὶ) προσεύχεσθε. All these instances turn out to be cases of the omission of only one of the parallel expressions. The omission in the first is due mainly to Origen (*see* Traditional Text, Appendix IV): in the three last there is Western evidence on both sides.

C. St. Luke yields us, (1) ii. 5, γυναικί and μεμνηστευμένη; (2) iv. 4, ἐπὶ παντὶ ῥήματι Θεοῦ or ἐπ' ἄρτῳ μόνῳ; (3) viii. 54, ἐκβαλὼν ἔξω πάντας (καὶ), or κρατήσας τῆς χειρὸς αὐτῆς; xi. 4, (ἀλλὰ) ῥῦσαι ἡμᾶς ἀπὸ τοῦ πονηροῦ, or μὴ εἰσενέγκῃς ἡμᾶς εἰς πειρασμόν. In all these cases, examination discloses that they are examples of pure omission of only one of the alternatives. The only evidence against this is the solitary rejection of μεμνηστευμένη by the Lewis Codex.

D. We now come to St. John. See (1) iii. 15, μὴ ἀπόληται, or ἔχῃ ζωὴν αἰώνιον; (2) iv. 14, οὐ μὴ διψήσῃ εἰς τὸν αἰῶνα or τὸ ὕδωρ ὃ δώσω αὐτῷ γενήσεται ἐν αὐτῷ πηγὴ ὕδατος, κ.τ.λ.; (3) iv. 42, ὁ Χριστός, or ὁ σωτὴρ τοῦ κόσμου; (4) iv. 51, καὶ ἀπήγγειλαν and λέγοντες; (5) v. 16, καὶ ἐζήτουν αὐτὸν ἀποκτεῖναι and ἐδίωκον αὐτόν; (6) vi. 51, ἣν ἐγὼ δώσω, or ὃν ἐγὼ δώσω; (7) ix. 1, 25, καὶ εἶπεν or ἀπεκρίθη; (8) xiii. 31, 32, εἰ ὁ Θεὸς ἐδοξάσθη ἐν αὐτῷ, and καὶ ὁ Θεὸς ἐδοξάσθη ἐν αὐτῷ. All these instances turn out to be single omissions:—a fact which is the more remarkable, because St. John's style so readily lends itself to parallel or antithetical expressions involving the same result in meaning, that we should expect conflations to shew themselves constantly if the Traditional Text had so coalesced.

How surprising a result:—almost too surprising. Does it not immensely strengthen my contention that Dr. Hort took wrongly Conflation for the reverse process? That in the earliest ages, when the Church did not include in her ranks so much learning as it has possessed ever since, the wear and tear of time, aided by unfaith and carelessness, made itself felt in many an instance of destructiveness which involved a temporary chipping of the Sacred Text all through the Holy Gospels? And, in fact, that Conflation at least as an extensive process, if not altogether, did not really exist.

§ 2. THE NEUTRAL TEXT.

Here we are brought face to face with the question respecting the Neutral Text. What in fact is it, and does it deserve the name which Dr. Hort and his followers have attempted to confer permanently upon it? What is the relation that it bears to other so-called Texts?

So much has been already advanced upon this subject in the companion volume and in the present, that great conciseness is here both possible and expedient. But it may be useful to bring the sum or substance of those discussions into one focus.

1. The so-called Neutral Text, as any reader of Dr. Hort's Introduction will see, is the text of B and ℵ and their small following. That following is made up of Z in St. Matthew, Δ in St. Mark, the fragmentary Ξ in St. Luke, with frequent agreement with them of D, and of the eighth century L; with occasional support from some of the group of Cursives, consisting of 1, 33, 118, 131, 157, 205, 209, and from the Ferrar group, or now and then from some others, as well as from the Latin k, and the Egyptian or other versions. This perhaps appears to be a larger number than our readers may have supposed, but rarely are more than ten MSS. found together, and generally speaking less, and often much less than that. To all general intents and purposes, the Neutral Text is the text of B–ℵ.

2. Following facts and avoiding speculation, the Neutral Text appears hardly in history except at the Semiarian period. It was almost disowned ever after: and there is no certainty—nothing more than inference which we hold, and claim to have proved, to be imaginary and delusive,—that, except as represented in the corruption which it gathered out of the chaos of the earliest times, it made any appearance.

3. Thus, as a matter of history acknowledged by Dr. Hort, it was mainly superseded before the end of the century of its emergence by the Traditional Text, which, except in the tenets of a school of critics in the nineteenth century, has reigned supreme ever since.

4. That it was not the original text of the Gospels, as maintained by Dr. Hort, I claim to have established from an examination of the quotations from the Gospels made by the Fathers. It has been proved that not only in number, but still more conclusively in quality, the Traditional Text enjoyed a great superiority of attestation over all the kinds of corruption advocated by some critics which I have just now mentioned[624]. This conclusion is strengthened by the verdict of the early versions.

5. The inferiority of the 'Neutral Text' is demonstrated by the overwhelming weight of evidence which is marshalled against it on passages under dispute. This glaring contrast is increased by the disagreement among themselves of the supporters of that Text, or class of readings. As to antiquity, number, variety, weight, and continuity, that Text falls hopelessly behind: and by internal evidence also the texts of B and ℵ, and still more the eccentric text of the Western D, are proved to be manifestly inferior.

6. It has been shewn also by evidence, direct as well as inferential, that B and ℵ issued nearly together from the library or school of Caesarea. The fact of their being the oldest MSS. of the New Testament in existence, which has naturally misled people and caused them to be credited with extraordinary value, has been referred, as being mainly due, to their having been written on vellum according to the fashion introduced in that school, instead of the ordinary papyrus. The fact of such preservation is really to their discredit, in-

stead of resounding to their honour, because if they had enjoyed general approval, they would probably have perished creditably many centuries ago in the constant use for which they were intended.

Such are the main points in the indictment and in the history of the Neutral Text, or rather—to speak with more appropriate accuracy, avoiding the danger of drawing with too definite a form and too deep a shade—of the class of readings represented by B and א. It is interesting to trace further, though very summarily, the connexion between this class of readings and the corruptions of the Original Text which existed previously to the early middle of the fourth century. Such brief tracing will lead us to a view of some causes of the development of Dr. Hort's theory.

The analysis of Corruption supplied as to the various kinds of it by Dean Burgon has taught us how they severally arose. This is fresh in the mind of readers, and I will not spoil it by repetition. But the studies of textual critics have led them to combine all kinds of corruption chiefly under the two heads of the Western or Syrio-Low-Latin class, and in a less prominent province of the Alexandrian. Dr. Hort's Neutral is really a combination of those two, with all the accuracy that these phenomena admit. But of course, if the Neutral were indeed the original Text, it would not do for it to be too closely connected with one of such bad reputation as the Western, which must be kept in the distance at all hazards. Therefore he represented it—all unconsciously no doubt and with the best intention—as one of the sources of the Traditional, or as he called it the 'Syrian' Text. Hence this imputed connexion between the Western and the Traditional Text became the essential part of his framework of Conflation, which could not exist without it. For any permanent purpose, all this handiwork was in vain. To say no more, D, which is the chief representative of the Western Text, is too constant a supporter of the peculiar readings of B and א not to prove its near relationship to them. The 'Neutral' Text derives the chief part of its support from Western sources. It is useless for Dr. Hort to disown his leading constituents. And on the other hand, the Syrio-Low-Latin Text is too alien to the Traditional to be the chief element in any process, Conflate or other, out of which it could have been constructed. The occasional support of some of the Old Latin MSS. is nothing to the point in such a. proof. They are so fitful and uncertain, that some of them may witness to almost anything. If Dr. Hort's theory of Conflation had been sounder, there would have been no lack of examples.

'Naturam expellas furca: tamen usque recurret.'

He was tempted to the impossible task of driving water uphill. Therefore I claim, not only to have refuted Dr. Hort, whose theory is proved to be even more baseless than I ever imagined, but by excavating more deeply than he did, to have discovered the cause of his error.

No: the true theory is, that the Traditional Text—not in superhuman perfection, though under some superhuman Guidance—is the embodiment of the original Text of the New Testament. In the earliest times, just as false doctrines were widely spread, so corrupt readings prevailed in many places.

Later on, when Christianity was better understood, and the Church reckoned amongst the learned and holy of her members the finest natures and intellects of the world, and many clever men of inferior character endeavoured to vitiate Doctrine and lower Christian life, evil rose to the surface, and was in due time after a severe struggle removed by the sound and faithful of the day. So heresy was rampant for a while, and was then replaced by true and well-grounded belief. With great ability and with wise discretion, the Deposit whether of Faith or Word was verified and established. General Councils decided in those days upon the Faith, and the Creed when accepted and approved by the universal voice was enacted for good and bequeathed to future ages. So it was both as to the Canon and the Words of Holy Scripture, only that all was done quietly. As to the latter, hardly a footfall was heard. But none the less, corruption after short-lived prominence sank into deep and still deeper obscurity, whilst the teaching of fifteen centuries placed the true Text upon a firm and lasting basis.

And so I venture to hold, now that the question has been raised, both the learned and the well-informed will come gradually to see, that no other course respecting the Words of the New Testament is so strongly justified by the evidence, none so sound and large-minded, none so reasonable in every way, none so consonant with intelligent faith, none so productive of guidance and comfort and hope, as to maintain against all the assaults of corruption

THE TRADITIONAL TEXT.

[620] Dr. Hort has represented Neutral readings by α, Western by β, as far as I can understand, 'other' by γ, and 'Syrian' (= Traditional) by δ. But he nowhere gives an example of γ.

[621] Introduction, p. 103.

[622] Cp. St. Luke xviii. 2, 3. Τις is used with ἐξ, St. Luke xi. 15, xxiv. 24; St. John vi. 64, vii. 25, ix. 16, xi. 37, 46; Acts xi. 20, xiii. 1, &c.

[623] Thus ἔπαινος is used for a public encomium, or panegyric.

[624] An attempt in the *Guardian* has been made in a review full of errors to weaken the effect of my list by an examination of an unique set of details. A correction both of the reviewer's figures in one instance and of .my own may be found above, pp. 144-153. There is no virtue in an exact proportion of 3:2, or of 6:1. A great majority will ultimately be found on our side.

www.ingramcontent.com/pod-product-compliance
Lightning Source LLC
LaVergne TN
LVHW091258080426
835510LV00007B/314